VISUAL QUICKSTART GUIDE

3D STUDIO MAX 3

Michele Matossian

Peachpit Press

Visual QuickStart Guide
3D Studio MAX 3
Michele Matossian

Peachpit Press
1249 Eighth Street
Berkeley, CA 94710
(510) 524-2178
(510) 524-2221 (fax)

Find us on the World Wide Web at: http://www.peachpit.com

Peachpit Press is a division of Addison Wesley Longman

Editors: Lisa Theobald and Valerie Perry
Production Coordinator: Kate Reber
Compositor: Owen Wolfson
Indexer: Valerie Perry

Notice of rights

Notice of liability

Trademarks

ISBN: 0-201-35350-4

0 9 8 7 6 5 4 3 2 1

Printed and bound in the United States of America

Dedication

For Chris, my wonderful husband, without whose support this book would never have been written

and

In memoriam to my loving grandmother, Katharine Hillix Kilbourne

and

To Robert D'Arista, the greatest art teacher of our time

Acknowledgements

I would like to thank the many people who contributed their time and talents to this work: Lisa Theobald, Kate Reber, David Duberman, Valerie Perry, Bob Prokopp, Marjorie Baer, and Nancy Dunn. In addition, I would like to thank my friends and family, especially Tim Rose, Wendy Sterndale, Donna Thomson, Barbara Brodsky, Ellen Caldwell, and all the members of the highly accomplished Matossian clan: Drs. Garo, Mary, Lou Ann, Viken, and Mark Matossian. Thank you one and all for your invaluable insights, love and support. May the Mother bless all beings and lead them into their true purpose.

With deepest appreciation,
Michele Matossian
July 22, 1999

TABLE OF CONTENTS

TABLE OF CONTENTS

INTRODUCTION

3D Studio MAX is one of the most powerful desktop 3D graphics programs available today. It is used for a wide variety of commercial and artistic applications, including architecture, computer games, film production, web design, forensics, medical visualization, scientific visualization, fine art, and virtual reality.

This book was written for artists, designers, students, teachers, working professionals, and anyone who dreams of building worlds. To guide you through the process of learning, the pages are filled with figures that illustrate step-by step instructions. Inline graphics and screen shots point you where you need to go. At the beginning of each chapter, the introduction presents the topic in practical terms. The section headings that follow present the theory you need just in time to do the tasks that follow. By studying both the theory and the mechanics, you will be equipped to not only push the right buttons, but to create, solve problems and invent solutions.

Like other Visual QuickStart Guides, this book is designed to be visually clear and easy to read, and it presumes no prior experience of the topic. If you are a beginner, the best thing to do is start at the beginning and work your way through the topics in order. Intermediate and advanced students will benefit from studying the working methods, as well as from the tips at the end of the tasks. To use this book as a "how to" reference, check the headings and tasks in the table of contents or look up the topic in the index.

To get the most out of this book, you should be familiar with the Windows environment and have access to an installation of 3D Studio MAX 3.0. You should also have a solid foundation in bitmap painting programs such as Adobe Photoshop.

There are as many ways to work in MAX as there are artists who use the program. Throughout the book, I have tried to select the easiest and most direct ways of using the program, while showing you the larger interface design. In a sense, you could say that this book is an interface to the interface: It filters out what you do not need to know, so you can concentrate on what you really do need.

You begin by creating a basic form, modifying its shape, applying texture and color to the surface, and placing it in the scene. This process can be compared to roughing out a form, sculpting the details, painting it, and placing it on a stage. Cameras and lights frame the scene and add light. Animation and special effects bring the scene to life. For final presentation, you can take pictures of the scene, or make a movie of events as they unfold over time.

The process of molding a form is called **modeling**. In the beginning, you will learn how to create simple geometric forms with just a few clicks of the mouse. As you go on,

you will learn to refine the model much as you would carve an intricate sculpture.

The next step, painting the object, is called **surface mapping**, or mapping for short. Mapping takes a 2D image called a map and applies it to an object in a process similar to wrapping a present. Maps can affect surface color and pattern as well as texture, reflectivity, and transparency.

After you have placed your cameras and lights, you may wish to take a picture to get a better idea of how your object looks. The process of taking a picture is called **rendering**. Rendering produces a 2D image of a 3D scene that is at a higher level of resolution than the normal screen display. If any special effects have been introduced, they will appear in the rendered image.

One of the most exciting aspects of 3D graphics is **animation**. To animate literally means to give life. In MAX, animation is easily achieved by changing an object over time. At the click of a button, the program computes all the "in-between" frames. You can animate modeling, mapping, lights, cameras, movement in space, and special effects.

By the end of this book, you will have learned how to create, model, map, animate, and render objects in 3D Studio MAX. Furthermore, you will have learned how to place cameras and lights, and you'll have been introduced to some of the many possible special effects. The final result is that you will be conversant in using 3D Studio MAX to create your own worlds and explore them.

Bon voyage!

GETTING STARTED

3D Studio MAX 3 is a software program designed to create the illusion of objects moving in space. Mastering it requires both visual thinking skills and the ability to think logically.

You can start by looking at three-dimensional graphics in visual terms. In two dimensions, images are flat and can be seen only from a single point of view. Because of this, they are experienced as being external to the viewer. In the world of 3D, you can immerse yourself in the depths and swim around, which gives you a tangible sense of space and time.

This chapter offers the opportunity to skim the surface of the program elements to become familiar with what you experience when you plunge into the program's depths.

Installing MAX 3

3D Studio MAX 3 is designed to run on an Intel compatible processor that has Windows NT 4.0 and Service Pack 4 installed. It can also run on top of a Windows 95 or Windows 98 operating system. See the sidebar "System Requirements" for more details.

The following steps guide you in setting up a typical installation of 3D Studio MAX 3. Setup takes a few minutes to copy files to your hard disk drive after you have made the selections in the installation screens.

To install 3D Studio MAX:

1. Prepare to install program files by closing any open programs, making sure sufficient free space is available on the hard disk drive, and gathering the serial number and CD Key located on the back of the 3D Studio MAX CD-ROM case.

2. Place the 3D Studio MAX 3 CD-ROM in the CD-ROM drive and double-click Setup.exe in the top-level directory.

3. Click 3D Studio MAX (**Figure 1.1**).

4. Follow the steps as prompted by the messages in the installation routine; accept the Typical installation option (**Figure 1.2**). Then click Next.

5. Click Yes to install DWG I/O files, Online Reference files, and Internet Explorer. (You need a browser for the MAX Help system.)

6. Click Finish to finish the MAX installation and restart your computer.

✔ Tip

■ If you are running Windows NT 4.0, you must install Service Pack 4 to use the MAX 3 Help system. Find Setup files in the Nt4sp4 folder on the MAX 3 CD-ROM.

Figure 1.1 Choose to install 3D Studio MAX from the Choose Setup Program dialog box.

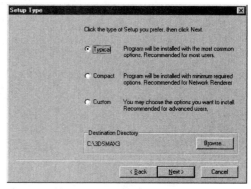

Figure 1.2 Choose Typical for the type of installation that most people need and to install the files that this book will expect you to have installed.

Authorizing MAX 3

Authorization is required to run MAX for more than 30 days from the date of installation.

To authorize the installation:

1. Collect your serial number and other registration information.

2. Call the Autodesk Registration and Authorization Department at 1-800-551-1491 from the USA and Canada to obtain an authorization code.

   To call from other countries, find the appropriate number to call or fax on Form A in the product literature.

3. From the Start button, choose Programs > Kinetix > Authorize 3D Studio MAX R3.

4. Enter your authorization code in the dialog box.

The first time you run MAX, it asks you to configure the display driver.

To configure the display driver:

1. Choose Start > Programs > Kinetix > 3D Studio MAX R3

2. In the 3D Studio MAX Driver Setup dialog box, choose a display driver.

   Unless you have a GLiNT card, Open GL card, or other hardware accelerators, stick with the default Heidi driver Software Z-Buffer. You can always change it later in Customize > Preferences > Viewports.

3. Click OK.

   Now launch 3D Studio MAX. Congratulations!

System Requirements

To run MAX R3 you will need the following hardware:

◆ An Intel-compatible processor that runs at a minimum speed of 150MHz. (3D Studio MAX 3 provides full support of multiple processor systems; a dual Pentium Pro or Pentium II system is recommended.)

◆ 64MB RAM (128MB or more is recommended).

◆ 205MB hard-disk drive space (for the typical installation, including AutoCAD *.dwg* file translators).

◆ 200MB hard-disk drive swap space (minimum; this program likes a lot of room).

◆ A mouse or other pointing device (the program is optimized for a Microsoft Intellimouse).

◆ A CD-ROM drive.

◆ A graphics card and SVGA monitor that supports a resolution of 1280 x 1024 pixels using True Color. Minimum requirement is 800 x 600 pixels at 256 colors. MAX 3 supports OpenGL and Direct3D hardware acceleration.

Optional hardware: sound card, speakers, TCP/IP network cabling, 3D hardware graphics accelerator, video input and output devices, a joystick, MIDI instruments, and a three-button mouse.

AUTHORIZING MAX 3

Accessing Technical Support

If you have any problems with your 3D Studio MAX installation or use, the following resources are available to help you:

◆ The Installation Notes in the Readme file located in the 3dsmax3 directory.

◆ The Authorized Dealer who sold you the product. To obtain the number of an Authorized Dealer, call 1-800-879-4233.

◆ The Kinetix Support Pages on the Web at *http://support.ktx.com/*. A well-referenced source of questions and answers.

◆ The Kinetix Product Support HelpFile in the MAX Help menu under Additional Help (**Figure 1.3**). Updated quarterly and posted on the Web.

◆ Kinetix Product Support: 1-415-547-2254, Monday through Friday, 6 a.m. to 5 p.m. Pacific Standard Time. Installation and configuration support is available for free for 10 consecutive business days. The charge is $65 per incident thereafter.

◆ Autodesk 24-hour FAX Support Information System at 1-415-446-1919. Select option 2 and enter 100# to recieve a fax of available support documents and their document numbers.

◆ The Autodesk Product Information Line at 1-800-964-6432.

For display problems, make sure that you have the latest display driver and video card BIOS installed by checking the technical support pages of your video-card manufacturer's Web site. If problems persist, contact the manufacturer directly.

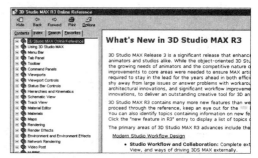

Figure 1.3 The Help System is an interactive system of reference accessed from the Menu Bar. You can open it from the Help menu within 3D MAX.

Touring the Interface

MAX 3 has hundreds, perhaps thousands, of commands. To save desktop real estate, many commands are initially hidden from view. Consequently, it can take a while to learn the lay of the land. This section of the chapter takes you on a tour of what you typically see as you work with MAX. Here you can learn how to use the special features of the program's user interface.

The MAX 3 interface is visually organized by function. Commands are layered in menus, toolbars, panels, modules, and dialog boxes to maximize the screen real estate without compromising workspace. Graphical icons and right-click menus supply handy shortcuts to the most commonly used commands.

The main user interface is organized into several regions, as shown in **Figure 1.4**.

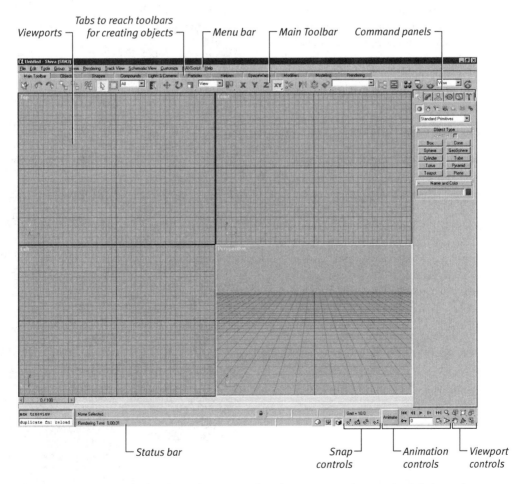

Figure 1.4 The MAX main display shows viewports, 11 drop-down menus on the menu bar, tabs to reach 11 moveable toolbars for creating objects, the Main Toolbar, six layered command panels, and a couple dozen more tools in the status bar underneath the viewports.

Elements of the MAX Interface

Special user interface features help make the program's tools accessible and easy to use. The special elements include:

◆ Tooltips (**Figure 1.5**) are pop-up labels that appear when you rest your cursor over an icon (before you click it). As part of the Help system, these pop-up labels for icons help you get to know the tools.

◆ Drop-down menus (**Figure 1.6**) on the menu bar work just as they do in any Windows program: menus drop down when you put the cursor on a menu title and click the mouse button. Elsewhere in program boxes, panels, toolbars, and drop-down menus are indicated by an inverted black triangle just to the right of the first menu item.

◆ Right-click menus (**Figure 1.7**) are extensive hidden menus that exist throughout MAX 3. They allow you to access commands for selected objects, viewports, viewport labels, toolbars, tool icons, command panels, and major modules such as the Schematic View. You access hidden menus by right-clicking. In some places you can also Ctrl+right-click to open different right-click menus that have context-sensitive commands.

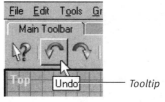

Tooltip

Figure 1.5 Tooltips, labels that appear when you hold down the mouse button when rolling over icons, help you figure out what icons represent.

Figure 1.6 When you find a little triangular arrow in a box, panel, or toolbar, you can click it to open a drop-down menu.

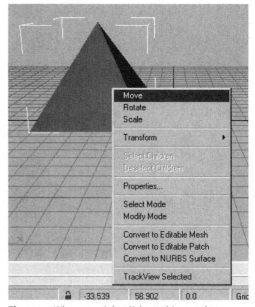

Figure 1.7 When you right-click an object and some elements of the MAX interface, a menu appears with commands that are useful at the time.

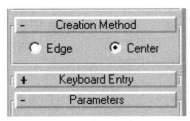

Figure 1.8 The creation-method rollout is open; the keyboard-entry rollout is closed.

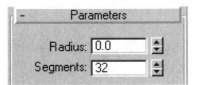

Figure 1.9 Press the spinner arrows to select from a list of parameters, or just type a parameter in the field.

Figure 1.10 You can find flyouts on the Main Toolbar, the status bar, and in the Material Editor, for example.

◆ Rollouts (**Figure 1.8**) collapse when you don't need them and expand when you want access to their commands. They show a plus sign (+) when they are closed; click the rollout title to open a rollout. They show a minus sign (–) when they are open; click a rollout title with a minus sign to close the rollout. A thin scrollbar to the right of the rollout provides an alternative means of scrolling. Rollouts appear in the command panels, the Material Editor, and the Render dialog box.

◆ Spinners (**Figure 1.9**), designated by a pair of little up- and down-facing triangular arrows, give you a quick way to change the value of the parameter. Press an arrow to open the spinner choices, or just type a parameter in the field. Right-clicking a spinner zeroes out the parameter.

◆ Flyouts (**Figure 1.10**) are sets of related tool icons that fit into the space for just one icon. Only one icon shows at a time until you press the flyout; then you can pick one of the hidden choices. You can recognize flyouts by the black triangle in the lower-right corner of the foreground icon.

✔ Tip

■ When the input field is selected you can change the parameter value from the keyboard: Type R and the amount you want to change (positive or negative).

TOURING THE INTERFACE

◆ Floaters (**Figure 1.11**) are modeless dialog boxes that "float" in the foreground and stay available as long as you need them.

◆ Floating and docking toolbars (**Figure 1.12**) for making MAX objects can float in the foreground or attach to the top, sides, or bottom of the interface. Drag a toolbar to detach it, move it, or dock it at an edge of the MAX display.

◆ Cursors (**Figure 1.13**) in MAX change to indicate the selected action. For example, if you click the Zoom button, the pointer changes to a magnifying glass as soon as you place it in a viewport. Cursors generally match the icon of the selected tool. Alternative cursors are used throughout the interface, especially in the toolbar buttons and view controls.

The Menu Bar

Eleven drop-down menus are available on the menu bar (**Figures 1.14 and 1.15**). The menus work just as those in any Windows program. Some menu commands lead to submenus that cascade off the side of the menu. Some commands on the menus have keyboard shortcuts listed to help you learn shortcuts for the commands you use most often.

Figure 1.11 Floaters, dialog boxes that stay in the foreground as long as you need them, are found on the Tools menu.

Figure 1.12 You can move some of the MAX toolbars and float or attach them to the side of the display.

Figure 1.13 The cursor changes shape to indicate what tool is active.

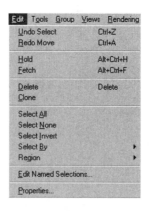

Figure 1.14 The Edit menu offers commands, keyboard shortcuts, and arrows that lead to submenus.

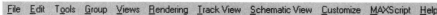

Figure 1.15 The MAX menu bar contains 11 menus that work just as any Windows menus do.

TOURING THE INTERFACE

The Main Toolbar

You can click the icons in the Main Toolbar to call up the most important tools, including the selection and transform tools (**Figure 1.16**). Several of the icons on the Main Toolbar act as flyouts that contain other related icons.

If you can't see all the icons along the top of your screen, drag the toolbar right or left by putting the cursor somewhere in the Main Toolbar where there is no icon. When the cursor turns into a hand, move it until the icon you want shows up.

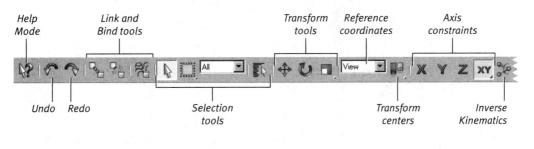

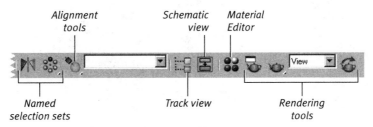

Figure 1.16 The Main Toolbar compactly contains dozens of tools.

The Viewports

The *viewports* are the main viewing area in the center of the interface (**Figure 1.17**). (*Chapter 2, "Navigation and Display," covers in detail how to work with the viewports and viewport controls.*)

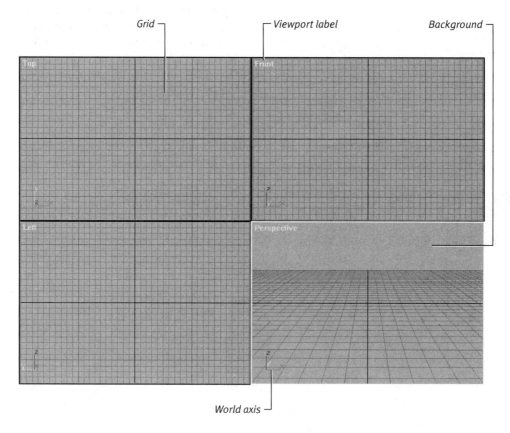

Grid ⌐   ⌐ Viewport label   Background ⌐

World axis ⌐

Figure 1.17 You can see four different views of your MAX scene at once or select just one view to fill the viewport.

Modify   *Motion*   *Utilities*
Create   *Hierarchy*   *Display*

Figure 1.18 MAX has six command panels that contain tools for creating, manipulating, and managing scenes. Click a tab to bring a panel to the foreground.

The Command Panels

The command panels give you access to the majority of modeling and animation commands. They also provide display controls and an assortment of utilities. Command panels are accessed by clicking tabs at the top of each panel (**Figure 1.18**).

Special Features

MAX has myriad command modules and dialog boxes, but three are worth introducing to beginners to suggest the depth, breadth, and flexibility of the program.

◆ The Schematic View (**Figure 1.19**) allows you to view and manipulate animation and material hierarchies in a flowchart format. This may not mean much now, but once you know how to create objects and their clones and compose them in a scene, you will understand how much power this view provides.

◆ The Asset Manager (**Figure 1.20**) allows you to browse your entire computer system for image files and scene files. You can drag files from the Asset Manager and drop them into MAX scenes. You can drag an image from the Asset Manager into the Material Editor, for instance.

◆ The Object Properties dialog box (**Figure 1.21**) provides handy access to essential controls for objects in a MAX scene.

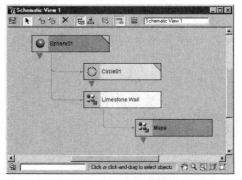

Figure 1.19 The Schematic View provides a big picture of objects in a scene and shows how they are related to one another.

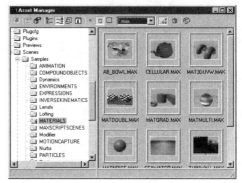

Figure 1.20 The Asset Manager lets you control the diverse elements you may use to compose 3D scenes.

Figure 1.21 The Object Properties dialog box acts as a clearinghouse for parameters for the selected object.

Figure 1.22 The Save File As dialog box allows you to save a MAX scene file.

Figure 1.23 The thumbnail in the Open File dialog box allows you to choose the right MAX scene file to open.

Managing Files

File management in 3D graphics is complicated by the many kinds of files and objects that you can manipulate. Consequently, such a complex program offers numerous preference settings. In this chapter, you learn just the basic file management commands and preference settings that get you started.

When you first initialize the program, a new untitled scene is displayed to view, which you can save. By default, you save scene files into the scenes directory of the 3dsmax3 folder.

The file extension for a 3D Studio MAX scene file is *.max.*

To save an untitled scene:

1. Choose File > Save.

The Save File As dialog box appears (**Figure 1.22**).

2. In the Save File As dialog box, type a name in the File Name field.

3. Click Save.

The file is named and saved in 3dsmax3\scenes, the default path for MAX scenes.

To open a scene:

1. Choose File > Open.

The Open File dialog box appears.

2. Click the name of the file you want to open.

A thumbnail image of the scene appears in the dialog box (**Figure 1.23**).

3. Click Open.

✔ Tip

■ MAX opens only one scene file at a time. If you are using Windows NT and have enough RAM, you can run multiple sessions of the program.

MANAGING FILES

13

To save as a new file or save into another directory:

1. Choose File > Save As.

The Save File As dialog box appears (**Figure 1.24**).

2. Navigate to the directory where you want to save the file.

3. Enter a new file name in the File Name field.

4. Click Save.

The file is saved under the new file name. The active view is saved as the thumbnail image for the new file. The other scene is preserved under its original name in the original directory.

✔ Tips

■ To increment a file name by one, click the plus sign (+) in the Save As dialog box.

■ If you like a scene but want to try out some changes, you can preserve it temporarily without saving it under a new name by choosing Edit > Hold. Retrieve the scene by choosing Edit > Fetch. You can fetch the Hold file even after a scene file has been saved, but you can hold only one scene at a time.

Figure 1.24 The Save File As dialog box allows you to rename your MAX scene file.

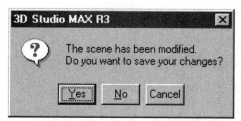

Figure 1.25 MAX runs only one scene at a time. If you have made changes to an open scene, you are asked if you want to save them before opening a new scene.

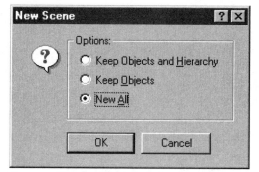

Figure 1.26 The New Scene dialog box lets you incorporate objects from the current scene into the new scene.

Creating a New Scene

The New command creates a new scene file; MAX offers the option of keeping elements from the previously loaded scene.

To create a new scene:

1. Choose File > New.

   If you have made changes to the current scene, you're asked whether you want to save your changes (**Figure 1.25**). If you have not made any changes to the current file, the New Scene dialog box appears (**Figure 1.26**) and you can skip to step 3.

2. If you have made changes to the current file, click Yes to bring up the Save File As dialog box and save your changes.

   or

   Click No to leave any changes unsaved.

   If you click No, the New Scene dialog box appears.

3. In the New Scene dialog box, click OK.

   A new, untitled scene is displayed.

MANAGING FILES

Resetting and Quitting the Program

The Reset command returns the program to its initial state. All objects, hierarchy, animation data, and materials are eliminated. A new untitled scene is displayed using the default settings and scene views.

The MAX interface is designed to be customized so that people who use the program can put the tools they use most often in a handy place. This book does not go into detail on how to customize the interface, but what you see on your screen may differ from what this book shows if someone has customized the interface. If you need to return the interface to its original state, choose Customize > Revert to Startup UI Layout.

Figure 1.27 Reset is the program's way of letting you know you are about to lose some changes unless you save.

To reset the program:

1. Choose File > Reset.

2. If necessary, save any changes you've made to the current file.

   If you opt not to save changes or if you have not made any changes to the scene, the Reset dialog box appears.

3. Click Yes in the Reset dialog box (**Figure 1.27**).

   The original MAX 3 settings are restored.

To exit the program:

1. Choose File > Exit.

2. If necessary, save changes to the current file.

   The program window closes and the program quits running.

✔ Tip

■ To quit the program, you can also close the program window.

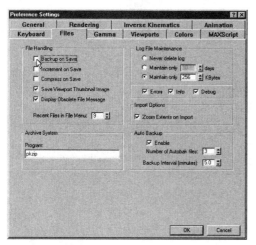

Figure 1.28 The Files panel of the Preference Settings dialog box. These settings govern saving, backing up, and archiving files.

Backing Up Files

Backing up files is crucial to the success of any project. Besides saving files manually, you can set a preference to back up files automatically.

Automatic Backup

The automatic backup process saves a limited number of backup files at set intervals of time. MAX automatically names the files Autobak1.mx, Autobak2.mx, Autobak3.mx, Autobak*N*.mx, where *N* is the maximum number of backup files you have set the program to save. When the number of backup files exceeds the maximum, the backup process saves over the oldest file starting with Autobak1.mx.

To back up files automatically:

1. Choose Customize > Preferences.

   The Preference Settings dialog box appears.

2. Click the Files tab.

   The Files panel appears (**Figure 1.28**).

3. Check Enable in the Auto Backup area.

4. Enter the maximum number of backup files to maintain, or use the default of three files.

5. Enter the backup interval in minutes, or use the default of five minutes.

6. Click OK.

To recover a file from automatic backup:

1. Choose File > Open.

2. Navigate to the 3dsmax3\Autoback directory.

3. In the File Type drop-down menu, choose All Files (*.*).

   The Auto Backup files appear in the list of files.

4. Click the Details icon in the upper-right corner of the dialog box.

   The modification dates of the Auto Backup files appear (**Figure 1.29**).

5. Double-click the most recently modified Autobak file to open the most recent backup file.

   Note that this is not necessarily the file name with the highest number, because the automatic backup process saves over old Autoback files sequentially.

6. Choose File > Save As.

   The file is renamed and placed in the scenes directory.

Details

Figure 1.29 When restoring from backup, click Details and choose to view all files to see the modification dates of all the Autobak files.

BACKING UP FILES

Figure 1.30 Check Backup on Save in the Files panel of the Preference Settings dialog box.

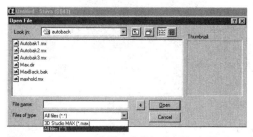

Figure 1.31 Choose All Files (*.*) in the Files of Type drop-down menu to see the MaxBack.bak file.

Backup on Save

Saving files is a good thing, right? Not when you save changes over work you had wanted to keep. Fortunately, you can set a preference in MAX that automatically backs up your file on Save. This nonincrementing file is saved in the 3dsmax3\Autoback directory.

To backup on save:

1. Choose Customize > Preferences.

2. Click the Files tab.

3. Check Backup on Save (**Figure 1.30**). MAX will now automatically back up your file every time you use Save.

To recover a file after a save:

1. Choose File > Open.

2. Navigate to the 3dsmax3\Autoback folder.

3. In the Files of Type drop-down menu, choose All Files (*.*) (**Figure 1.31**).

4. Double-click MaxBack.bak.
   The previous saved version of your file appears.

5. Choose File > Save As.
   The file is renamed and placed in the scenes directory.

BACKING UP FILES

Changing the Default Path for Scenes

Designated paths cause the program to look for certain types of files in specific directories and folders. Configuring custom paths can help you work more efficiently on a project when you need to organize files in different locations.

Bitmaps with Multiple Paths

Bitmaps—as opposed to MAX scenes—can have multiple paths, which MAX searches in this order:

1. The path of the image file last loaded.

2. The directory of the current scene.

3. The subdirectories below the current scene.

4. The paths listed in the Bitmaps panel of the Configure Path dialog box, starting at the top of the list (**Figure 1.32**).

To configure a path for saving scenes:

1. Choose File > Configure Paths.

   The Configure Paths dialog box appears (**Figure 1.33**).

2. Select the Scenes path and click Modify.

3. In the Choose Directory for Scenes dialog box that appears, navigate to choose a folder.

   or

   Click Create New Folder and name the folder.

4. Double-click the desired folder and click Use Path.

5. Click OK.

   The program uses the new folder whenever you attempt to open a scene file, and it saves scene files to the designated folder instead of 3dsmax3\Scenes, the default path for MAX scenes.

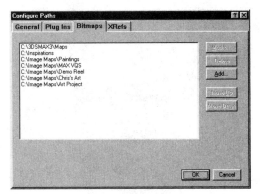

Figure 1.32 The Bitmaps panel of the Configure Paths dialog box allows you to add paths for finding bitmaps. Paths are searched from the top of the list on down.

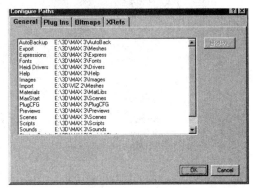

Figure 1.33 The Configure Paths dialog box tells the program where to find files.

Figure 1.34 The initial scene before merging it with another file.

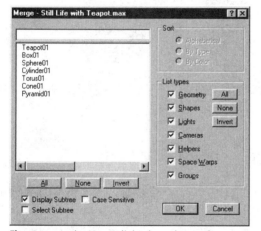

Figure 1.35 In the Merge dialog box, choose the objects that you want to add to your scene.

Figure 1.36 The scene after merging in the teapot.

Adding Objects to Scenes

By merging files you can bring into your current scene objects from other scenes, along with their materials and animation data. This means you can create animations in separate files and then combine them.

You can also replace one object with another. The substitute object takes on the properties and animation data of the object it replaces. This comes in handy when you want to create an animation with simple objects and then substitute more complex ones.

To merge objects into a scene:

1. Open a scene file (**Figure 1.34**).

2. Choose File > Merge.

3. Select and open the file that contains the objects you want.

   The Merge dialog box appears with a list of objects in the scene file (**Figure 1.35**).

4. Click an object name and click OK.

   The chosen object appears in the scene (**Figure 1.36**).

To replace objects in a scene:

1. Open a scene file (**Figure 1.37**).

2. Choose File > Replace.

3. In the dialog box that appears, open the scene that has the object you want to substitute into your file. Important: The substitute object must have the exact same name as the object you are replacing or you will not be able to access the file.

4. Select the objects you want to replace (**Figure 1.38**).

5. In the dialog that appears, click Yes to replace materials along with the objects or No to bring in objects only (**Figure 1.39**).

   The replacement objects appear in the scene (**Figure 1.40**).

Figure 1.37 The initial scene before replacing the vase.

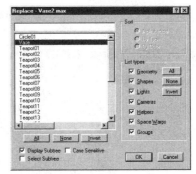

Figure 1.38 In the Replace dialog box you choose the substitute objects for your scene.

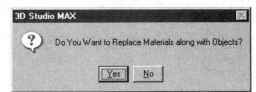

Figure 1.39 When you replace objects, you can replace the materials that control the surface's appearance at the same time or simply bring in the objects alone.

Figure 1.40 Here the substitute object shows more detail.

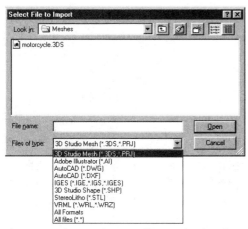

Figure 1.41 When you import a file, start by choosing a file type from the Select File to Import dialog box.

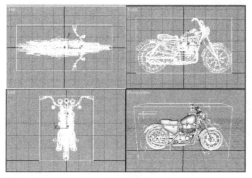

Figure 1.42 The imported files appear in the MAX viewports.

Importing and Exporting

You can import files in eight file formats: 3D Studio Mesh (.3DS, .PRJ), Adobe Illustrator (.AI), AutoCAD (.DWG) and AutoCAD (.DXF), IEGS (.IGE, .IGS, .IGES), 3D Studio Shape (.SHP), StereoLitho (.STL), and VRML (.WRL, .WRZ).

Exporting files causes MAX to translate the native *.max* scene information into universal 3D file formats such as *.3ds* or *.dxf*. Because these universal files are usually less robust, some of the scene information may change or disappear. Generally speaking, MAX warns you of impending changes, and it preserves essential name, hierarchy, animation, material, and mesh information.

To import a file:

1. Choose File > Import.

   The Select File to Import dialog box appears.

2. Select a file format from the Files of Type menu (**Figure 1.41**).

3. Double-click the name of the file you want to import.

4. In the dialog box that appears, choose Completely Replace Current Scene.

5. Click OK to accept the default settings.

   The imported files appear on the screen (**Figure 1.42**).

To export a file:

1. Choose File > Export. The Select File to Export dialog box appears.

2. Select an export file format from the Save As Type menu (**Figure 1.43**).

3. Choose a directory to hold the exported file.

4. Name the file and click Save.

✔ Tip

■ If you like a scene but want to try out some changes, you can preserve it temporarily without saving it under a new name by choosing Edit > Hold. Retrieve the scene by choosing Edit > Fetch. You can fetch the Hold file even after a scene file has been saved.

Figure 1.43 When you export a file, you select a file and an export file format.

NAVIGATION AND DISPLAY

2

Working in 3D graphics requires good spatial awareness. Painters, sculptors, photographers, lighting and set designers, architects, and builders can easily adapt their spatial awareness to 3D graphics. A background in dance, martial arts, acting, or sports also helps you work in virtual space.

Even if you have no experience to help you understand how 3D space works, in this chapter you will learn how to orient yourself in 3D space and how to navigate that space using the viewport controls. This provides a foundation for all of your 3D modeling and animation work.

Getting Oriented

Viewports are like cameras that look at a scene. The image that appears in each viewport is called a *view*. To find just the right view to work with, viewports can be "flown" around a scene like a plane. But, like any good pilot, you need a system of reference to orient yourself and measure your position in space.

When you drive a car, a road map provides a two-dimensional system of reference. This includes a scale of distance in miles or kilometers and an indication of the cardinal directions of north, east, south, and west (**Figure 2.1**).

When you fly through space, you need a three-dimensional system of reference. Pilots use polar coordinates and altitude to stay on course. Navigating in 3D space is probably more like flying a spaceship than a plane because you are traveling through a universe rather than around a planet. To explain how this works, we need to take a page out of your old geometry book.

In planar geometry, space is measured using two perpendicular axes named X and Y. By assigning regular intervals along their lengths, rectangular coordinates *(x, y)* can be established for any position in space. The point at which the axes intersect is called the *origin*, because it is the point from which measurement originates. The coordinates of the origin are *(0,0)* (**Figure 2.2**).

In 3D geometry, a third axis called the Z axis is used to measure depth. The Z axis runs perpendicular to both the X and Y axes and intersects them at the origin. In this system, every position in space has three coordinates: *(x, y, z)*. Thus the coordinates of the origin in 3D space are *(0,0,0)* (**Figure 2.3**).

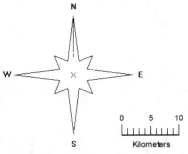

Figure 2.1 In a two-dimensional road map, the system of reference includes distance and direction.

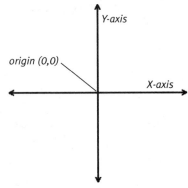

Figure 2.2 Rectangular coordinates measure space using perpendicular axes that meet at the origin.

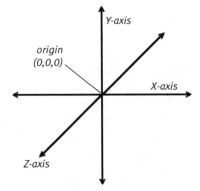

Figure 2.3 Adding the Z axis to rectangular coordinates makes it possible to measure depth.

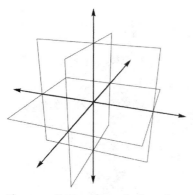

Figure 2.4 The world coordinate system uses a fixed system of reference to define world space.

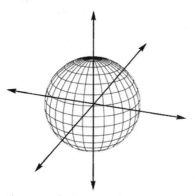

Figure 2.5 The local coordinate system uses a relative system of reference to define object space.

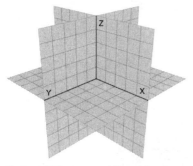

Figure 2.6 The home grid is made of three intersecting grids that are aligned to the *XY, YZ,* and *ZX* planes of the world coordinate system.

When the *X, Y,* and *Z* axes are assigned to a fixed position and orientation in 3D space, they can be used to measure the position and orientation of every object in a scene. This absolute frame of reference is called a *world coordinate system*. When 3D space is defined by a world coordinate system, it is referred to as *world space* (**Figure 2.4**).

When the axes of a 3D coordinate system are tied to an object, they can be used to measure changes in orientation and scale of that object relative to its previous coordinates. This relative system of reference is called a *local coordinate system*. When 3D space is defined by a local coordinate system, it is referred to as *object space* (**Figure 2.5**).

Because it takes two lines to define a plane, the axes of the world coordinate system can be used to define three planes: the *XY, YZ,* and *ZX* planes. When these three planes are divided by lines at regular intervals, they form three perpendicular grids that intersect at the origin. The combination of these three intersecting grids is called the *home grid*. The home grid is useful for navigating 3D space because it indicates the position and orientation of the world coordinate system (**Figure 2.6**).

To allow you to see the objects you're building, MAX shows only one plane of the home grid.

GETTING ORIENTED

Looking Around

Viewports can show views of a scene from fixed directions or from positions that you define. How objects are displayed on the screen depends in part on the type of view you select.

Six views face the scene from fixed directions: the Front, Back, Left, Right, Top, and Bottom views. The name of each view follows the convention of stage directions, so that the Right view looks at the scene *from* the right. Together, these six views are known as the *orthogonal views,* because they squarely face the planes of the home grid (**Figure 2.7**).

If you rotate an orthogonal view so that it faces the home grid from a nonperpendicular angle, it becomes known as a *User view* (**Figure 2.8**). Other views that can be rotated to different angles include the *Perspective, Camera,* and *Light* views.

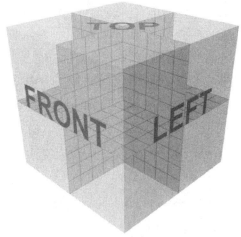

Figure 2.7 The orthogonal views face the origin from six fixed directions to help you keep track of your orientation in space.

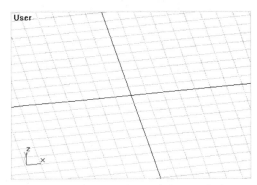

Figure 2.8 Rotating an orthogonal view results in a User view, which is simply a custom view.

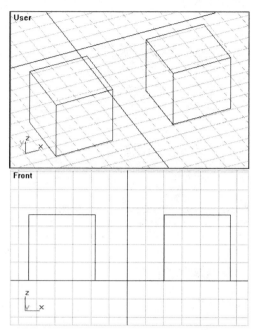

Figure 2.9 Two identical cubes appear true to size in these two types of axonometric views. Parallel lines remain parallel as they recede.

Both User views and orthogonal views are called *axonometric* views because they use parallel projection to draw the scene. This affects the appearance of objects in two important ways. First, objects always appear true to size no matter how far away they are from the viewer. Second, parallel lines (including parallel edges of objects) always appear to be parallel no matter how far they project into space (**Figure 2.9**).

In contrast to axonometric views, *perspective views* use perspective projection to draw the scene. Objects in perspective views appear to get smaller as they recede in the distance, and parallel lines appear to converge. Views that use perspective projection include the Perspective, Camera, and Light views (**Figure 2.10**).

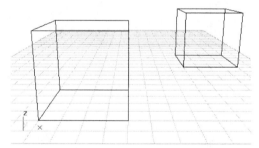

Figure 2.10 The same cubes in the perspective views appear to get smaller as they recede. Parallel sides and parallel grid lines appear to converge.

LOOKING AROUND

Using Viewports

If you want to change views in a viewport, you must first make it the active viewport. When a viewport is activated, the boundary around it turns white. Only one viewport can be active at a time.

The viewport label also gives you access to a drop-down menu that you can use to choose commands for controlling the viewport.

To activate a viewport:

◆ Right-click in the viewport.

The boundary of the viewport turns white, indicating that the viewport has been activated (**Figure 2.11**).

✔ Tips

■ Technically, you can left-click to select a viewport, but left-clicking can cause you to also select or deselect objects unintentionally. Right-clicking is a better habit to develop.

■ Each viewport label also functions as a menu.

■ To toggle the display of the grid, choose Show Grid in the right-click viewport menu, or press G on your keyboard.

To use a viewport menu:

1. Right-click the viewport label to open the menu (**Figure 2.12**).

2. Left-click to select a menu item.

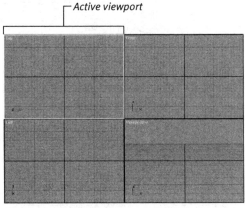

Active viewport

Figure 2.11 Clicking a viewport activates it. Here, the Top viewport is active, as indicated by its white border.

Figure 2.12 Open a viewport menu to select a view.

Table 2.1

View-Change Keyboard Shortcuts	
KEY	VIEW
F	Front view
K	Back view
R	Right view
L	Left view
T	Top view
B	Bottom view
P	Perspective view
U	User view
C	Camera view
$	Light view
G	Grid view
E	Track view
W	Minimize/Maximize view
D	Disable/Enable view
Shift-Z	Undo view change
Shift-A	Redo view change

Selecting Objects: A Preview

When learning to manipulate views as described in this chapter, you may need to select an object. That topic is covered in detail in the next chapter, but the basics are very simple. First, you open a file that has objects in it—for instance, a tutorial file or one of the *3D Studio MAX 3: Visual QuickStart* files downloaded from the Web. Click the Select Object tool on the Main Toolbar, as shown in **Figure 1.4** in the previous chapter. Then click the object you want to select. To deselect an object, just click somewhere else in the scene—someplace that doesn't have any objects.

To change a view:

1. Open the viewport menu by right-clicking the viewport label.

2. Choose Views > [view name].
   The view changes.

✔ Tip

■ To undo a view change, choose Views > Undo from the menu bar or press Shift + Z. To redo a view change, choose Views > Redo or press Shift + A.

Changing a view with keyboard shortcuts

For convenience, all of the view-change commands have keyboard shortcuts, summarized in **Table 2.1**. Most shortcuts use the first letter of the name of the view, so memorizing them is very easy.

To change a view with keyboard shortcuts:

1. Activate the view you want to change.

2. Type the shortcut key for the desired view.

✔ Tip

■ If you type *E* to display a Track View and no amount of typing can change the view back, you must change the Track View in the Layout panel, as described in the next section.

USING VIEWPORTS

Changing the Viewport Layout

3D Studio MAX 3 initially opens with four equal viewports showing the Top, Front, Left, and Perspective views. The proportion of the viewports and combination of the views they display is called the *viewport layout*. You can change the layout in the Viewport Configuration dialog box.

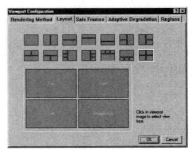

Figure 2.13 The layout panel of the Viewport Configuration dialog box.

To change the viewport layout:

1. Use any viewport menu to choose Configure.

   The Viewport Configuration dialog box appears.

2. Click the Layout tab.

   The Layout panel appears (**Figure 2.13**).

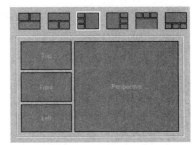

Figure 2.14 When you select a layout from the 14 choices, it fills the preview area of the panel.

3. Select a layout from the 14 choices at the top of the panel.

   A diagram that previews the new layout appears in the lower part of the panel (**Figure 2.14**).

4. Click the diagram, if necessary.

   If you want to change the view in any of the viewports, click a viewport in the diagram and then select a view from the menu (**Figure 2.15**).

5. Select a view, if necessary.

   The diagram updates to reflect the view change.

Figure 2.15 Click the preview diagram to open a pop-up menu where you select a view for each viewport.

6. Click OK.

   The new layout appears (**Figure 2.16**).

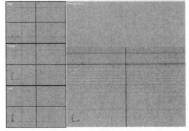

Figure 2.16 The new layout appears in the viewport.

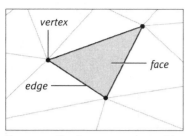

Figure 2.17 The three components of the mesh that represent the surface of a 3D object are faces, vertices, and edges.

Figure 2.18 An object displayed in smooth mode.

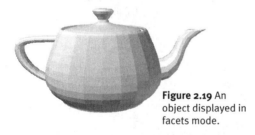

Figure 2.19 An object displayed in facets mode.

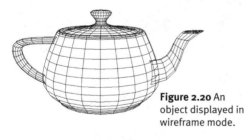

Figure 2.20 An object displayed in wireframe mode.

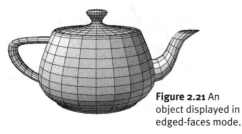

Figure 2.21 An object displayed in edged-faces mode.

Choosing a Display Mode

Another factor that affects the appearance of objects is the level of rendering, also known as the *viewport display mode*. *Rendering* is simply the process of drawing an image of a scene to the screen. In MAX, there are two methods of rendering: using the fast, interactive viewport renderer and using the slower, high-resolution scanline renderer. The renderer that affects viewport display modes is the interactive viewport renderer.

Three-dimensional graphics programs can represent the surface of an object as a web of continuous polygons called a *mesh*. The polygons that make up the mesh surface are called *faces*. The faces are triangular surfaces made up of three *vertices* and three *edges* that connect them (**Figure 2.17**). Depending on the level of resolution that you choose, viewports can display the vertex, edge, and face structure of a mesh in different ways:

◆ Smooth display modes use the highest level of resolution. They show light falling across the faces of a mesh as if it were a smooth surface. They can also display materials, the surface textures applied to the outside of objects (**Figure 2.18**).

◆ Facets display modes use the next highest level of resolution. They show light falling across the faces of a mesh as if each one were the facet of a gem. They can also display materials (**Figure 2.19**).

◆ Wireframe display modes use a low level of resolution that delineates faces by tracing their edges only. They do not display materials (**Figure 2.20**).

◆ Edged-faces modes add edge rendering to either smooth or facets display modes (**Figure 2.21**).

◆ Bounding-box display modes use the lowest level of resolution. Bounding boxes display objects as the edges of a box that is just big enough to enclose the object (**Figure 2.22**).

To change the display mode:

1. Open the viewport menu.

2. Choose a display mode from the menu (**Figure 2.23**).

   Objects in the viewport change to the new mode of display (**Figure 2.24**).

✔ Tips

■ You can set up keyboard shortcuts to toggle display modes. Look in Customize Preferences > Keyboard and check out the shortcut commands for Edged Faces, Shade Selected, and Wireframe toggle.

■ Vertex display can be turned on by checking Vertex Ticks in the Display Properties rollout of the Display panel (**Figure 2.25**).

■ Press the number 1 on your keyboard if at any time you need the program to redraw the interface.

Figure 2.22 An object displayed in bounding-box mode.

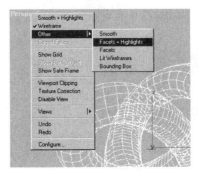

Figure 2.23 Choosing a display mode from the viewport menu.

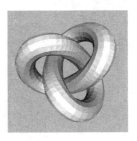

Figure 2.24 Objects change to the new mode of display.

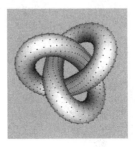

Figure 2.25 An object in smooth mode with Vertex Ticks turned on.

Figure 2.26 Viewport Window Controls for navigating axonometric views.

Figure 2.27 Viewport Window Controls for navigating Perspective views.

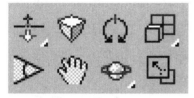

Figure 2.28 Camera Viewport Controls allow you to manipulate cameras and navigate camera views.

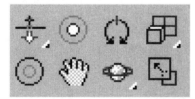

Figure 2.29 Light Viewport Controls allow you to manipulate spotlights, directional lights, and navigate their views.

Navigating with Views

Viewport navigation buttons allow you to look around a scene by manipulating the viewports. Each of the three sets of viewport navigation buttons appears automatically to match the view in the active viewport:

◆ Viewport Window Controls allow you to navigate axonometric views, including Front, Back, Left, Right, Top, Bottom, and User views (**Figure 2.26**). In Perspective views, the controls are nearly identical; the Region Zoom button changes to Field-of-View control (**Figure 2.27**).

◆ Camera Viewport Controls manipulate Cameras and Camera views. They are similar to the controls for Perspective views (**Figure 2.28**).

◆ Light Viewport Controls are used for manipulating spotlights and directional lights as well as the views seen from those lights. They are similar to the controls for Camera views (**Figure 2.29**).

Table 2.2 outlines the function of each viewport control button. *(See Chapter 10, "Cameras," and Chapter 11, "Lights," for more information about the controls for Light and Camera viewports.)*

Table 2.2

Viewport Window Controls		
BUTTON	NAME	DESCRIPTION
🔍	Zoom	Zooms in to or out from the viewport.
	Zoom All	Zooms in to or out from all viewports.
	Zoom Extents	Centers all objects in the viewport.
	Zoom Extents Selected	Centers selected objects in the viewport.
	Zoom Extents All	Centers all objects in all viewports.
	Zoom Extents All Selected	Centers selected objects in all viewports.
	Field-of-View	Changes the angle of the perspective view. Changes to the Region Zoom button when an axonometric view is active.
	Region Zoom	Enlarges selected area to fill the viewport. Changes to the Field-of-View button when a Perspective view is active.
	Pan	Moves the view parallel to the view plane.
	Arc Rotate	Rotates the view around its current center.
	Arc Rotate Selected	Rotates the view around selected objects.
	Arc Rotate Subobject	Rotates the view around selected sub-objects.
	Min/Max Toggle	Toggles between the viewport layout and a full screen display of the active view.

NAVIGATING WITH VIEWS

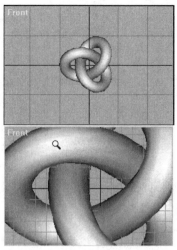

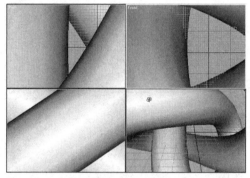

Figure 2.30 Dragging the Zoom tool increases or decreases the viewport magnification.

Figure 2.31 Zoom All magnifies all four viewports at once.

Viewport Names

For convenience, this book refers to viewports by the name of the view that they currently display. For example, the Perspective viewport is the viewport that currently displays the Perspective view, and the Front viewport is the viewport that displays the Front view. Properly speaking, however, all viewports are simply viewports, which can display any view that you choose.

Zooming a Viewport

The most common way that MAX users navigate a viewport is by zooming in to get closer to detail or zooming out to look at the big picture of a scene. MAX provides several ways to zoom viewports, giving you the flexibility you need to work efficiently in the views.

To zoom a viewport:

1. Click the Zoom tool.
   The cursor changes to a Zoom cursor.

2. Drag up and down in any viewport.
   The viewport zooms in and out around the center of the view (**Figure 2.30**).

✔ Tips

- To zoom in and out around the cursor, press the bracket keys, [and] (you can also use the IntelliMouse wheel to zoom). Zooming around a cursor can be set as a program preference in the Viewports panel of the Preference Settings rollout.

- To zoom all four viewports at once, use the Zoom All tool (**Figure 2.31**).

ZOOMING A VIEWPORT

To zoom in on an object in a scene:

1. [icon] Select an object (**Figure 2.32**).

2. [icon] Click Zoom Extents Selected.

   The active viewport zooms up to the selected object (**Figure 2.33**).

✔ Tip

■ To zoom all of the viewports so the selected object fills the viewport, open the [icon] Zoom Extents All flyout and choose [icon] Zoom Extents All Selected.

When you zoom in on an object in a complex scene, it may be difficult to see and work with the object because of other background or overlapping objects. In that case, isolate the object temporarily while you work with it.

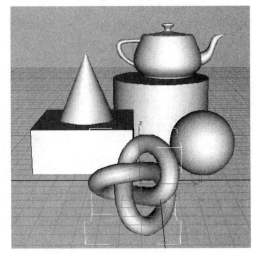

Figure 2.32 You can select an object in a scene and then zoom in on it.

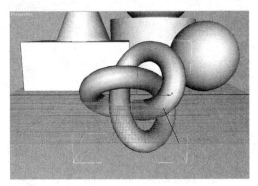

Figure 2.33 After you select an object in the scene, click Zoom Extents Selected to zoom in so that the object fills the view.

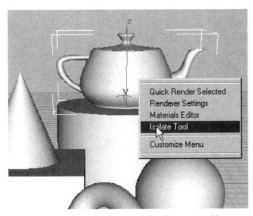

Figure 2.34 You find the Isolate Tool command by opening an object's menu: hold down the Ctrl key while you right-click the object.

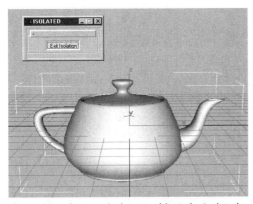

Figure 2.35 When you isolate an object, the Isolated floater appears where you can exit isolation mode.

To isolate an object:

1. Select an object.

2. Ctrl + right-click the object to open its menu, and then choose Isolate Tool (**Figure 2.34**).

   The object becomes isolated and the Isolated floater appears in the viewport (**Figure 2.35**).

3. When you have finished with operations that require the object to be isolated, choose Exit Isolation from the Isolated floater.

✔ Tip

■ You can also select an object and then click Isolate on the Modeling toolbar.

Zooming in on a scene

If a scene is only partly visible in a viewport, you can zoom in on the scene *and* fit it in the viewport in a single move.

To zoom in on a scene:

1. Open a file with multiple objects displayed in a scene, but not centered in the viewport (**Figure 2.36**).

2. ▣ Choose Zoom Extents from the Zoom Extents Selected flyout.

   The display is redrawn so that the whole scene fits in the viewport (**Figure 2.37**).

✔ Tips

- ▦ To fit the scene in all four viewports, click Zoom Extents All.

- To center a viewport around the cursor, type *I*.

To zoom a region:

1. ▣ Click the Region Zoom tool.

2. Drag a region in any axonometric viewport (**Figure 2.38**).

3. When you release the mouse button, the viewport zooms in on the selected region (**Figure 2.39**).

✔ Tip

- The Region Zoom tool does not appear in the Perspective viewport controls. To use Region Zoom in a Perspective view, change the Perspective view to a User view by pressing U. After you are finished, press P to restore the Perspective view.

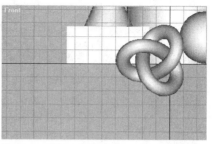

Figure 2.36 Here, objects in a scene do not fit neatly in the viewports.

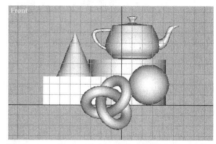

Figure 2.37 Zoom Extents makes the scene fit in the active viewport.

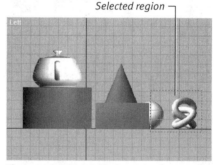

Selected region

Figure 2.38 Drag to select a region for zooming in an axonometric view.

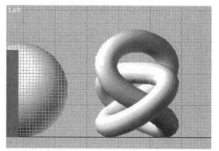

Figure 2.39 The result of zooming the region.

Figure 2.40 The Perspective viewport before using the Field-of-View tool.

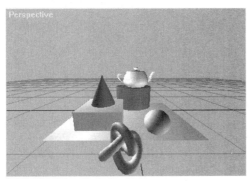

Figure 2.41 After using the Field-of-View tool, the viewport display changes magnification and perspective.

Changing the Field of View

The Field-of-View tool lets you zoom and change perspective in a single move. It works only in the Perspective and Camera viewports.

To change the field of view:

1. Activate a Perspective viewport (**Figure 2.40**).

2. ▷ Click the Field-of-View tool.

3. ▷ Drag the Field-of-View cursor up or down in the Perspective viewport.

   The viewport changes magnification and perspective (**Figure 2.41**).

✔ Tip

■ To undo a viewport change, choose Views > Undo or press Shift + Z. To redo a viewport change, choose Views > Redo or press Shift + A.

Panning and Rotating a Viewport

Besides zooming, the most common way MAX users manipulate the viewport is by moving it from side to side, or *panning* the viewport.

You can also rotate a viewport to improve the view of a scene.

To pan a viewport:

1. 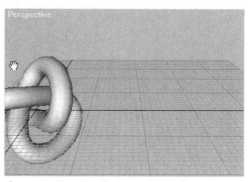 Click the Pan tool.

2. Drag the pan cursor across any viewport.

   The viewport moves across the scene (**Figure 2.42**).

✔ Tip

- To zoom and pan at faster speeds, hold down the Ctrl key while using these tools.

- The IntelliMouse wheel zooms the viewport when you are in Pan mode.

- Holding down the Alt key in Pan mode switches to Arc Rotate.

Figure 2.42 Dragging the hand-shaped Pan tool moves the viewport across a scene.

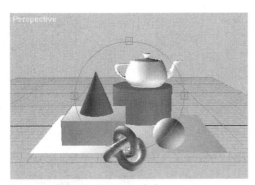

Figure 2.43 The Arc Rotate tool places a green navigation circle in the viewport.

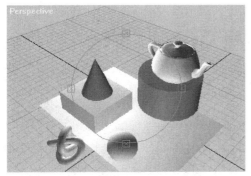

Figure 2.44 Rotate the viewport by dragging in the circle.

Figure 2.45 Rotating the viewport by dragging around the circle.

To rotate a viewport:

1. Click the Arc Rotate tool.

   A green circle appears in the active viewport. It has four square handles positioned around the circle (**Figure 2.43**).

2. Drag inside the circle.

   The view rotates around the object in a motion similar to a track ball (**Figure 2.44**).

3. Drag the perimeter of the circle.

   The view rotates parallel to the screen, like a disk spinning upon a platter (**Figure 2.45**).

✔ Tips

- Drag the handles of the arc-rotate circle to rotate the view vertically or horizontally.

- Rotating an orthogonal view changes that view to a User view.

- The Arc Rotate Selected tool, found in the Arc Rotate flyout, rotates a view around a selected object. This is often the best rotation tool to use.

- Pressing Ctrl speeds up navigation in axonometric views. Pressing Alt slows down navigation in all views.

- Temporarily switch to Arc Rotate from any tool by pressing Alt while clicking the middle mouse button.

- Temporarily switch to Arc Rotate from Pan by pressing Alt while clicking the left mouse button.

- Press V on the keyboard to enable the Arc Rotate tool.

Maximizing a Viewport

When you want to see your scene on a large scale, you should maximize the viewport rather than zooming. The active viewport fills the screen; the other viewports disappear.

To maximize a viewport:

1. ▦ Click the Min/Max toggle button.

    The active viewport enlarges to fill the display area (**Figure 2.46**).

2. ▦ Click the Min/Max toggle again.

    The original viewport layout is redrawn (**Figure 2.47**).

✔ Tip

■ The keyboard shortcut for the Min/Max toggle is W.

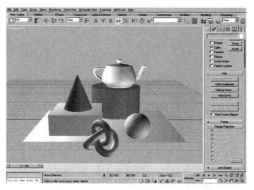

Figure 2.46 Clicking the Min/Max tool enlarges the viewport to fit the entire display area.

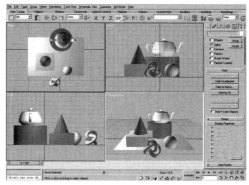

Figure 2.47 Clicking the Min/Max tool a second time returns the viewports to the previous layout.

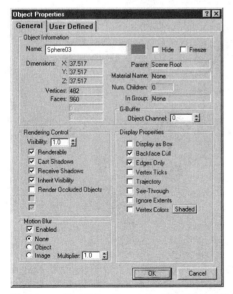

Displaying Objects

In this chapter, you have learned how to control the display of objects using the right-click viewport menu and the viewport controls. But the mother lode of display commands is yet to come. The Display command panel has six rollouts that affect surface color, visibility, selection, complexity, and link display. This is where you show or hide hidden parts of a scene such as the trajectory of an animated object or the edges that divide coplanar faces. This is also where you can hide and unhide objects categorically or by selecting them individually (**Figure 2.48**).

For your convenience, most of the commands that are listed in the Display panel can also be found in a floating dialog box called the Display Floater. Because this dialog box is modeless, you can control display without switching command modes to open the Display panel. You access the Display Floater by choosing Tools > Display Floater.

Finally, the Object Properties dialog box allows you to affect the display of a selected object only. It includes the same Display Properties group that is found in the Display panel, plus commands for hiding, freezing, and rendering (**Figure 2.49**). It also includes important information about the object such as its name, color, dimensions, and the number of vertices and faces of an object.

Figure 2.48 Use the Display command panel's rollouts to hide and show scenes and objects.

Figure 2.49 The Object Properties dialog box allows you to affect the display of a selected object.

DISPLAYING OBJECTS

Hiding Objects

Hiding objects helps you to manage complex scenes by simplifying the viewport display and speeding up redraw time. Hidden objects disappear from view and cannot be selected until they are unhidden.

To hide an object:

1.  Select an object (**Figure 2.50**).

2. Click the tab of the Display command panel.

   The Display command panel appears (**Figure 2.51**).

3. In the Hide rollout, click Hide Selected.

   The selected object disappears (**Figure 2.52**).

To unhide an object:

◆ In the Hide rollout, click Unhide All.

   The hidden object reappears.

✔ Tips

■ Hide Unselected hides unselected objects.

■ Hide by Name brings up a list of objects to hide (**Figure 2.53**).

■ Hide by Hit allows you to hide objects by clicking them.

■ Unhide by Name brings up a list of hidden objects to unhide.

■ The Hide by Category rollout allows you to hide objects according to object type.

■ MAX hides frozen objects only if you check Hide Frozen Objects in the Hide rollout.

■ Press 5 on your keyboard to open the Unhide by Name dialog box.

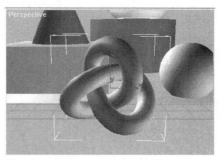

Figure 2.50 Select an object for hiding.

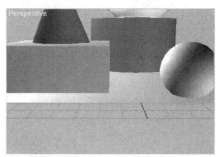

Figure 2.51 The Display command panel contains commands that affect object display, including hiding and freezing.

Figure 2.52 Clicking Hide Selected causes the object to disappear.

Figure 2.53 The Hide Objects dialog box allows you to hide objects by name.

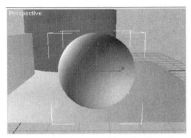

Figure 2.54 Select an object for freezing.

Figure 2.55 The Freeze rollout allows you to freeze objects so they cannot be selected.

Figure 2.56 The object turns dark gray when it freezes.

Figure 2.57 The Freeze Objects dialog box allows you to freeze objects on the list.

Freezing Objects

Freezing prevents objects from being manipulated while you're still able to view them on the screen. When objects are frozen, they turn dark gray and cannot be selected until they are unfrozen.

To freeze an object:

1. Select an object (**Figure 2.54**).

2. Open the Display command panel.

3. Open the Freeze rollout.
   The Freeze rollout appears (**Figure 2.55**).

4. In the Freeze rollout, click Freeze Selected.
   The object freezes (**Figure 2.56**).

To unfreeze an object:

◆ In the Freeze rollout, click Unfreeze All.
   The object becomes unfrozen.

✔ Tips

■ Freeze Unselected freezes all visible objects that are unselected and unfrozen.

■ Freeze by Name brings up a list of unhidden and unfrozen objects to freeze (**Figure 2.57**).

■ Freeze by Hit allows you to freeze objects by clicking on them.

■ Unfreeze by Name brings up a list of frozen objects to unfreeze

■ Unfreeze by Hit allows you to unfreeze objects by clicking them.

■ Press 6 on your keyboard to freeze a selection of objects.

■ Press 7 on your keyboard to unfreeze all frozen objects.

FREEZING OBJECTS

Using Grids

By illustrating the position and orientation of the world coordinate system, the home grid provides you with a 3D system of reference for navigating space (**Figure 2.58**). The home grid also serves as a construction plane for objects. This means that objects are oriented to sit on the visible grid of the viewport in which they are created. Objects that are created in different views may be oriented at 90° or 180° angles to each other because different views display different planes of the home grid (**Figure 2.59**).

What if you want to build objects on a plane that's not on the home grid? A *grid object* allows you to construct a grid anywhere in space that can be activated and used as a construction plane (**Figure 2.60**).

Another option is the *AutoGrid* feature, which creates a temporary construction plane on the surface of any object (**Figure 2.61**).

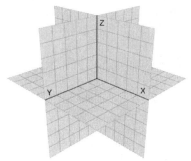

Figure 2.58 The home grid provides a 3D system of reference for navigating space.

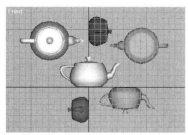

Figure 2.59 Objects built on the home grid can be constructed at right angles to each other.

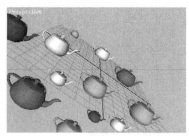

Figure 2.60 Objects built on a grid object can be constructed anywhere in space.

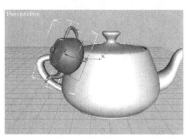

Figure 2.61 Objects built on AutoGrids can be constructed on the surfaces of other objects.

USING GRIDS

Figure 2.62 You define grid objects in the Grid Object creation rollout.

To create a grid object:

1. Access the Helpers Toolbar.

2. ▦ Click the Grid Object tool.

   The Grid Object creation rollout appears (**Figure 2.62**).

3. In the Front viewport, drag diagonally to create a grid of any size (**Figure 2.63**).

   The grid is given a default name.

   The *XY* plane of the grid aligns to the home grid of the Front viewport and appears to stand vertically in the Perspective viewport. Although the grid looks small, the grid object is actually infinite in size (**Figure 2.64**).

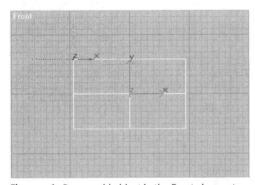

Figure 2.63 Drag a grid object in the Front viewport.

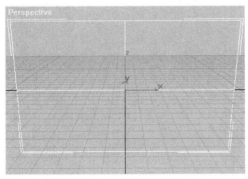

Figure 2.64 The grid object as it appears in the Perspective viewport.

To activate a grid object:

◆ Choose Views > Grids > Activate Grid Object.

The grid object becomes active and grid line subdivisions appear. The home grid becomes inactive and grid line subdivisions disappear (**Figure 2.65**).

To activate the home grid:

◆ Choose Views > Grids > Activate Home Grid.

The home grid becomes active and the grid object becomes inactive. The grid line subdivisions of the grid object disappear.

✔ Tip

■ You can also activate a grid by right-clicking in a viewport background and selecting the Activate Grid menu (**Figure 2.66**).

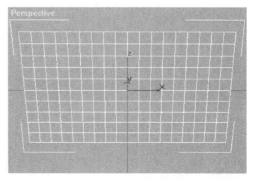

Figure 2.65 The activated grid object displays grid-line subdivisions.

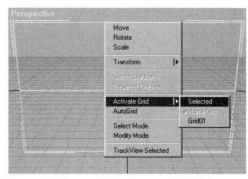

Figure 2.66 You can also activate a grid with the viewport menu.

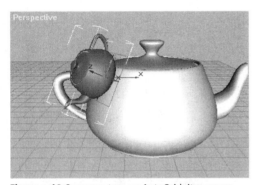

Figure 2.67 The AutoGrid command is found in the viewport menu.

Figure 2.68 Once you turn on AutoGrid, it appears as you move creation-tool cursors over object surfaces or another grid.

To turn on AutoGrid:

1. Right-click on a viewport background (**Figure 2.67**).

2. Select AutoGrid.

   An AutoGrid appears fleetingly during object creation whenever the cursor passes over the surface of an object or another grid (**Figure 2.68**).

✔ Tip

■ Once you have AutoGrid turned on, you can create a permanent grid object instead of an AutoGrid by holding down the Alt key while creating an object.

Customizing the Grid Units

The grid displays grid lines at intervals of 10 inches by default, with major (thicker) lines every tenth line. You can change this *grid spacing* to different size intervals and units of measurement. You can also turn off the grid display if you find the grid lines distracting.

What about units of measurement? By default, MAX uses generic system units equal to one inch. If you are building a highway, however, it makes more sense to measure distance in kilometers or miles. This is why MAX allows you to set specific units of measure, including metric, U.S. Standard, and custom units.

To set units of measurement:

1. Choose Customize > Units Setup.

   The Units Setup dialog box appears (**Figure 2.69**).

2. Choose a system of measurement: Metric, U.S. Standard, Custom, or Generic Units.

3. Choose a scale from the drop-down menu for that system, if applicable (**Figure 2.70**).

4. If you are creating a custom unit of measurement, assign it a name and size.

5. Click OK.

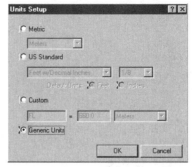

Figure 2.69 The Units Setup dialog box is accessed from the Customize menu.

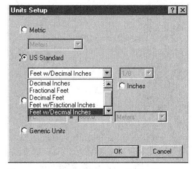

Figure 2.70 Choosing a scale for the system of measurement.

Figure 2.71 You can make grid spacing settings in the Grid and Snap Settings dialog box.

Figure 2.72 The Home Grid panel of the Grid and Snap Settings dialog box.

Figure 2.73 You can toggle on or off the grid display with the viewport menu.

To set grid spacing:

1. Choose Customize > Grid and Snap Settings.

   The Grid and Snap Settings dialog box appears (**Figure 2.71**).

2. Click the Home Grid tab (**Figure 2.72**).

3. In the Grid Spacing field, enter the size of the interval you want to have between grid lines.

4. Close the dialog box.

To toggle the grid display:

1. Open any viewport menu (**Figure 2.73**).

2. Select Show Grid.

   The grid display turns off if the grid is turned on, or on if it the grid is turned off (**Figure 2.74**).

3. Select Show Grid again to reverse the setting.

![The viewport after the grid display has been turned off, showing a wireframe building.](Camera01)

Figure 2.74 The viewport after the grid display has been turned off.

CUSTOMIZING THE GRID UNITS

Using Snaps

Once grid units and grid spacing have been established, you can set *snaps*. Snaps help you build objects to exact specifications by causing the cursor to jump to the grid spacing intervals. This comes in handy for object creation, as well as for positioning, rotating, and scaling objects.

To turn on snaps for object creation:

◆   Click 3D Snap.

The 3D snap option is enabled. The cursor snaps to grid intersections and a blue snap icon appears at the tip of the cursor (**Figure 2.75**).

During object creation, the cursor jumps in space along the *Z* axis of the grid to the distance set by the grid spacing interval. You can't position the cursor at any point in between when the snap option is turned on.

To change snap settings:

1. Choose Views > Snaps to Right-click on the 3D Snap tool.

The Grid and Snap Settings dialog box appears (**Figure 2.76**).

2. In the Snaps panel, check the boxes for the snap targets you want to use.

3. Close the Grids and Snap Settings dialog box.

The blue snap icon changes to match the icons next to the snap targets as it snaps to those targets in the scene (**Figure 2.77**).

✔ Tips

■ During object creation, the base of the object snaps to the grid and the height of the object snaps along its vertical axis at intervals equal to the grid spacing.

■ Press S on your keyboard to toggle the snap button on and off.

Figure 2.75 The blue snap icon appears at the tip of the cursor when it snaps to a target. Here, the cursor jumps to grid intersections.

Figure 2.76 The Grid and Snap Settings dialog box allows you to choose snap targets.

Figure 2.77 The blue snap icon changes to indicate the type of target to which it is snapping.

CREATING OBJECTS

Still life of object primitives, Michele Matossian.

Everything in nature can be represented as geometric forms. As the French painter Paul Cézanne once wrote, "Interpret nature in terms of the cylinder, the sphere, the cone...." He also is reported to have said, "The study of art is badly conducted. Today a painter must learn everything for himself, for there are no longer any but very bad schools, where one becomes warped, where one learns nothing. One must first of all study geometric forms: the cone, the cube, the cylinder, the sphere. When one knows how to render these things in their form and their planes, one ought to know how to paint."

Today, 3D artists use geometric forms called objects to create and animate entire worlds. Starting with a foundation of "the cone, the cube, the cylinder, the sphere," you can combine and manipulate basic objects to create highly complex and realistic scenes.

This chapter covers how to create objects with just a few clicks of the mouse. In addition to 3D objects such as cubes and spheres, you will learn to create flat shapes and linear objects such as circles, text, and arcs. By the end of the chapter, you will have learned to render images.

About Creating Objects

The easiest way to create objects is to start with simple predefined forms called *primitives*. Primitives in 3D Studio MAX 3 include the Sphere, Box, Cone, Tube, Torus, and others.

You define the dimensions of primitives by numerical *creation parameters*. You set creation parameters either interactively by dragging the shape in the viewport or by entering them in a command panel.

As you create each object, a small set of axes called an *axis tripod* appears at the object's pivot point. It indicates the pivot point of the object and the origin of the object's local coordinate system (**Figure 3.1**). Some objects, such as spheres, have a pivot point in the middle by default. Some, such as cones and boxes, have the pivot point on their flat bases by default.

This chapter covers the two most basic types of geometric objects that MAX can create: *mesh objects,* which are three-dimensional forms, and *spline objects,* which are essentially two-dimensional shapes that you can manipulate as part of a three-dimensional scene.

Once you know how to create objects, you need to know how to delete them. It's a very simple matter of selecting the object and clearing it. *For more selecting techniques, see Chapter 4, "Selecting Objects."*

To delete an object:

1. Select an object with the Select Object tool from the Main Toolbar.

2. Press the Delete key.

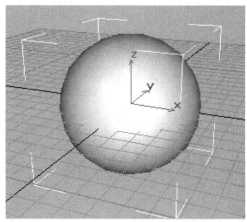

Figure 3.1 The axis tripod is located at the object's origin.

The Utah Teapot

Students often ask me why the Teapot is included among the standard primitives. After all, how many forms are based on teapots? Well, back in 1970s at the University of Utah, Martin Newell created an elegant wireframe model of a teapot. His colleague, James Blinn, used the teapot to experiment with different methods of surface rendering. Soon, images of reflecting teapots were appearing everywhere. Eventually, the "Utah Teapot" became so identified with 3D graphics that it became immortalized as a symbol for the field.

3D Studio MAX Object Types

MAX offers many types of objects. Basically, everything that you create is an object, and all objects can be affected by commands. Some types of objects can be rendered to an image as part of the scene. Other objects cannot be rendered; instead, they assist you in modeling, animating, or rendering the rest of the scene.

- Standard primitives, basic geometric mesh objects.

- Extended primitives, more complex geometric mesh objects.

- Splines, open, and closed linear objects.

- Patches, Bézier spline curves, and surfaces.

- NURBS, nonuniform rational b-spline curves and surfaces used mostly to create organic forms.

- Compound objects, combinations of two or more objects.

- Particle systems, numerous small objects, and the nonrendering apparatus that emits them.

- Dynamics objects, mesh objects that interact with the motion of other objects.

- Architectural objects, predefined architectural forms, such as doors and windows.

Nonrendering objects include:

- Lights, nonrenderable objects that shine light into scenes.

- Cameras, nonrenderable objects that define a view of the scene.

- Helpers, nonrenderable objects that help create, measure, animate, and link other objects.

- Space warps, nonrenderable objects that deform other objects within a defined field.

- Bones, a hierarchical system of linked objects used to animate other objects.

Creating Mesh Objects

Mesh objects, three-dimensional geometric forms, are defined by a triangular mesh surface. MAX provides two types of primitives for creating mesh objects:

◆ *Standard primitives* create the basic geometric forms, such as a Sphere, Box, Torus (the doughnut-shaped object), and Cone (**Figure 3.2**).

◆ *Extended primitives* create more specialized forms, such as the C-Ext, the Torus Knot, and the Hedra (**Figure 3.3**).

The Create command panel contains the commands for creating standard primitives and extended primitives, in the Geometry category of the panel. Shortcuts to the commands are on the Objects Toolbar (**Figure 3.4**).

There are two ways to produce a simple mesh object: by the keyboard or by a single click-and-drag sequence. The dragging method gives you direct visual feedback as you create the object; it's probably the best method for beginners. The section "Creating Objects with the Keyboard," later in this chapter, covers the alternate method, which is more precise.

Figure 3.2 MAX uses ten standard primitives to make basic geometric forms.

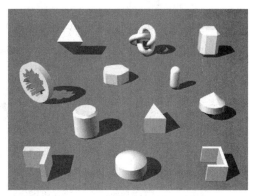

Figure 3.3 Twelve extended primitives make more specialized forms.

Figure 3.4 The Objects Toolbar provides buttons for quickly selecting mesh primitive tools.

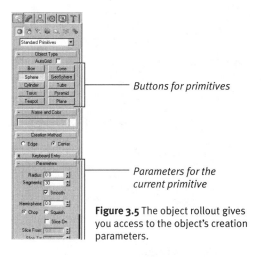

— *Buttons for primitives*

— *Parameters for the current primitive*

Figure 3.5 The object rollout gives you access to the object's creation parameters.

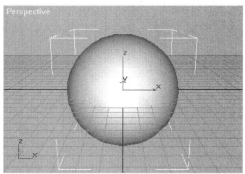

Figure 3.6 The quickest way to create a mesh object is to click and drag.

Creating Objects in a View

Technically, you can create mesh objects in any view, but I recommend specific views in the steps. For instance, the Perspective view usually gives the best visual feedback for creating most mesh objects. On the other hand, the Top view works best for creating flat spline shapes. If you do decide to work in a different view, develop the habit of creating all the objects in the same view because the view determines the orientation of an object's axis.

To create a mesh object by dragging:

1. On the Objects Toolbar, click the button for the object you want to create.

The Standard Primitives menu appears in the Create command panel, with the rollouts for the tool you selected (**Figure 3.5**).

2. In the rollout, set the creation method you prefer, or just accept the default.

Different tools offer different choices for creating objects. For instance, you can choose to create either a box or a cube with the Box tool and choose to drag a cone's base either from the center or from the edge.

3. In the Perspective viewport, drag to create the object or its base; release the mouse button when the object or base is the right size (**Figure 3.6**).

4. Click to set other dimensions, if necessary.

Different objects need different numbers of clicks and drags to produce them.

5. Before you start making another object, adjust the object's parameters, if necessary.

✔ Tip

■ Move the cursor to another position in the viewport and drag again to create another object of the same type.

Adjusting the creation parameters of a mesh object

After you create an object, you can easily adjust its parameters. If the object is still selected, you can make the adjustments directly in the Create panel. If you have started creating a new object (which happens as soon as you click in a viewport again), you will need to reselect the object you want to adjust and open the Modify panel.

To adjust the creation parameters of a mesh object:

1. Change the viewport display to wireframe.

2. Change the dimensions of the selected object in the Parameters rollout by entering new values in the input fields or by dragging the spinners to the right of each field.

   If the object is no longer selected,  choose the Select Object tool in the Main Toolbar and click the object to select it. Next, click the Modify tab to open the Modify panel so that the original creation parameters appear (**Figure 3.7**). Then change the dimensions as indicated above.

3. Drag the Segments spinner(s) to change the density of the mesh surface.

   The surface of the object divides into more faces as you increase the number of segments (**Figure 3.8**). This causes the surface to appear smoother when shaded.

4. Change other parameter settings as needed. For example, to change the base alignment of a Sphere or GeoSphere so that the object sits on top of the grid, click Base to Pivot (**Figure 3.9**).

   If any of these parameters are not visible, place the cursor on a non-input area and drag the panel with the 🖑 panning hand. You can also drag the thin scroll bar just to the right of the Parameters rollout.

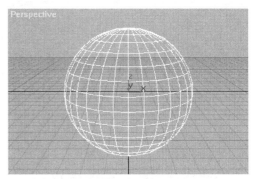

Figure 3.7 The object's original creation parameters can also be found in the Modify panel.

Figure 3.8 Increasing the number of segments increases the density of the mesh, so that the surface looks smoother.

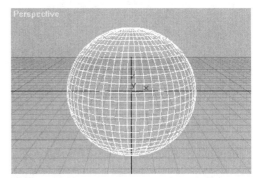

Figure 3.9 Clicking Base to Pivot makes a Sphere or GeoSphere sit on top of the grid.

CREATING MESH OBJECTS

Creating Objects with Standard Primitives

You can learn how to use all of the standard primitives by learning about the basic primitives presented in this section. Make objects from the rest of the standard primitives the same way you do the Sphere, the Box, the Cone, and the Tube. In general, you click first to set the radius or base and then click again to set the height or other dimensions as needed.

Creating a sphere

The simplest object to create is the sphere, which you create by defining its radius.

To create a sphere:

1. Click the Sphere button on the Objects Toolbar.

2. In the Perspective viewport, position the cursor where you want the center of the sphere and then drag.

3. Release the mouse button when the sphere is big enough.

4. Adjust parameters, if necessary, before creating any other objects.

Creating a box

A box takes two clicks to create; the drag builds the base of the box. Then you click to set the height.

To create a box:

1. 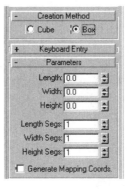 Click the Box button on the Objects Toolbar.

   The Box rollout appears (**Figure 3.10**).

2. In the Perspective viewport, drag diagonally to form the base of the box.

3. Release the mouse button to set the length and width of the box.

   The base of the box sits squarely on the grid (**Figure 3.11**).

4. Without clicking, move the cursor upward in the viewport.

5. Click to set the height (**Figure 3.12**).

6. Adjust parameters, if necessary, before creating any other objects.

✔ Tips

- To create a box that hangs below the grid plane, drag down in the viewport in step 4.

- To create a box that has a square base, hold down the Ctrl key as you drag to create the base. In this method, the first click sets the center of the base, and dragging causes the base to grow equally in all directions.

- To create a cube, choose Cube in the Creation Method rollout.

Figure 3.10 The Box rollout has parameter inputs for length, width, and height.

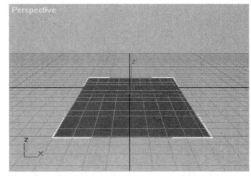

Figure 3.11 Drag to set the length and width of the box.

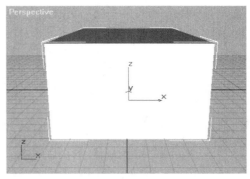

Figure 3.12 Then click to set the height.

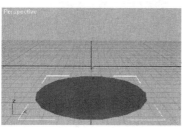

Figure 3.13
The parameters for the Cylinder primitive include dimensions and settings for making slices out of the cylinder.

Figure 3.14 Drag to make the base of the cylinder.

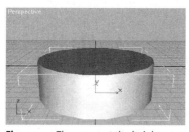

Figure 3.15 Then you set the height.

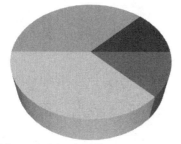

Figure 3.16 Use the Slice parameters to make separate wedges of a cylinder "pie."

Creating a cylinder

You create a cylinder with three moves: After you click the Cylinder button, the first drag sequence sets the radius of the base, and then you click to set the height.

To create a cylinder:

1. Click the Cylinder button in the Objects Toolbar.

   The Cylinder rollout appears (**Figure 3.13**).

2. In the Perspective viewport, drag the base of the cylinder.

3. Release the mouse button to set the base radius (**Figure 3.14**).

4. Without clicking, move the cursor up in the viewport.

5. Click to set the height (**Figure 3.15**).

✔ Tip

- Check the Slice On box and then set the Slice From and Slice To parameters (in degrees) to create wedges of the cylinder "pie" (**Figure 3.16**).

Creating a cone

You make a cone with three moves: you drag to set the radius of the base, click to set the height, and click again to set the radius of the top.

To create a cone:

1. Click the Cone tool on the Objects Toolbar.

   The Cone rollout appears. (**Figure 3.17**).

2. In the Perspective viewport, position the cursor where you want the center of the base and then drag the base of the cone.

   You can also draw the base from edge to edge by choosing Edge on the Creation Method rollout.

3. Release the mouse button when the base is the right size (**Figure 3.18**).

4. Without clicking, move the cursor upward in the viewport.

5. Click to set the height (**Figure 3.19**).

6. Without clicking, move the cursor downward in the viewport to establish the radius for the top.

   If you want to close up the point at the top of the cone, drag downward from the top till it closes up.

7. Click to set the radius of the top (**Figure 3.20**).

✔ Tips

- You can make the radius of the top wider than the radius of the base by dragging upward in the viewport in step 6.

- To slice the cone, choose Slice On from the Parameters rollout and adjust the values of the Slice From and Slice To parameters.

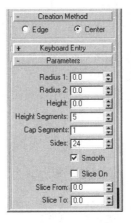

Figure 3.17 The Cone rollout has parameter inputs for height and two radii.

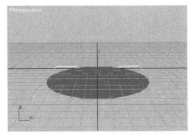

Figure 3.18 Drag to set the base radius of the cone.

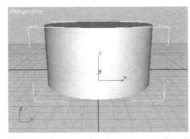

Figure 3.19 Move the cursor upward and click to set the height of the cone.

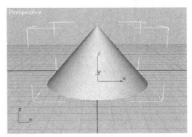

Figure 3.20 Move the cursor down and click to complete the cone.

Figure 3.21
The Tube rollout includes parameters for two radii and a height.

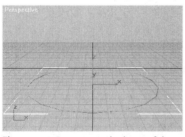

Figure 3.22 Drag to set the base of the tube.

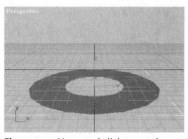

Figure 3.23 Move and click to set the second radius.

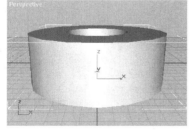

Figure 3.24 Move and click to set the height and complete a tube.

Creating a tube

A tube has two radii, one for the inner wall and one for the outer wall. The difference between them sets the thickness of the wall of the tube. After you establish the two radii, you click to set the height.

To create a tube:

1. Click the Tube button on the Objects Toolbar.

    The Tube rollout appears (**Figure 3.21**).

2. In the Perspective viewport, drag the base of the tube (**Figure 3.22**).

    By default you drag from the center of the base, but you can change the setting in the Creation Method rollout to drag from the edge.

3. Release the mouse button to set the first radius.

4. Move the mouse toward (or away from) the center of the tube.

5. Click to set the second radius (**Figure 3.23**).

6. Move the cursor upward in the viewport.

7. Click to set the height (**Figure 3.24**).

CREATING OBJECTS WITH STANDARD PRIMITIVES

Creating a teapot

One of the easiest objects to create is also the most complex. The teapot has preset proportions for a body, handle, spout, and lid. All that you need to do is drag a radius.

To create a teapot:

1. Click the Teapot button in the Objects Toolbar.

   The Teapot rollout appears (**Figure 3.25**).

2. In the Perspective viewport, drag a teapot of any size.

   The entire teapot grows outward and upward from the grid (**Figure 3.26**).

3. Release the mouse button to set the radius.

   For variations, try turning off (unchecking) the body, handle, spout, or lid in the parameters rollout (**Figure 3.27**).

✔ Tip

- Why can you see through the inside of the teapot? In order to save memory and time, mesh objects are rendered only on the outside. To render a mesh object on the inside, you must either change the surface normals or apply a two-sided material. *(For more information, see Chapter 7, "Modifying Objects," or Chapter 12, "Maps and Materials.")*

Figure 3.25 The Teapot rollout has a radius parameter input and checkboxes for including the body, handle, spout, and lid.

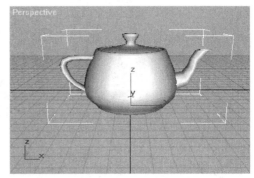

Figure 3.26 Drag to set the radius of a teapot.

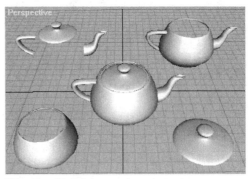

Figure 3.27 Variations on a teapot.

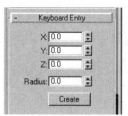

Figure 3.28 You can type exact position coordinates and dimension parameters in the keyboard-entry rollout. Here, the rollout is for a sphere.

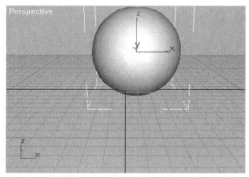

Figure 3.29 A sphere created from the keyboard with X = 10, Y = 20, Z = 30, and Radius = 40.

Creating Objects with the Keyboard

When dragging doesn't offer enough precision, create objects by specifying their locations and other settings from the keyboard. You may find that it's a more convenient method than dragging; people who type quickly often prefer to keep their hands on the keyboard.

To create a mesh object with the keyboard:

1. Activate the Perspective viewport.

2. Select an object from the Objects Toolbar.
   The corresponding rollout appears in the Create command panel.

3. Click the Keyboard Entry title bar of the object rollout (**Figure 3.28**).

4. Enter *x*, *y*, and *z* values to position the object.
   By default the coordinates are all set to zero.

5. Set any necessary dimension parameters.
   For instance, in the case of a sphere, you type the radius. For a box, you type length, width, and height.

6. Click Create.
   The object appears, in the location you specified in the coordinates (**Figure 3.29**).

✔ Tip

■ Use the Tab key to move between entry fields.

Creating a box using the keyboard-entry method

This example shows how to put into practice the general instructions in the previous task to create a box. Also try the keyboard method for creating other objects from standard primitives.

To create a box using the keyboard-entry method:

1. Activate the Perspective viewport.

2. [icon] Click the Box button on the Objects Toolbar.

3. Open the Box Keyboard Entry rollout (**Figure 3.30**).

4. Enter location coordinates.

5. Enter length, width, and height dimensions.

6. Click Create.

   A box appears in the viewport (**Figure 3.31**).

✔ Tip

■ The keyboard-entry method can be used to create a 3D bar chart by changing the *x* position and height of each successive box (**Figure 3.32**).

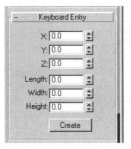

Figure 3.30 You type exact position coordinates and dimensions for a box in the Box primitive's keyboard-entry rollout.

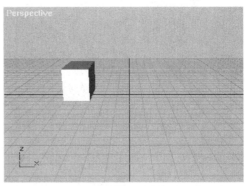

Figure 3.31 A box created from the keyboard, made with an *x* value of -40, length = 40, width = 20, and height = 25. It appears just to the left of the origin on the grid.

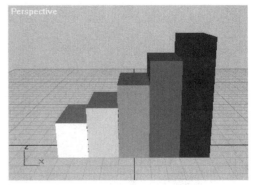

Figure 3.32 Create a bar chart easily with the keyboard-entry method.

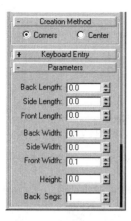

Figure 3.33 The C-Ext rollout has length and width parameters for all three sides.

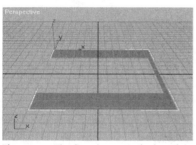

Figure 3.34 The first drag sets the lengths of the walls, which have a default thickness.

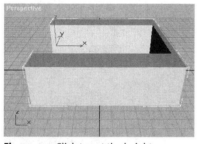

Figure 3.35 Click to set the height.

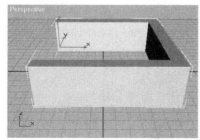

Figure 3.36 Move the cursor up and click to set the width of the walls.

Using Extended Primitives

Extended primitives are slightly more complex objects than standard primitives. Additional parameters for slicing, rounding off corners, or creating a more complex base can be set using a few more clicks of the mouse.

Creating a C-Ext

A C-Ext looks like an office cubicle. You set the thickness, or width, of the walls after you establish the length and height.

To create a C-Ext:

1. Click the C-Ext button on the Objects Toolbar.

   The C-Ext rollout appears (**Figure 3.33**).

2. In the Perspective viewport, drag diagonally to create the base of the C-Ext (**Figure 3.34**).

   You can drag from the center instead by choosing Center from the Creation Method rollout.

3. Release the mouse button to set the length of the back, side, and front of the base.

   The initial width, or thickness, of the walls is assigned by default.

4. Move the cursor up and click to set the height (**Figure 3.35**).

5. Move the cursor up and click to set the width of the walls.

   The three sides all adopt the same width (**Figure 3.36**).

✔ Tip

■ To constrain the base of the C-Ext to sides of equal length, hold down the Ctrl key as you drag the base.

Creating a Torus Knot

The Torus Knot is similar to the Torus in that it has two radii: one for the base, and one for the cross section.

To create a Torus Knot:

1. ⬡ Click the Torus Knot button in the Objects Toolbar.

   The Torus Knot rollout appears (**Figure 3.37**).

2. Activate the Top viewport and change the viewport display to Smooth + Highlights.

3. In the Top viewport, position the cursor where you want the center of the Torus Knot and then drag out from the center.

   A three-lobed knot, the default, appears in the viewport as you drag.

4. Release the mouse button to set the radius of the base (**Figure 3.38**).

5. Slowly move the cursor up or down to establish the cross-section radius.

6. Click to set the radius of the cross section (**Figure 3.39**).

✔ Tip

■ The P parameter of the Base Curve controls the number of times the Torus Knot winds around the center. Q controls the number of lobes it makes as it winds. In combination, the two parameters work together as a ratio, often creating surprising results (**Figure 3.40**).

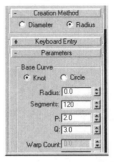

Figure 3.37 The Torus Knot rollout has inputs for the radius of the base and the radius of the cross section.

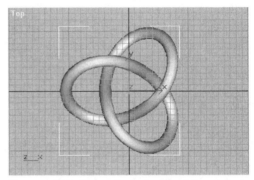

Figure 3.38 Drag to set the first radius. A three-lobed Torus appears by default.

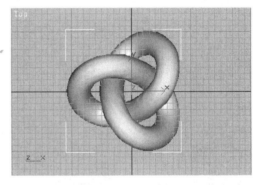

Figure 3.39 Next set the radius of the cross section.

Figure 3.40 Varying the P and Q parameters can yield surprising results. In this illustration, Segments = 2000, $P = 6$, and $Q = 18.5$.

USING EXTENDED PRIMITIVES

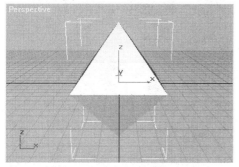

Figure 3.41 The Hedra rollout has no keyboard-entry rollout. Here you see the Hedra parameters.

Figure 3.42 The most basic parameter of a polyhedron is its radius. Here, a Hedra is being dragged into view.

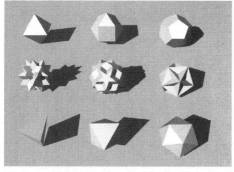

Figure 3.43 Examples of each of the families of Hedra.

Figure 3.44 A Star1 Hedra with $P = .38$ and $Q = .62$

Creating a polyhedron

A Hedra is so complicated that it does not have a keyboard-entry method. The real fun of using this object is playing with the different parameters.

To create a polyhedron:

1. Click the Hedra button on the Objects Toolbar.

   The Hedra rollout appears (**Figure 3.41**).

2. In the Perspective viewport, drag a Hedra (**Figure 3.42**).

   Make a big polyhedron to see the results of your experimentation with the Hedra settings.

3. Release the mouse button to set the radius.

4. Select a family in the parameters rollout.

   The Hedra dramatically changes form (**Figure 3.43**).

5. Drag the P and Q spinners for family parameters up and down.

   The edges of the polyhedron change position (**Figure 3.44**).

6. Change the axis-scaling parameters to make the points more or less prominent.

USING EXTENDED PRIMITIVES

Creating a ChamferBox

A ChamferBox is a box with the edges filed down. The first two clicks create the box, and then you set the chamfer, or filed edge.

To create a ChamferBox:

1. Click the ChamferBox button in the Objects Toolbar.

   The ChamferBox rollout appears (**Figure 3.45**).

2. In the Perspective viewport, drag diagonally to make the base of the ChamferBox (**Figure 3.46**).

3. Release the mouse button to set the base length and width.

4. Move the cursor and click to set the height (**Figure 3.47**).

5. Move the cursor up again and click to set the fillet, or filed edge (**Figure 3.48**).

✔ Tips

- Uncheck Smooth in the Parameters rollout to see the actual shape better.

- The ChamferBox is a useful replacement for the standard box because most real-world objects have rounded edges and corners.

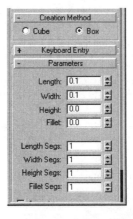

Figure 3.45
The ChamferBox rollout has length, width, and height parameters as well as fillet.

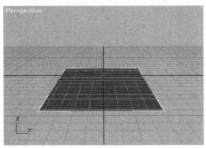

Figure 3.46 First drag to create the base.

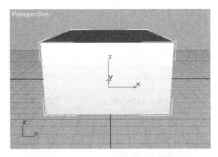

Figure 3.47 Next click to set the height.

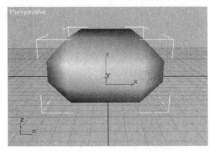

Figure 3.48 Click again to set the fillet.

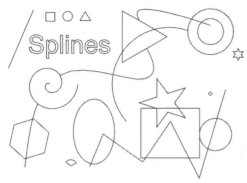

Figure 3.49 Spline objects are composed of straight and curved lines.

Figure 3.50 The Splines menu contains 11 different object types.

Figure 3.51 The Shapes Toolbar provides buttons that give you quick access to spline tools.

Creating Splines

A *spline* is a curvable line that forms open or closed shapes. Splines are composed of vertex points and line segments that connect them (**Figure 3.49**).

The term *spline* dates back to the 18th century, when shipbuilders and architects used a long, narrow, and flexible strip of wood or metal called a spline. The spline was weighted and used as an aid for drafting curved lines, such as the hull of a ship.

In 3D graphics, designers use splines to create planar objects, text, animation paths, and as the basis for creating geometry objects. Spline primitives include simple shapes like circles, rectangles, and lines. (Although splines are technically primitives, the program refers to them as *shapes* to distinguish them from three-dimensional primitives.) They also include more complex shapes such as the Helix and text.

The Splines menu is found in the Shapes branch of the Geometry category (**Figure 3.50**). Shortcuts to the Shape commands are found on the Shapes Toolbar (**Figure 3.51**).

It works best to create splines in orthogonal viewports so that you can evaluate their proportions in two dimensions. The exception is the Helix, the only spline that may be created in three dimensions.

As with mesh objects, splines can be created either by dragging or from the keyboard. The keyboard method gives you more precise control over the location and dimensions of the spline.

Finally, you adjust a spline in the same way as a mesh object, which is by using the modify panel.

To create a spline by dragging:

1. 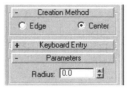 Click a spline button on the Shapes Toolbar.

   The corresponding object's rollout appears in the command panel (**Figure 3.52**).

2. In the Top viewport, position the cursor where you want to start the spline then drag to create it (**Figure 3.53**).

3. Release the mouse button when the spline is the right size.

✔ Tip

■ Where you place the cursor to start the spline depends upon which creation method is selected. For instance, you can draw circles from the edge or from the center. Use the default or click the alternate in the Creation Method rollout of the command panel.

To create a spline by keyboard entry:

1. 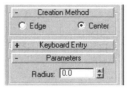 Select a spline tool from the Shapes Toolbar.

2. Activate the Top viewport.

3. Open the keyboard-entry rollout and enter *x, y,* and *z* coordinates for the location of the spline.

4. Enter any necessary dimension values (**Figure 3.54**).

5. Click Create.

   A spline appears in the Top viewport (**Figure 3.55**).

✔ Tip

■ To create more circles in different places, just change the *x, y,* or *z* parameters and click Create.

Figure 3.52 The Circle rollout has only one parameter.

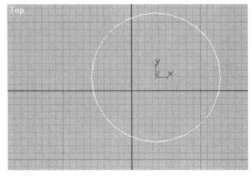

Figure 3.53 Drag a spline to set its radius.

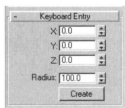

Figure 3.54 This keyboard-entry rollout allows you to type in the exact position and dimension parameter for a circle.

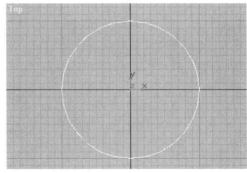

Figure 3.55 A spline created from the keyboard, with coordinates that match the origin and with a radius of 100.

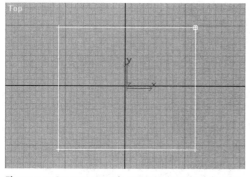

Figure 3.56
The Rectangle rollout has parameters for length and width.

Figure 3.57 Drag a rectangle to set its length and width.

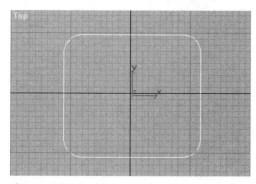

Figure 3.58 You make a rectangle with rounded corners by increasing the corner-radius parameter.

Making Closed Splines

You can make a variety of closed geometric figures with spline tools. This section demonstrates how to make two of the closed splines: the Rectangle and the NGon.

Other closed shapes like the ellipse, donut, and star have similar parameters; you can make them by following similar procedures. For example, the ellipse is dragged out to set its length and width, and a donut is simply two concentric circles.

To create a rectangle:

1. ▢ Click the Rectangle button on the Shapes Toolbar.

   The Rectangle rollout appears (**Figure 3.56**).

2. Choose the edge creation method in the rollout.

   You can draw rectangles from the center, if you prefer, but it's easier for most people to visualize rectangles when drawn from the edge.

3. In the Top viewport, position the cursor where you want to start the rectangle and drag diagonally from the upper left-hand corner to the lower right-hand corner (**Figure 3.57**).

4. Release the mouse button when the rectangle is the right size.

✔ Tip

■ To round the corners of a rectangle, increase the Corner Radius parameter (**Figure 3.58**).

Creating an NGon

NGons create regular polygons of up to 100 sides.

To create an NGon:

1.  Click the NGon button in the Shapes Toolbar.

   The NGon rollout appears (**Figure 3.59**).

2. In the Top viewport, position the cursor where you want the center of the NGon and drag outward to make the NGon.

   A regular hexagon appears in the viewport (**Figure 3.60**).

3. Release the mouse button to set the radius.

4. Change the number of sides, if necessary. By default, the number of sides is six.

✔ Tips

■ An NGon is a good way to make an equilateral triangle. Just set the Sides parameter to 3.

■ You can create a "snowflake" by setting the radius and corner-radius parameters to extremely high values (**Figure 3.61**).

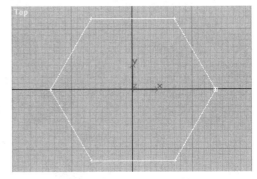

Figure 3.59 The NGon rollout allows you to create regular polyhedra of up to 100 sides.

Figure 3.60 Dragging an NGon in the Top viewport. The default number of sides is six.

Figure 3.61 Create a figure like this with the NGon tool, drastically increasing the radius and corner radius parameters. In this example, Radius = 60, Sides = 12, and Corner Radius = 1152.

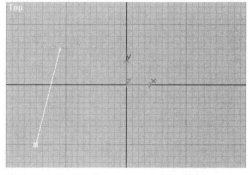

Figure 3.62 The Line rollout has parametric inputs for the type of vertex points used to create the line.

Making Open Splines

You create open shapes like lines and arcs by defining points along their paths. This process may be familiar if you have used two-dimensional drawing programs such as Adobe Illustrator, CorelDRAW, or Macromedia FreeHand.

To create a line:

1. ▨ Click the Line button on the Shapes Toolbar.

   The Line rollout appears (**Figure 3.62**).

2. Set the line's beginning point by clicking in the Top viewport.

3. Move the cursor to a new position and click to complete a line segment (**Figure 3.63**).

4. Continue clicking points in new positions to create more line segments (**Figure 3.64**).

5. Right-click to end the line.

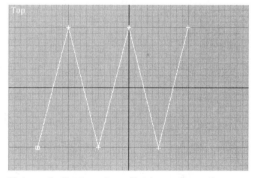

Figure 3.63 Setting the end point of the line.

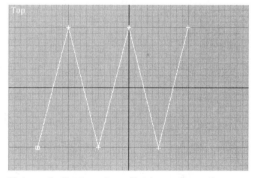

Figure 3.64 Create a zigzag line by moving and clicking a zigzag pattern.

✔ Tips

- To create a curved line, select Drag Type Smooth in the Creation Method rollout. Then click and drag to set vertex points. The line smoothes out automatically (**Figure 3.65**).

- To create a closed shape from line segments, click the last point on top of the first point. When the Spline dialog box asks, "Close the Spline?" click Yes (**Figure 3.66**).

- *To learn how to edit the shape of a line, see Chapter 8, "Editing Objects."*

- *To adjust the shape of a line, see "To convert a vertex" and "To adjust a vertex" in Chapter 8, "Editing Objects." The move, rotate, and scale tools are found in the Main Toolbar. They are explained in depth in Chapter 5, "Object Transforms."*

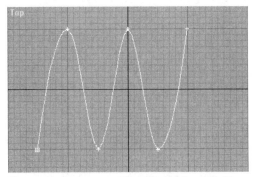

Figure 3.65 Create a wavy line after setting Initial Type and Drag Type to Smooth.

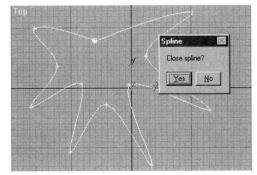

Figure 3.66 To create a closed shape, click to place the last point on top of the first one. Then click Yes to close the spline.

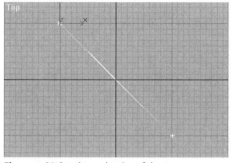

Figure 3.67 The Arc rollout has parametric inputs for radius and degrees of arc.

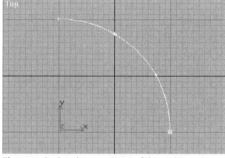

Figure 3.68 Set the end point of the arc.

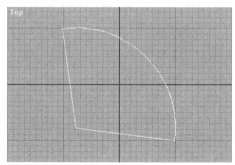

Figure 3.69 Set the curvature of the arc.

Figure 3.70 Check the Pie Slice parameter to create a closed shape like a slice of pie.

To create an arc:

1. Click the Arc button in the Shapes Toolbar.

   The Arc rollout appears (**Figure 3.67**).

2. Make sure that End-End-Middle is selected in the Creation Method rollout.

3. In the Top viewport, position the cursor where you want the arc to begin.

4. Drag from the beginning point to the end point.

   The click sets the beginning point; releasing the mouse button sets the end point. It still looks like a straight line (**Figure 3.68**).

5. Without clicking, slowly move the cursor along the line toward the middle of the arc.

6. Move the cursor to either side of the line.

   The arc appears to stick to the cursor (**Figure 3.69**).

7. Click to set the curvature of the arc.

✔ Tips

- To create a closed form called a pie slice, check the Pie Slice parameter (**Figure 3.70**).

- The Center-End-End creation method allows you to establish a center point and radius before drawing the arc around the center.

MAKING OPEN SPLINES

Creating a helix

The Helix is the only spline that has three-dimensional parameters. Watch it change in all four viewports as you create it.

To create a helix:

1. ▒ Click the Helix button in the Shapes Toolbar.

   The Helix rollout appears (**Figure 3.71**).

2. In the Perspective viewport, drag the base of the helix. Release the mouse button to set the first radius (**Figure 3.72**).

3. Move the cursor upward and then click to set the height (**Figure 3.73**).

   The end of the helix rises from the grid plane to that height.

4. Move the cursor up or down in the viewport and click to set the second radius (**Figure 3.74**).

   The helix is complete.

5. Adjust the number of turns and the bias amount, if necessary.

Figure 3.71 The Helix rollout has two radii and a height parameter.

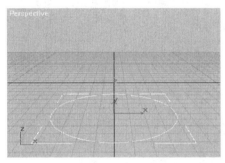

Figure 3.72 Set the first radius of a helix.

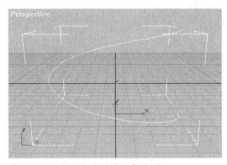

Figure 3.73 Set the height of a helix.

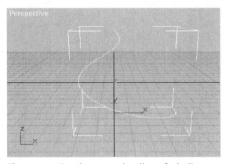

Figure 3.74 Set the second radius of a helix.

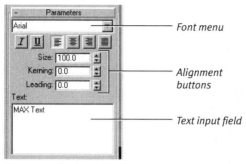

Font menu

Alignment
buttons

Text input field

Figure 3.75 The Text rollout has settings for different fonts and styles of text.

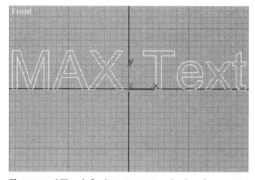

Figure 3.76 The default text appears in the view.

Figure 3.77 Changing the default text to the name of my business.

Creating Text

Text is often used to make 3D logos. To create text, you start with a default object and adjust its settings interactively.

To create text:

1. Click the Text button in the Shapes Toolbar.

   The Text rollout appears.(**Figure 3.75**).

2. Click in the center of the Front view.

   The words *MAX Text* fill the viewport (**Figure 3.76**). This is the default text, which you will replace. The default size is 100%, or about 400 generic units in width.

3. In the Text input field, select and delete the default text. Then type in the text you want.

   This text replaces the default text in the scene (**Figure 3.77**).

4. Adjust the Size parameter.

   The text shrinks or grows, based on a percentage of the original size.

5. Choose a font from the font drop-down list.

   The text changes to the new font.

6. Use the alignment buttons to align, center, and justify multiple lines of text.

7. If you want to italicize or underline the text, click *I* for italics or **U** for underline.

8. Spread out the text with more space between letters by increasing the kerning amount (**Figure 3.78**).

Zoom out of the viewport if you need more room.

9. To spread out multiple lines of text vertically, increase the Leading parameter.

10. Click Zoom Extents Selected to see the results.

✔ Tips

■ Use the Leading parameter to vertically space multiple lines of text.

■ Use the alignment buttons to left-align, center, right-align, or justify multiple lines of text.

■ Applying an Extrude modifier makes the text appear three dimensional. *(See Chapter 7, "Modifying Objects.")*

■ Lofting also can make text look three dimensional. *(See Chapter 9, "Compound Objects.")*

Figure 3.78 The result of centering and kerning the text.

MAKING OPEN SPLINES

Figure 3.79 The Section rollout with Infinite checked in Section Extents.

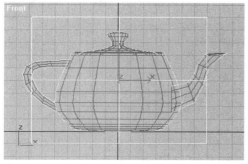

Figure 3.80 Dragging a section causes a yellow line to appear at the "waterline" of the teapot.

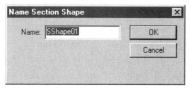

Figure 3.81 Clicking Create Shape brings up the Name Section Shape dialog box.

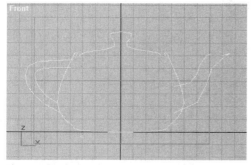

Figure 3.82 The resulting cross-section shape.

Making Cross Sections

Use sections to make two-dimensional cross sections of three-dimensional objects. A *section* is basically an infinite plane that slices anything in its path. When a section cuts a mesh object, it creates a cross section that is a spline.

To create a section:

1. In the Perspective viewport, create a mesh object using keyboard entry.

   Leave *x*, *y*, and *z* at zero.

2. Click the Section button in the Shapes Toolbar.

   The Section rollout appears (**Figure 3.79**).

3. In the Front viewport, drag a section of any size.

   A yellow line appears where the section bisects the object (**Figure 3.80**).

4. In the Section Parameters rollout, click Create Shape.

   The Name Section Shape dialog box appears (**Figure 3.81**).

5. Click OK to accept the default name or type a new name.

   A cross section of the object is created.

✔ Tip

■ To get a better look at the teapot cross-section shape, select and delete the teapot (**Figure 3.82**).

Changing an Object's Name and Color

Figure 3.83 Highlight the name in the Name and Color rollout; then type a new name.

Every object in a scene has a name. Default names are based on the object type and the order in which it was created, so that the first, second, and third sphere that you create are named Sphere01, Sphere02, and Sphere03. To make it easier to identify objects, you can assign them descriptive names.

By default, 3D Studio MAX randomly assigns colors to objects as you create them. You can easily choose your own colors and assign them at any time.

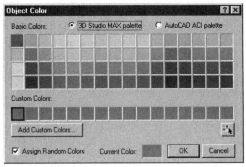

Figure 3.84 The Object Color dialog box allows you to pick colors.

To assign a name to an object:

1. Create or select an object.

2. In the Name and Color rollout of the Create panel, highlight the name— Sphere01, in this example.

3. Type a new name (**Figure 3.83**).

To assign a color to an object:

1. Create or select an object.

2. In the Name and Color rollout of the Create panel, click the color swatch next to the name.

   The Color Selector dialog box appears (**Figure 3.84**).

3. Click a swatch to pick color and click OK.

   The object changes to the new shade.

✔ Tip

■ To assign the same color to objects as you create them, uncheck Assign Random Colors in the Object Color dialog box.

Figure 3.85 A 640 x 480 pixel image of a teapot rendered line by line in the virtual frame buffer.

Rendering Objects

Once you have created an object, you can take a picture of it using the scanline renderer. This is the simplest form of rendering in MAX.

Scanline rendering takes place in a special window called a *virtual frame buffer*. From this window, you can save the resulting image in a wide variety of image file formats.

Rendering a mesh object

Mesh objects are automatically smoothed and shaded when rendered by the scanline renderer.

To render a mesh object:

1. Create or select a mesh object, such as a teapot, in any viewport.

2. Click the Quick Render button in the Main Toolbar.

    The virtual frame buffer appears. The active view of the object is drawn line by line in the window against a black background. The default size of the image is 640 x 480 (**Figure 3.85**).

    Once you have rendered an image to the frame buffer, you must save the image if you want to keep it. *See "To save a rendered image to a file," later in this chapter.*

RENDERING OBJECTS

Rendering a spline object

Splines are nonrendering by default. This means that they are not rendered by the scanline renderer unless you set them as such.

To render a spline object:

1.  Create a spline object.

2. Click Zoom Extents to center it in the viewport.

3. In the General rollout, check Renderable and set a thickness for the spline (**Figure 3.86**).

4. Click Quick Render.

   The spline object is rendered in the virtual frame buffer (**Figure 3.87**).

✔ Tip

■ To make a spline appear solid (**Figure 3.88**), apply an Extrude modifier. *(See Chapter 7, "Modifying Objects.")*

Figure 3.86 Use the General rollout of a spline object to make the spline render at a certain thickness. Here the setting is 1.

Figure 3.87 A rendered text object.

Figure 3.88 A rendered text object that has been slightly extruded.

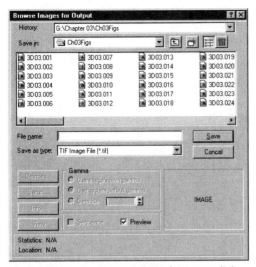

Figure 3.89 Use the Browse Images for Output dialog box to save an image directly from a virtual frame buffer.

Saving a rendered image

The simplest way to save a rendered image is to do it directly from the virtual frame buffer. You can save images in a wide variety of output files.

To save a rendered image to a file:

1. With a rendered image in the virtual frame buffer, click the Save Bitmap button in the virtual frame buffer.

   The Browse Images for Output dialog box appears (**Figure 3.89**).

2. Choose a name, file format, and directory in which to save your file and click OK.

   The image is saved to a file. You can open and manipulate the image in any 2D paint program.

✔ Tip

■ You cannot print out 2D rendered images from MAX. To print a saved image, open the file in a 2D paint program, such as Adobe Photoshop, and choose File > Print.

RENDERING OBJECTS

To view a rendered image file:

1. Choose File > View File.

   The View File dialog box appears (**Figure 3.90**). Note the similarity to the Browse Images for Output dialog box.

2. Select a file.

   A thumbnail of the image appears in the dialog box (**Figure 3.91**).

3. Click Open.

   A full-scale image appears in its own virtual frame buffer (**Figure 3.92**).

✔ Tip

■ The Browse Images for Output dialog box can also be used to view images by selecting an image file and clicking View. Use whichever one is more convenient.

Figure 3.90 Use the View File dialog box to view external 2D image and animation files.

Figure 3.91 The thumbnail of the image file.

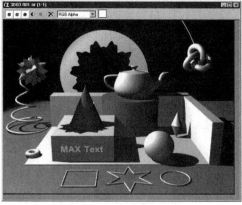

Figure 3.92 MAX displays the image.

SELECTING OBJECTS

Objects work as the basic building blocks of scenes. When you create an object, it is assigned a name, a form, and attributes of display. By applying a series of commands to an object, you can further tailor it to meet your needs.

In order to apply commands to an object, you must first *select* it. When you select an object, it tells the program what commands can be applied to it, based upon the type of object it is. Commands that you can apply to the object in its current state are enabled. Commands that you cannot use with the object are grayed out.

In Chapter 2, you learned how to hide and freeze objects so that they cannot be accidentally selected. This chapter explains how to select objects and how to use selection filters to choose just the objects you need.

About Selecting

MAX provides a simple method for selecting objects individually. The program also offers many ways to select multiple objects: by region, by name, by type, by color, and by size. The variations on selecting provide great flexibility and power. You can select objects easily, and you can also select with great precision the objects that you need to work on together.

You can place objects in groups or named selection sets so that you can repeat a selection of multiple objects. Selection sets leave individual objects more accessible; you can temporarily or permanently free individual objects from a group, but it takes more steps.

Once you have made a selection, you can lock it so that you can't accidentally deselect it while you work.

Finally, you can make a selection and then invert it, choosing instead all the unselected objects in a scene.

Figure 4.1 Unselected objects in a scene.

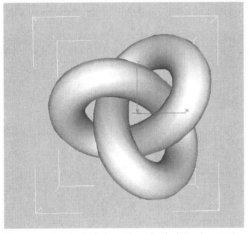

Figure 4.2 A selected object in a shaded display mode.

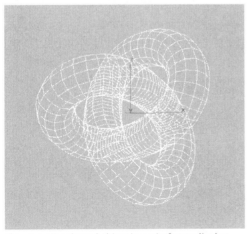

Figure 4.3 A selected object in a wireframe display mode.

Selecting an Individual Object

The objects you make with MAX usually just start the process of creating a 3D scene. If you want to do anything else with an object, first you must select it.

The most basic way to select objects is one at a time.

To select an object:

1. Open or create a scene file with an object (**Figure 4.1**).

2. ⬚ Choose Select Object from the Main Toolbar.

3. Click an object.

   The object is selected.

   In shaded viewports, the corners of a white bounding box appear around the object to show that it is selected (**Figure 4.2**).

   In wireframe viewports, the selected object turns white (**Figure 4.3**).

To deselect an object:

1. Start with a selected object.

2. ⬚ Click outside the object with the Select Object tool.

   Just click the background of any viewport.

   In shaded display modes, the bounding box corners disappear. In wireframe display modes, the color of the object changes back to its assigned color.

✔ Tips

- To add to a selection, hold down the Crtl key and click OK.

- To subtract from a selection, hold down the Alt key and click the object to deselect.

Selecting Objects by Region

Region selection is the easiest way to select multiple objects. Region selection is accomplished by dragging a window around the objects you want to select. Everything inside the window is selected, no matter how far away it is in space.

You can select regions by *window* or by *crossing*. When you select by window, the region must completely surround an object in order to select it. When you select by crossing the region need only cross the edge of an object in order to select it. Practice both window and crossing selection until you become proficient in each.

Region selection can take place with three different window shapes, which are listed below.

To select an object by region:

◆ Rectangular selection region selects objects within a rectangular area (**Figure 4.4**). This is the default.

◆ Circular selection region selects objects within a circular area (**Figure 4.5**).

◆ Fence selection region selects objects within a polygon-shaped area (**Figure 4.6**).

The circular and fence selection regions work well for selecting objects at the sub-object level, in preparation for editing.

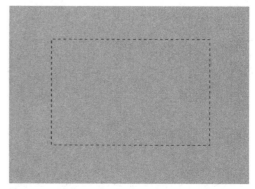

Figure 4.4 Region selections come in three shapes. The rectangular selection is the default shape.

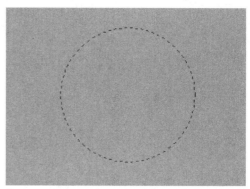

Figure 4.5 You can also drag a circular region to select objects.

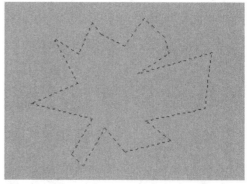

Figure 4.6 You point and click to make a polygon-shaped region for selecting specific objects.

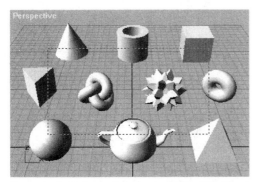

Figure 4.7 Dragging a window selection region around some objects.

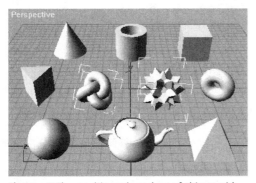

Figure 4.8 The resulting selected set of objects with everything fully enclosed by the selection region.

To select objects by window:

1. Open or create a scene with some objects.

2. ⬚ Choose the Select Object tool on the Main Toolbar.

3. ⬚ Click the Window/Crossing toggle in the status bar to enable Window Selection.

4. Accept the default rectangular region or switch to the ⬚ circular or ⬚ fence selection in the Selection Region flyout.

5. Drag a selection region around some objects (**Figure 4.7**).

6. Release the mouse.

   The objects entirely enclosed by the selection window are selected (**Figure 4.8**).

✔ Tip

■ The ⬚ Selection Filter menu next to the Region Selection button allows you to limit the types of objects you select, as explained in the section "Selecting by Name," later in this chapter.

To select objects by crossing:

1. Open or create a scene with some objects.

2. ▫ Choose the Select Object tool on the Main Toolbar.

3. ▫ Click the Window/Crossing toggle in the status bar to enable the Crossing Selection.

4. Accept the default rectangular region or switch to ▫ circular or ▫ fence selection in the Selection Region flyout.

   The task on the next page explains in detail how to make a fence selection.

5. Select the objects by dragging a region across them (**Figure 4.9**).

   The objects that are crossed by the selection region are selected (**Figure 4.10**).

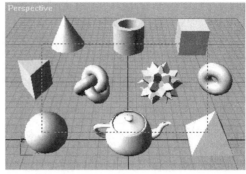

Figure 4.9 Dragging a selection across some objects.

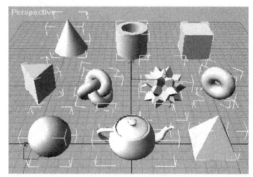

Figure 4.10 The resulting selection of objects touched by the selection region.

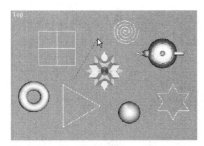

Figure 4.11 You start a fence selection by making the first line segment for the polygon-shaped selection region.

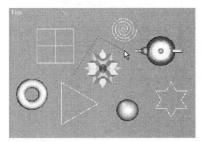

Figure 4.12 Make the second segment of the fence selection.

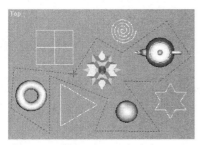

Figure 4.13 If you want to close the selection, bring the end of the last segment close to the starting point until the cross-hair cursor appears.

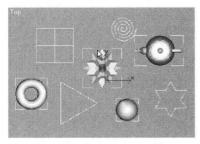

Figure 4.14 The objects selected by the fence: Torus, Hedra, Teapot, and Sphere.

Selecting objects with a fence

Fence selection allows you to select objects with an open or closed polygon region.

To select objects with a fence:

1. ▧ Choose Fence Selection Region from the Selection Region flyout.

2. Drag the first segment of the fence next to an object you want to enclose.

3. Release the mouse button to set the end of the first segment (**Figure 4.11**).

4. Move the cursor to define the next segment.

   A "rubber band" line stretches from the end of the first segment to the cursor.

5. Click to set the end of the second segment (**Figure 4.12**).

6. Continue moving the mouse and clicking until you have completely fenced in your selection.

7. To close the fence, move the cursor close to the first point that you set, so that a cross-hair cursor appears and then release (**Figure 4.13**).

   or

   To create an open fence, double-click the mouse button anywhere in the viewport.

   The objects enclosed by the fence are selected (**Figure 4.14**).

✔ Tip

- Double-clicking a fence is usually easier than closing it.

Selecting Objects by Name

The Select Objects dialog box allows you to select objects from a list of names. You can sort the list or filter out certain types of objects to help you make the selection you need.

To select an object by name:

1. Open or create a scene that has some objects in it.

2.  Click the Select by Name button in the Main Toolbar.

   or

   Press the H key.

   The Select Objects dialog box appears with a list of all selectable objects in the scene (**Figure 4.15**).

Figure 4.15 In the Select Objects dialog box you can select objects by name and type.

3. If necessary, switch to a different sorting order.

   You can sort by type, color, size, or alphabetically by name. The default is alphabetical order.

4. Click the name of an object.

5. Click OK.

   The object is selected.

Figure 4.16 The Edit menu provides another way to reach object-selection tools.

✔ Tips

- If you have a lot of objects, you may want to list only some of them in the Select Objects dialog box, as explained on the next page.

- To bring up a selection-list floater that stays open while you work, choose Tools > Selection Floater.

- Selection commands are also available in the Edit Menu (**Figure 4.16**).

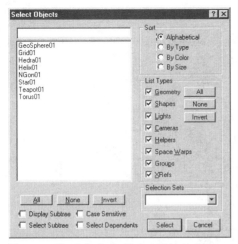

Figure 4.17 By default, the Select Objects dialog box lists all the objects in a scene. Here the scene contains eight objects.

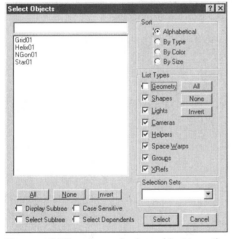

Figure 4.18 When you uncheck an object type, the objects of that type disappear from the list. Here, the mesh objects disappear when you uncheck Geometry, leaving only four objects on the list.

Figure 4.19 Use any selection filter boxes in menus, command panels, or dialog boxes the same way.

To filter a selection list:

1. ![icon] With a scene open, click the Select by Name button in the Main Toolbar.

   or

   Press the H key.

   The Select Objects dialog box appears, listing all the objects in the scene (**Figure 4.17**).

2. In the List Types group, uncheck the types of objects you want to remove from the list.

   The list shortens to show only the checked object types (**Figure 4.18**).

✔ Tips

- Look for object filters in any dialog box or menu that allow you to hide, freeze, link, bind, pick, or select objects (**Figure 4.19**).

- You can filter objects for selection in the viewports using the ![icon] Selection Filter drop-down menu in the Main Toolbar.

Using Named Selection Sets

Often, it's necessary to select a certain set of objects repeatedly. To make the process of repeat selection easier, assign the objects to a named selection set. If you always want to select the objects as a group—rather than individually—group the objects in a set, as explained in the next section of this chapter.

To create a named selection set:

1. Open or create a scene that has some objects in it.

2. ▨ Select some objects (**Figure 4.20**).

3. In the Main Toolbar, click the Named Selection Sets field (**Figure 4.21**).

4. Type a name for the set and press Enter.

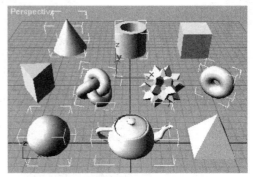

Figure 4.20 Select objects for the set.

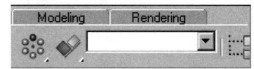

Figure 4.21 Type a name in the Named Selection Sets input field on the Main Toolbar.

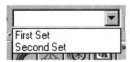

Figure 4.22 Choose a selection set from the drop-down menu on the Main Toolbar.

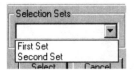

Figure 4.23 You can also choose a named selection set from the Selection Sets list of the Select Objects dialog box.

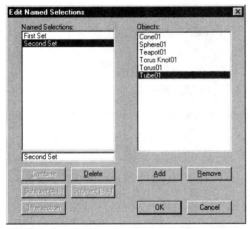

Figure 4.24 In the Edit Named Selection Sets dialog box you can combine sets, add objects to sets, or remove objects from sets.

To select a named selection set:

1. Open the Named Selection Set drop-down menu on the Main Toolbar (**Figure 4.22**).

2. Choose one of the named selection sets from the menu.

   The objects in the set are selected.

✔ Tip

■ ▣ You can also select named selection sets from the Selection Sets part of the Select Objects dialog box (**Figure 4.23**).

■ 3D Studio MAX 3 provides you with a powerful editor for adding objects to named selection sets, subtracting objects from sets, and recombining entire sets. Open the editor by selecting Edit > Edit Named Selections (**Figure 4.24**).

Working with Groups

Grouping combines objects into a single unit called a group. You can select, transform, modify, and animate grouped objects as if they were a single object. Grouped objects cannot be selected individually unless you open or dissolve the group.

If you want to work with the objects together only part of the time and expect to select individual objects sometimes, create a named selection set instead of making a group, as described on the previous page.

To define a group:

1. Open or create a scene with some objects.

2. Select the objects to group (**Figure 4.25**).

3. Choose Group > Group.
   The Group dialog box appears
   (**Figure 4.26**).

4. Name the group or accept the default name, Group01.

5. Click OK.

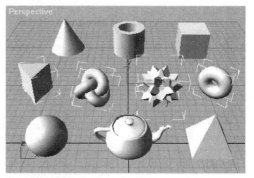

Figure 4.25 Select some objects to group.

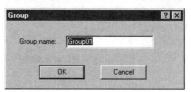

Figure 2.26 Name the group in the simple Group dialog box.

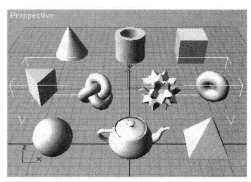

Figure 4.27 A bounding box surrounds the selected group.

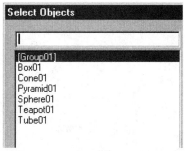

Figure 4.28 The Select Object dialog box distinguishes groups by putting their names in brackets.

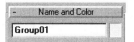

Figure 4.29 Command panels show group names in boldface.

To select a group:

1. ▣ Choose the Select Object tool from the Main Toolbar.

2. Click any member of the group.

   A single bounding box appears around the group to show that it's selected (**Figure 4.27**).

✔ Tips

■ Group names appear in brackets in the Select Objects dialog box. Individual objects enclosed in a group do not appear (**Figure 4.28**).

■ Group names appear in boldface in the command panel (**Figure 4.29**).

■ To add an object to a group, select the object and choose Group > Attach. Then click the group to attach it to.

■ To nest a group within a group, select the group and choose Group > Group; then select the objects for the nested group.

To open and close a group:

1. [cursor] Select a group.

2. Choose Group > Open.

   A pink bounding box encloses the group (**Figure 4.30**).

3. When you have finished working with objects in the group, close it again by choosing Group > Close.

   The pink bounding box disappears and the group closes; you can no longer select individual objects in the group (**Figure 4.31**).

To detach an object from a group:

1. Open the group.

2. Select the object to subtract from the group.

3. Choose Group > Detach.

To ungroup a group:

1. [cursor] Select a group.

2. Choose Group > Ungroup.

   The group dissolves (**Figure 4.32**).

✔ Tip

- To ungroup nested groups all at once, choose Group > Explode.

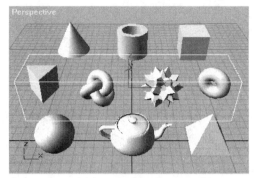

Figure 4.30 A pink bounding box appears when a group is open. Objects in an open group can be individually selected.

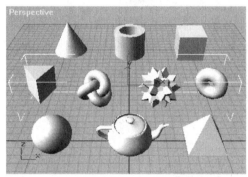

Figure 4.31 The pink bounding box disappears when the group is closed. Objects in a closed group can only be selected as a group.

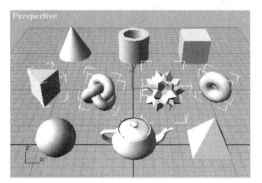

Figure 4.32 Ungrouping a group dissolves it and leaves the objects individually selected.

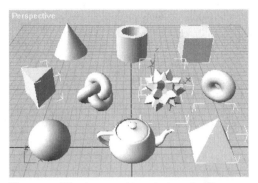

Figure 4.33 When you want to select most of the objects in a scene but not all, select backward. Start by selecting the few objects you don't want to work with. Here, the Prism, Cube, Hedra, and Pyramid are selected.

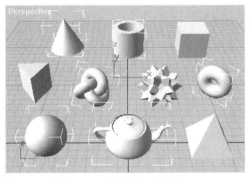

Figure 4.34 When you invert the selection, you deselect the few and instead select the many objects you left out of the original selection.

Locking and Inverting Selections

Locking a selection shields selected objects from being deselected accidentally. It's a way of creating a temporary selection set.

One other important selecting technique works for both individual and multiple selection techniques: inverting a selection. In a scene with multiple objects, you can select the one object or the few objects that you don't want to select and then reverse the selection to leave them out and select everything else.

To lock a selection:

1. Select one or more objects.

2. Click Lock Selection Set in the Status Bar Controls.

   or

   Press the spacebar.

To unlock a selection:

◆ Click Lock Selection Set in the Status Bar Controls.

   or

   Press the spacebar.

Inverting a selection

Select Invert is one of a number of useful selection commands on the Edit menu. Most of the commands also appear on the Main Toolbar, but Select Invert appears only on the Edit menu and in the Select Objects dialog box.

To invert a selection:

1. Select some objects (**Figure 4.33**).

2. Choose Edit > Select Invert.

   The selection is inverted so that everything *except* the objects you selected in step 1 are now selected (**Figure 4.34**).

TRANSFORMING OBJECTS 5

Affine transformations are mathematical functions that transform geometric forms in such a way that parallel lines remain parallel. Transformations include *translation* (moving along a straight line), *rotation* (rotating around a pivot point), *scaling* (enlarging or reducing), *reflection* (mirroring), and *shearing* (slanting). Each of these transformations can be expressed as an algebraic equation or computed in a matrix.

The three most common transformations in 3D graphics are translation, rotation, and scaling. In 3D Studio MAX, translation, rotation and scaling are called the *move, rotate*, and *scale transforms*.

Fortunately, MAX takes care of computing transforms for you in a composite matrix that updates constantly. This matrix keeps track of the position, rotation, and scale of an object with respect to a reference point. Although you cannot access the transform matrix directly, you can use *type-in transforms* to enter new values.

This chapter covers the three basic transforms as well as more complex transforms that allow you to create object clones in geometric arrangements.

About Transforms and Coordinate Systems

A transform command changes the coordinates of an object with respect to a system of reference. The three basic transforms of move, rotate, and scale change the position, orientation, and size of objects.

Objects must be selected in order to be transformed. For convenience, the three basic transform tools allow you to select and transform an object in one move. You can also use any multiple-selection technique *(see Chapter 4, "Selecting Objects")* to select several objects and then use the transform tool on all the selected objects at once.

MAX updates the geometry matrix after every transform; you cannot recall individual transforms after you save a scene.

MAX has seven types of reference coordinate systems that define the orientation of the axes. They allow you to transform objects in relation to the absolute frame of reference of the world coordinates, as well as to other relative frames of reference, such as the local coordinates of an object.

You can choose only one reference coordinate system at a time. When a reference coordinate system is selected, the axis tripods and transform axes of all objects in the scene align to the orientation of that system. Remember that unless you have turned it off deliberately, the world axis in the lower-left corner of each viewport always indicates the orientation of the world coordinate system.

The default reference coordinate system is View. View coordinates use screen coordinates in orthogonal views and world coordinates in all other views. This can be confusing at first. For example, if you move an object along the Y axis in an orthogonal view it appears to move up and down relative to the screen.

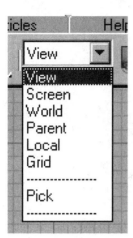

Figure 5.1 The Reference Coordinate System drop-down list allows you to choose a system of reference for each transform.

In contrast, if you move the object along the Y axis of the Perspective view, it moves in and out relative to the screen. To keep track, remember that the X and Y axes always lie on the visible grid, and the Z axis is perpendicular to the grid.

To choose a coordinate system:

1. Open the Reference Coordinate System drop-down list in the Main Toolbar (**Figure 5.1**).

2. Choose one of the seven options.

   The sidebar "Coordinate System Choices" explains the differences among the options.

Coordinate System Choices

The axes of each coordinate system are aligned as follows:

◆ **Screen** X and Y are parallel to the display screen; Z is perpendicular to the screen.

◆ **World** X, Y, and Z align to the world coordinate system.

◆ **View** Combination of Screen and World. X and Y lie on the visible grid plane of the active view; Z is perpendicular to the grid.

◆ **Parent** X, Y, and Z align to the local coordinates of an object's parent. If the object is not linked to a parent, it is a child of the world and uses world coordinates.

◆ **Local** X, Y, and Z align to the local coordinates of an object.

◆ **Grid** X, Y, and Z align to the coordinate system of the active grid.

◆ **Pick** X, Y, and Z align to the local coordinate system of any object in the scene that you pick.

ABOUT TRANSFORMS AND COORDINATE SYSTEMS

Setting the Transform Axis

The direction in which MAX executes a transform command is determined by the transform axis, also called the axis of constraint. Each transform has a default axis of constraint when you open the program, but you can also set a different constraint axis, which remains in effect until you change it again. For instance, the default transform axis for a move is *XY* (on the plane of the grid) and for rotate, it's *Z*.

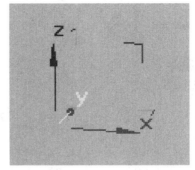

Figure 5.2 The Transform Gizmo indicates the direction of the current transform.

You can also constrain two axes for limiting transforms on a plane.

When you choose a transform tool, every axis tripod in your selection changes to a *Transform Gizmo,* the tripod axis with some extra corners that act like handles for selecting the two axes for a plane. The transform axis for the current transform turns yellow (**Figure 5.2**). The axis of constraint indicates the direction in which an object can be transformed.

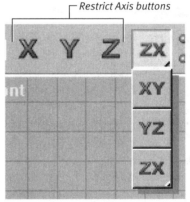

Figure 5.3 The Restrict Axis buttons allow you to select the direction for a transform.

To constrain transforms along a single axis:

1. Click one of the Restrict Axis buttons (**Figure 5.3**) on the Main Toolbar.

   With these buttons you can constrain transforms to the positive or negative direction of the *X, Y,* or *Z* axis.

2. Select a transform tool and perform the transform in the direction you have constrained.

✔ Tip

■ Use keyboard shortcuts for selecting a constraint axis: press F5 to constrain the *X* axis, F6 for *Y,* or F7 for *Z*.

SETTING THE TRANSFORM AXIS

Restrict to Plane flyout ⌐

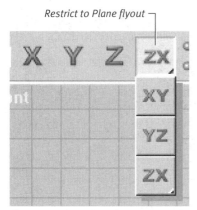

Figure 5.4 You can use the Restrict to Plane buttons to limit transforms to a plane.

Figure 5.5 When you select a transform tool and then an object, the axis tripod turns into the Transform Gizmo.

To constrain transforms to a plane:

1. Open the Restrict to Plane flyout and choose a plane (**Figure 5.4**).

2. Select a transform tool and perform the transform.

✔ Tip

■ A keyboard shortcut for selecting the plane of constraint is F8, which cycles through *XY, YZ,* and *ZX.* You can also cycle through the dual axis constraints by pressing the tilde (~) key.

To change an object's axis of constraint:

1. ⊹ ↻ ▢ Choose a transform tool from the Main Toolbar.

2. Click an object.

   The object is selected and the axis tripod changes to a transform gizmo (**Figure 5.5**).

3. Roll the cursor over the transform axis.

   The *X, Y,* and *Z* axes highlight in yellow as the cursor rolls over them.

4. When the axis that you want to constrain turns yellow, click it.

   The default axis constraint is overridden, and you can drag the object in the direction of the highlighted axis to transform the object in that direction. If you want to switch to a dual axis, click the corner of the transform gizmo that highlights the axes and define the plane you want.

✔ Tip

■ The depth axis can be very difficult to select onscreen. Use the Restrict Axis buttons on the Main Toolbar instead to select it.

■ Press F5 to constrain the *X* axis, F6 for *Y,* or F7 for *Z.* F8 cycles through *XY, YZ,* and *ZX.*

SETTING THE TRANSFORM AXIS

Moving Objects

The move transform changes the position of an object by translating it along the axes of the current system of reference. As you try out move transforms, experiment with changing the reference coordinates to see how each coordinate system affects the direction of movement.

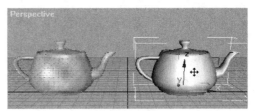

Figure 5.6 This move transform repositions the teapot to the right.

To move an object:

1. Choose the Select and Move tool from the Main Toolbar.

2. Select one or more objects.

3. Choose a transform axis from the Main Toolbar or use the default *XY* axis.

4. Position the cursor over a selected object. The cursor changes to a ✥ move cursor.

5. Drag the object in the direction of the current transform axis.

   The object is selected and moved (**Figure 5.6**).

✔ Tips

■ Practice moving an object in each view to develop your sense of 3D spatial relationships.

■ Select an object before transforming it if you want to see the axis tripod to help you keep track of directions.

■ Locking a selection allows you to transform an object without clicking it directly.

■ In orthogonal views, you cannot drag objects perpendicular to the view plane.

Those Ghostly Objects

In this chapter, to show the before-and-after view of transforms, two views of an object appear in some figures. The ghostly image represents the object before transformation; the more substantive image represents the results of the transform.

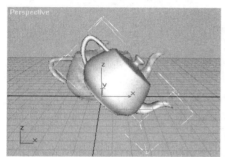

Figure 5.7 The Center flyout allows you to choose the center of rotation and scaling.

Figure 5.8 This transform rotates a teapot in *Y* in the Perspective viewport.

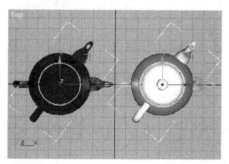

Figure 5.9 Rotating teapots around their individual pivot points.

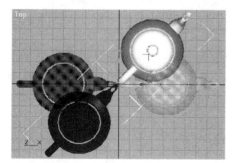

Figure 5.10 Rotating teapots around the center of the selection.

Rotating Objects

The rotate transform changes the orientation of an object in space by rotating it around its pivot point. An object's pivot point for rotation and scaling is located at the origin of its axis tripod. (You can change an object's pivot point in the Hierarchy command panel.)

You can also select and rotate groups of objects, choosing a pivot point beforehand for the entire group of objects.

To rotate an object:

1. Choose the Select and Rotate tool from the Main Toolbar.

2. Select multiple objects and then choose the Select and Rotate tool from the Main Toolbar.

3. Choose a transform axis from the Main Toolbar, or use the default *Z* axis.

4. Change the center of rotation, if necessary, with the Center flyout, located just to the right of Reference Coordinate system drop-down menu (**Figure 5.7**).

5. Place the cursor over an object.
   The cursor changes to a ✛ rotate cursor.

6. Drag the cursor up or down in the viewport.
   The object rotates around its pivot point along the axis of constraint (**Figure 5.8**).

✔ Tip

- When you have selected multiple objects, you can rotate them around their individual pivot points (**Figure 5.9**), around the center of the selection (**Figure 5.10**), or around the origin of the current system of reference.

ROTATING OBJECTS

111

Scaling Objects

The scale transform changes the size of an object along its axes. MAX has three scale tools:

◆ The Select and Uniform Scale tool selects and scales objects equally in all three axes, regardless of the current axis constraints.

◆ The Select and Non-Uniform Scale tool selects and scales objects in up to two axes, resulting in a change in its proportions.

◆ The Select and Squash tool selects and scales objects up in one or two axes and inversely scales objects in the remaining axes, resulting in a deformation of proportions in which the volume remains constant.

To uniformly scale an object:

1. ▫ Choose the Select and Uniform Scale tool from the Main Toolbar.

   or

   Select multiple objects and then choose the Select and Uniform Scale tool from the Main Toolbar.

2. Place the cursor over an object.

   The cursor changes to a ✛ uniform scale cursor.

3. Change the center of scaling, if necessary, with the Transform Center flyout, located just to the right of Reference Coordinate system drop-down menu (**Figure 5.11**).

4. Drag up or down in the viewport.

   The object uniformly increases in size as you drag up and decreases in size as you drag down (**Figure 5.12**).

Figure 5.11 You can change the center for scaling with the Transform Center flyout.

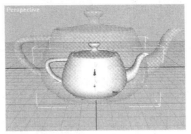

Figure 5.12 Uniform Scale tool scales an object equally in all three axes.

Picking a Center of Rotation or Scaling

When you move an object, MAX calculates the move transform using the coordinates of the object's pivot point. When you rotate or scale an object, you can pick other centers of rotation or scaling with the Use Center flyout in the Main Toolbar. Like axis constraints for transforms, centers of rotation and scaling stick with their respective transforms until you change them.

▣ **Pivot Point Center** enables rotation or scaling around the pivot point of each selected object.

▣ **Selection Center** enables rotation or scaling around the selection center of an object or a selection set. This is also the geometric center of the selection.

▣ **Transform Coordinate Center** enables rotation or scaling around the origin of the reference coordinate system selected in the drop-down list immediately to the left of the Use Center flyout.

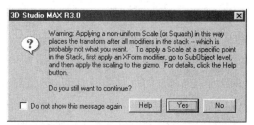

Figure 5.13 The Non-Uniform Scale Warning alerts you that transforms are evaluated after modifiers. In most cases, you can just click Yes.

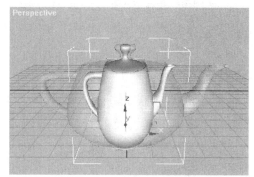

Figure 5.14 The Non-Uniform Scale tool scales an object disproportionately in up to two axes.

To non-uniformly scale an object:

1. Choose the Select and Non-Uniform Scale tool from the Scale flyout.

   or

   Select multiple objects and then choose the Select and Non-Uniform Scale tool from the Scale flyout.

   A warning appears to let you know that the transform is evaluated after the modifier stack (**Figure 5.13**). *(For more about the modifier stack, see Chapter 7, "Modifying Objects.")*

2. Click Yes to ignore the warning.

   You can disable the warning by checking Do Not Show This Message Again. Or choose Customize > Preferences > General and uncheck Display NU Scale Warning.

3. Place the cursor over the object you want to scale.

   The cursor changes to a ▦ non-uniform scale cursor.

4. Drag up or down in the viewport.

   The object increases in size along the axis or axes of constraint as you drag up and decreases in size along the axis or axes of constraint as you drag down (**Figure 5.14**).

SCALING OBJECTS

To squash an object:

1. 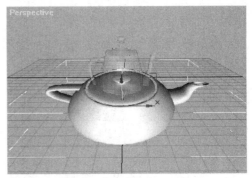Choose the Select and Squash tool from the Scale flyout.

   or

   Select multiple objects and then choose the Select and Squash tool from the Scale flyout.

   If you have not disabled it, the Non-Uniform Scale warning appears.

2. Click Yes to ignore the warning.

   You can disable the warning by checking Do Not Show This Message Again. Or choose Customize > Preferences > General and uncheck Display NU Scale Warning.

3. Choose an axis of constraint from the Main Toolbar, or use the default *XY* axis.

4. Place the cursor over an object.

   The cursor changes to a squash cursor.

5. Drag up in the viewport to enlarge or down in the viewport to reduce the size of the object.

   As you drag up, the object increases in size along the axis of constraint and proportionally decreases in size along the unconstrained axes. As you drag down, the object decreases in size along the axis of constraint and proportionally increases in size along the unconstrained axes (**Figure 5.15**).

Figure 5.15 The Squash tool scales an object disproportionately in all three axes while conserving its overall volume.

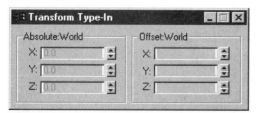

Figure 5.16 The Transform Type-In dialog box allows you to transform an object precisely, either absolutely in relation to the world coordinates or relative to its current position.

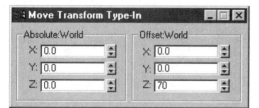

Figure 5.17 To move an object in relation to its current location, type offset amounts on the right side of the Move Transform Type-In dialog box.

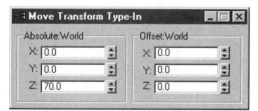

Figure 5.18 After you press Enter, the position coordinates update.

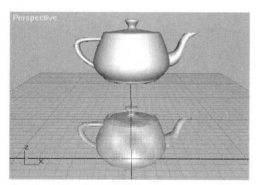

Figure 5.19 The object moves to its new position, in this case 70 units above its previous site.

Transforming with Precision

Type-in transforms allow you to transform objects by entering numbers from the keyboard. You can offset an object a relative amount from its current position using the current system of reference, or you can transform it in absolute terms using the world coordinate system if you know the exact final transformed position for the object (**Figure 5.16**).

✔ Tip

- Press F12 to open the Transform Type-In dialog box. If you have a specific tool selected, it opens the corresponding dialog box.

To type in a relative move transform:

1. Select one or more objects.

2. ✛ Choose Select and Move from the Main Toolbar.

3. Choose Tools > Transform Type-In.
   or
   Right-click the Select and Move button.
   The Move Transform Type-In dialog box appears.

4. In the Offset area, enter the amount to change the position of the object in each axis (**Figure 5.17**).
   You can use positive or negative values.

5. Press Enter.
   The Absolute coordinates of the object update, and the Offset amount resets to 0 (**Figure 5.18**). The object moves to its new position (**Figure 5.19**).

To type in an exact move transform:

1. Select one or more objects

2. ⊕ Choose Select and Move from the Main Toolbar.

3. Choose Tools > Transform Type-In.
   or
   Right-click the Select and Move button. The Move Transform Type-In dialog box appears.

4. In the Absolute fields, enter the exact location for each axis of the world coordinate system (**Figure 5.20**).

5. Press Enter.
   The object moves to its new position.

To type in a rotate transform:

1. Select one or more objects.

2. ↻ Choose Select and Rotate from the Main Toolbar.

3. Choose Tools > Transform Type-In.
   or
   ↻ Right-click the Select and Rotate button.
   The Rotate Transform Type-In dialog box appears.

4. Enter a new orientation (in degrees) in the Absolute fields (in world coordinates) or enter the number of degrees to rotate the object in the Offset area (**Figure 5.21**).
   Choose the rotation axis by typing in the desired axis field.

5. Press Enter.
   The Absolute coordinates of the object update, and the Offset amount resets to 0 (**Figure 5.22**). The object aligns to the new orientation (**Figure 5.23**).

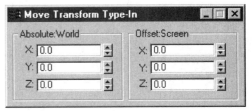

Figure 5.20 To move an object to an exact position in world coordinates, type the transformed position in the fields on the left of the Move Transform Type-In dialog box.

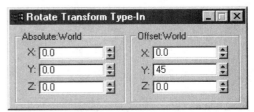

Figure 5.21 Using the Rotate Transform Type-In to offset the orientation of an object 45° in Y.

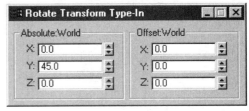

Figure 5.22 After you press Enter, the rotation values update.

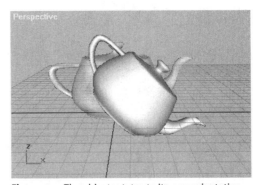

Figure 5.23 The object rotates to its new orientation.

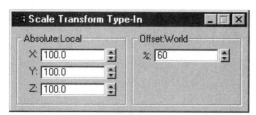

Figure 5.24 Preparing to reduce the size of an object to 60 percent of its original size.

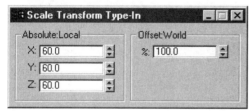

Figure 5.25 After pressing Enter, the scale percentages update.

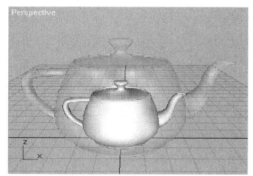

Figure 5.26 The object resizes, in this case scaling to 60 percent of the original size.

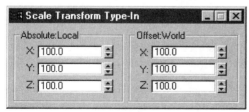

Figure 5.27 The Scale Type-In Transform dialog box for non-uniform scaling and squashing has additional inputs for offset scaling each axis.

To type in a scale transform:

1. Select one or more objects.

2. ▣ Choose Select and Uniform Scale from the Main Toolbar.

3. Choose Tools > Transform Type-In.

   or

   ▣ Right-click the Select and Uniform Scale button.

   The Scale Transform Type-In dialog box appears.

4. Enter the percentage amount to scale the object (**Figure 5.24**).

   Enter the same amount for each axis to scale the object uniformly. Use different amounts to squash the object.

5. Press Enter.

   The Absolute size of the object updates to a percentage, and the Offset amount resets to 100% (**Figure 5.25**). The object scales to new percentages (**Figure 5.26**).

✔ Tip

- If you prefer to type the offset for each axis, choose Select and Non-Uniform Scale or Select and Squash from the Scale flyout. The Scale Type-In Transform dialog box updates to include offset entry fields for each axis (**Figure 5.27**).

TRANSFORMING WITH PRECISION

Snapping Transformations

Just as you can use the grid to snap objects to precise locations, you can snap transformations to precise locations on the grid.

Snaps constrain cursor movement, and therefore transforms, to preset targets or options. You can snap move transforms to the grid or to object components. You can snap rotate transforms to degree increments, and scale transforms to a percentage of the original object size (**Figure 5.28**).

Move snaps are "relative" by default, meaning that objects move the exact distance of the grid interval. If an object is offset from the lines of the grid, it maintains that offset during a relative snap. If you prefer, you can change the settings to perform a transform that snaps one of the object's vertices to a grid intersection.

Also by default, snaps ignore transform axis constraints. If you prefer, you can enable them.

You can also temporarily override the snap settings for an object by using Shift-right-click menu for the object and momentarily changing the snap status or the snap targets.

To snap a move:

1. ⊕ Choose the Select and Move tool from the Main Toolbar.

2. ⋰ Turn on 3D Snap by clicking the 3D Snap Toggle in the Status Bar Controls.

   The cursor snaps to grid intersections as you move it across the grid (**Figure 5.29**).

3. Move an object.

   The object snaps from one grid intersection to another as you drag it. You can't drag an object perpendicular to the grid; the object sticks to the grid (**Figure 5.30**).

Figure 5.28 The snap locks on the Main Toolbar activate snaps.

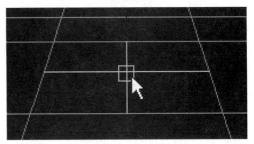

Figure 5.29 As the cursor snaps to a target, the snap marker for that target appears. Here, the snap target is Grid Points.

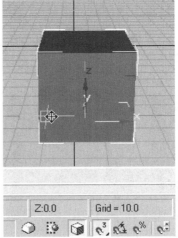

Figure 5.30 Snapping a move; the object snaps to the grid.

Figure 5.31 The Grid and Snap Settings dialog box appears when you right-click on the 3D Snap button.

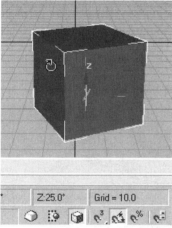

Figure 5.32 Rotating a cube with angle snap limits the rotation to five-degree increments by default.

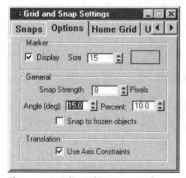

Figure 5.33 Adjust the amount of an angle snap, or other settings, in the Grid and Snap Settings Options panel.

Setting snap targets

Snap targets tell the program two things: the target to which it should snap a cursor or object and the part of an object you want to be snapped.

To set snap targets:

1. Right-click on the 3D Snap button.

   The Grid and Snap Settings dialog box appears (**Figure 5.31**).

2. In the Snaps panel, check the snap targets you want to enable. Uncheck the snap targets you do not want the program to use.

   The snap targets are set for all three transforms.

✔ Tip

■ To perform absolute snaps, which snap the corner of an object to a grid intersection, set your snap targets to Grid Points and Vertex.

To snap a rotation:

1. Choose the Select and Rotate tool from the Main Toolbar.

2. Turn on Angle Snap by clicking the Angle Snap Toggle in the Status Bar Controls.

3. Rotate an object.

   The object snaps to increments of five degrees as it rotates (**Figure 5.32**).

✔ Tips

■ To change the snap angle, right-click the Angle Snap Toggle and enter a new value for Angle Snap in the Options panel of the Grid and Snap Settings dialog box (**Figure 5.33**).

(continues on next page)

SNAPPING TRANSFORMATIONS

- To rotate an object around a vertex or edge, turn on 3D Snap and enable Vertex and Edge in the Snaps panel of the Grid and Snaps Settings dialog box (**Figure 5.34**).

To snap a scale:

1. Choose the Select and Uniform Scale tool from the Main Toolbar.

2. Turn on Percent Snap by clicking on the Percent Snap button in the Status Bar Controls.

3. Scale an object.

   The object snaps to increments of 10% (**Figure 5.35**).

✔ Tip

- The percent snap increment can be set in the Options panel of the Grid and Snap Settings dialog box. This can be accessed quickly by right-clicking on the Percent Snap button (**Figure 5.36**).

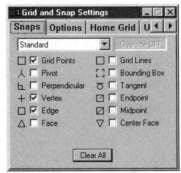

Figure 5.34 Set the snap targets for the objects. Use these settings to rotate an object around a vertex or edge.

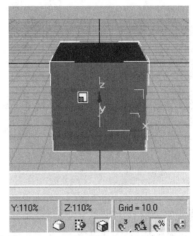

Figure 5.35 Scaling the cube with percent snap limits the scale action to 10% increments by default.

Figure 5.36 Adjust the percent snap increment in the Grid and Snap Settings Options panel.

Figure 5.37 The Options panel allows you to increase the strength of a snap, as well as set snap angles and percentages, snap to frozen objects, and use axis constraints.

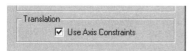

Figure 5.38 Check Use Axis Constraints, the default.

To strengthen snaps:

1. Choose Customize > Grid and Snap Settings.

2. Click the Options tab (**Figure 5.37**).

3. Use the Snap Strength spinner or type a value to increase the "magnetism" of the grid points.

To enable transform axis constraints with snaps:

1. Choose Customize > Grid and Snap Settings.

2. Click the Options tab.

3. Check Use Axis Constraints, which is the default (**Figure 5.38**).

SNAPPING TRANSFORMATIONS

Aligning Objects

The Mirror, Array, and Align commands are "advanced transforms" that can precisely move, rotate, or scale objects in various combinations (**Figure 5.39**). Because the Mirror and Array tools also contain options for cloning objects, they are discussed in the following sections.

The Align tool precisely aligns the position, orientation, or scale of one or more objects to another object.

To align objects:

1.  Select one (or more) objects to align (**Figure 5.40**).

   MAX calls this the *current object*.

2. Choose the Align tool from the Main Toolbar.

3. Click a second object, also known as the *target object*.

   The Align Selection dialog box appears (**Figure 5.41**).

4. Accept the default alignment reference point—the center of each object—or choose another option for each object.

   Minimum and Maximum refer to the dimensions of the object's bounding box.

5. Check the position, orientation, and scale of each axis in the target object to which you want to align the current object.

   As you check each axis, the current object aligns with that axis of the target object (**Figure 5.42**).

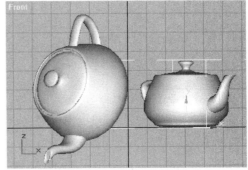

Figure 5.39 The "advanced transforms" include the Mirror, Array, and Align commands found in the Main Toolbar.

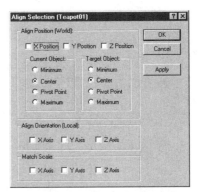

Figure 5.40 Select the object you want to align.

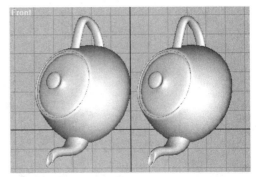

Figure 5.41 In the Align Selection dialog box, you align the position, orientation, and scale of objects.

Figure 5.42 These two teapots align in all ways except the *X* position.

ALIGNING OBJECTS

Figure 5.43 When you use the Normal Align tool, a blue surface-normal symbol appears where you click an object.

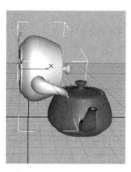

Figure 5.44 The surface normals of the two objects align; the objects appear to stick together.

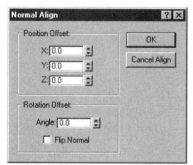

Figure 5.45 In the Normal Align dialog box you set the rotation and position offsets for the normal aligned objects.

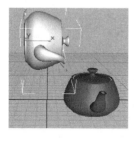

Figure 5.46 Normal aligned objects can be offset so that they're aligned but not touching.

In Chapter 9 you'll learn how to combine objects, but there's a form of alignment called *aligning normals* that makes objects appear to stick together even though they remain separate objects. In geometry, *normal* means perpendicular, so normal alignment lines up the surfaces of objects so that they kiss.

To align objects to stick together (normal align):

1. Select an object.

2. Choose the Normal Align tool from the Align flyout.

3. Click the surface of the first object with the normal align cursor.

    A blue surface-normal symbol appears where you click the surface (**Figure 5.43**).

4. Click the surface of the second object.

    A green surface-normal symbol appears where you click the surface. The first object aligns to the surface of the second object by aligning the blue and green surface normals in a straight line (**Figure 5.44**). The Normal Align dialog box also appears (**Figure 5.45**).

5. If necessary, enter values in the dialog box to offset the first object.

    To offset the first object from the second along the lengths of the surface normals, enter a new value for Z in the Position Offset group. To offset the position of the first object in a perpendicular direction from the two surface normals, enter new Position Offset values for X and/or Y (**Figure 5.46**).

(continues on next page)

ALIGNING OBJECTS

6. If necessary, change the Angle value in the Rotation Offset area of the dialog box to rotate the first object around the surface normals.

   To rotate the object 180 degrees along the length of the surface normals, check Flip (**Figure 5.47**).

7. To clear settings and start over, click Cancel.

8. When you're satisfied with the settings, click OK.

✔ Tips

■ Hold down the Ctrl key while dragging spinners to make them change faster. Hold down the Alt key while dragging spinners to make them change slower.

■ ↻ Use the Place Highlight tool in the Array flyout to align a selected light to the surface normal of an object: simply click the surface of the object.

■ 📷 Use the Align Camera tool in the Array flyout to align a selected camera to the surface normal of an object: simply click the surface of the object.

Aligning an object to a view

The Align to View tool in the Align flyout allows you to align an object perpendicularly to the view plane of a view using the object's pivot point center and local axes for reference.

To align an object to a view:

1. ▸ Select an object (**Figure 5.48**).

2. 🔲 Choose the Align to View tool from the Align flyout.

   The Align to View dialog box appears with an axis of alignment already selected (**Figure 5.49**).

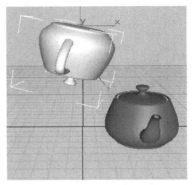

Figure 5.47 You can also rotate objects around the surface normals.

Figure 5.48 To align an object to a view, start by selecting the object.

Figure 5.49 In the Align to View dialog box you can select an axis of alignment.

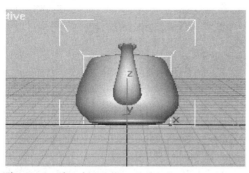

Figure 5.50 The object aligns to the view.

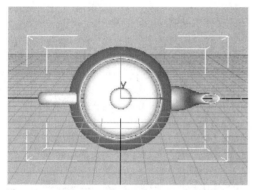

Figure 5.51 When you change the axis of alignment, the object immediately changes in the view.

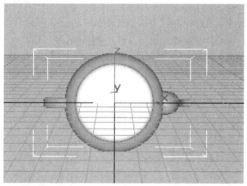

Figure 5.52 You can also flip objects in relation to the view.

The object aligns to the view in the selected axis (**Figure 5.50**).

3. Change the axis of alignment, if necessary, in the View Align dialog box (**Figure 5.51**).

4. To flip an object 180 degrees in the axis of alignment, check Flip in the dialog box (**Figure 5.52**).

5. Click OK.

✔ Tip

- ▣ Use the Align to View tool to align the current view to the surface normal of an object: simply click the surface of the object.

ALIGNING OBJECTS

Cloning Objects

Cloning creates objects that look exactly like the original. Clones can be created singly or in multiples, and they can be placed in different spatial configurations. Commands for creating clones include the Clone command, the transform commands, and the array commands.

You can make three types of clones in 3D Studio MAX 3:

◆ A *copy* is a duplicate object that you can modify independently of the original. This is the default clone type.

◆ An *instance* is a duplicate object that shares all its modifiers with the original.

◆ A *reference* is a duplicate object that shares some of its modifiers with the original but not all of them.

For a full explanation of clone types, and why you use them, see the sidebar on this page.

Clone Types

Copies inherit all of the attributes of the original object, but are completely independent thereafter. Changes to the original do not affect its copies, and changes you make to copies do not affect the original.

Instances share the same master object and modifiers but do not share transforms, space warps, or object properties. You can animate one instance to affect them all. This is great for creating flocks of birds, swarms of bees, schools of fish, or any other objects that needs to look alike and move together simultaneously.

References are also partially dependent objects that have more freedom than instances. References share the same master object as the original, but they share modifiers only under certain conditions. In the simplest terms, when you create a reference, modifiers applied before you create the reference are shared. Modifiers you apply afterward affect only the selected object. *(See Chapter 7, "Modifying Objects," for a full explanation.)*

Since you can control which modifiers are passed on and which ones are not, it is easy to create variations on a theme with references. References are like multiple casts made from a mold. You can apply different decorations to each cast of the sculpture, or you can change the original mold.

You can also make a reference of a reference, like making a new mold out of one of the casts. You can make references of instances to create variations of a multi-object animation, such as birds that veer from a flock, bees that split into smaller swarms, or fish that pause to look at the camera.

Figure 5.53 Choose the type of clone and name the new object.

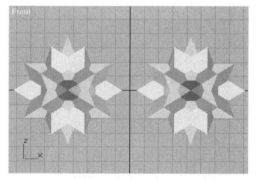

Figure 5.54 Comparing a clone to the original.

Cloning an object

The simplest way to make a clone is to use the Edit > Clone command. This method creates a clone in the exact same position as the original.

To clone an object:

1. ▶ Select an object.

2. Choose Edit > Clone.

   The Clone Options dialog box appears (**Figure 5.53**). The Copy option is enabled by default; until you know how to use the modifier stack, make copies rather than the other types of clones. *(For more about modifying objects, see Chapter 7, "Modifying Objects.")*

3. Type a name or accept the default, which is the name of the original object with a numbered suffix.

4. Click OK.

   The clone occupies the same spot as the original. To see the clone, move it away from the original (**Figure 5.54**).

Object Data Flow

Objects can be modified, transformed, warped, shadowed, or mapped. As an object is changed, its data is passed from one command subroutine to another. MAX evaluates these commands in *Object data flow* order:

1.) A **master object** is the basic definition of an object including its creation parameters, position, orientation, and scale. **2.)** **Modifier** commands typically deform the structure of objects. **3.)** **Transform** commands change the position, orientation, and scale of objects. **4.)** **Space warps** are objects that act on other objects, causing them to deform as though they were passing through a force field. **5.)** **Object properties** include an object's name, color, display properties, and rendering properties, including its ability to cast and receive shadows.

Note that the order of evaluation of commands may differ from the order of their application. For example, if you scale an object and subsequently modify it, the scaling data is not passed to the modifiers for evaluation. This can create some unexpected results, especially if the scale transforms deform the object unevenly. The typical workarounds are to change an object's creation parameters instead of scaling it or to apply scale commands as modifiers by using an XForm modifier. *(See "Applying Xform Modifiers" in Chapter 7.)*

Making a series of clones

The transform commands can be used to create a series of clones if you hold down the Shift key before transforming an object. This is called Shift-cloning an object.

The Select and Move tool can be used to create a series of clones spaced evenly along a line.

To make a series of clones:

1. Choose a transform tool from the Main Toolbar.

2. Hold down the Shift key.

3. Drag an object.

   A second object is dragged out of the first one (**Figure 5.55**).

4. Release the mouse button and the Shift key.

   The Clone Options dialog box appears. This time there is place to enter the number of copies (**Figure 5.56**).

5. Enter a value for Number of Copies.

6. Click OK.

   The copies appear, lined up with the first clone that you dragged. Each one is spaced the same distance apart as the first clone is from the original. You can now rename the copies and place them anywhere in the scene (**Figure 5.57**).

✔ Tip

■ To Shift-clone an object in place so that it overlaps the original completely, simply click the object instead of dragging it.

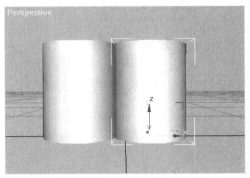

Figure 5.55 Shift-cloning a cylinder with the Select and Move tool.

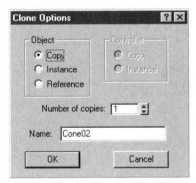

Figure 5.56 In the Clone Options dialog box, you enter the number of copies that you want to make.

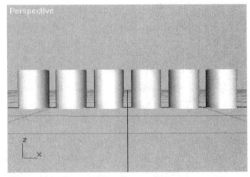

Figure 5.57 The resulting clones of a move transform are always spaced an even distance apart.

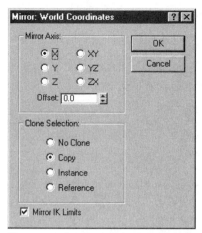

Figure 5.58 The Mirror dialog box allows you to choose the axes of mirror reflection and the resulting clone type.

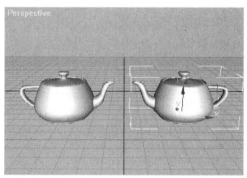

Figure 5.59 The result of mirroring an object and offsetting its clone in *X*.

Figure 5.60 Use the mirror commands repeatedly to create patterns.

Mirroring Objects

The Mirror tool reflects an object along one or two of its axes. It can also create a clone that is an exact mirror image of the original.

To mirror an object:

1. Select an object.

2. Choose the Mirror tool on the Main Toolbar.

   The Mirror dialog box appears (**Figure 5.58**).

3. Choose a mirror axis or use the default.

4. Enter an Offset value to specify how far away the mirrored clones will be.

5. Set Clone Selection to Copy.

   A mirrored copy of the object is created, offset in the direction of the mirror axis (**Figure 5.59**).

✔ Tips

■ To mirror an object without creating a clone, choose No Clone.

■ Try mirroring with different axes *(X, Y, Z, XY, YZ,* and *ZX)* and observe the results.

■ To create multiple clones of mirrored objects, create an object and mirror it. Then select the object and its clone and mirror them together. Repeat this process until you get the number of clones that you need (**Figure 5.60**).

MIRRORING OBJECTS

Making Arrays

The Array tool creates an arrangement of clones by moving, rotating, or scaling an object in up to three dimensions. You can arrange clones in a line, a grid, a *lattice* (an array of clones that are arranged in a three-dimensional grid), a circle, or a spiral.

A radial array is a one-dimensional array of clones arranged in a circle. You can create a radial array anywhere on the grid.

Creating a 3x3x3 lattice array

The Array tool creates an array of clones by moving, rotating, or scaling an object in up to three dimensions. Clones can be arranged in a line, a grid, a lattice, a circle, or a spiral.

A *lattice array* is an array of clones that are arranged in a three-dimensional grid.

To create a 3x3x3 lattice array:

1. ⬚ Select an object.

2. ⬚ Choose the Array tool.

    The Array dialog box appears (**Figure 5.61**).

3. In the Move row in the Incremental area, enter *X = 100* (**Figure 5.62**).

    This will space each element in the array 100 units apart in *X*.
    In the Array Dimensions area, choose 3D, and then enter the following:

    > *1D Count = 3*
    > *2D Count = 3*
    > *3D Count = 3*

    This will make a total of 3x3x3 = 27 clones.

4. In the 2D row of the Incremental Row Offsets section, enter *Y = 100*.

    This will space each element in the array 100 units apart in *Y*.

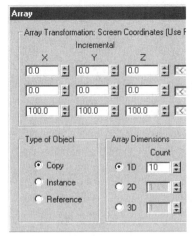

Figure 5.61 The Array dialog box allows you to create a one-, two-, or three-dimensional array.

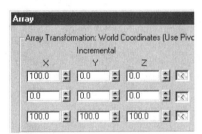

Figure 5.62 You can combine move, rotation, and scale transforms in a single array.

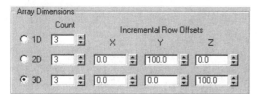

Figure 5.63 Entering the Incremental *Z* parameter.

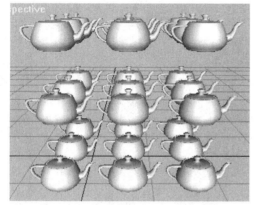

Figure 5.64 Use Zoom Extents All for a look at the array.

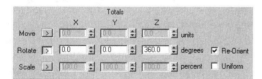

Figure 5.65 These parameters create an array of clones in a 360-degree circle.

5. In the 3D row of the Incremental Row Offsets section, enter *Z = 100*.

   This will space each element in the array 100 units apart in *Z* (**Figure 5.63**).

6. Click OK.

   A lattice array of 27 objects is created. Use Zoom Extents All to get a better look (**Figure 5.64**).

✔ Tips

- To create a two-dimensional grid of clones, choose Count = 2D.

- To create a line of clones, choose Count = 1D.

To create a radial array:

1. Decide on the center point for the array and place an object near the center point.

2. Choose Use Transform Coordinate Center from the Transform Center flyout.

3. Choose View from the Reference Coordinate drop-down list.

4. Choose the Array tool from the Main Toolbar.

5. In the Array dialog box that appears, choose 1D, if it's not already selected.

6. In the Array Dimensions area, enter a count in the top count field.

7. In the Rotate row, click the arrow button to the right of the world Rotate.

8. In the Totals area enter *Z = 360* (**Figure 5.65**).

   The objects surround the center point completely in a circular array. Enter fewer degrees to clone the object in an arc.

   (continues on next page)

9. Click OK.

A radial array of clones appears (**Figure 5.66**).

✔ Tips

- Try out array settings and then click Undo. This undoes the array creation but leaves the last settings in the Array dialog box. You can then update them. To clear all settings, choose Reset All Parameters.

- To create a radial array around an object, choose Pick from the Reference Coordinate Center drop-down, and click the object you want in the center.

- To make the clones face the same direction, uncheck Re-Orient.

- To create a spiral array, assign a value to Z in the Move row (**Figure 5.67**).

Creating a snapshot array

The Snapshot tool creates multiple clones by taking "multiple exposures" of an animated object over time. *(For more about animation, see Chapter 6, "Basic Animation.")*

To create a snapshot array:

1. ⬚ Select an animated object.

2. In the Display panel, check Trajectory in the Display Properties rollout if you want to see the animation's path before making the array.

The trajectory of the object appears (**Figure 5.68**).

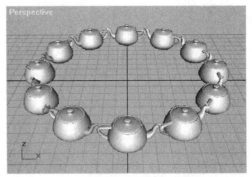

Figure 5.66 This radial array of 12 teapots is centered around the world origin.

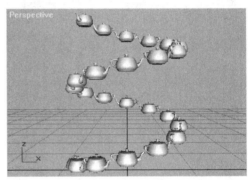

Figure 5.67 This spiral array is the result of assigning a value to Z in the Move row.

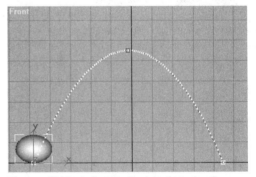

Figure 5.68 The trajectory displays the animation path of this bouncing ball.

MAKING ARRAYS

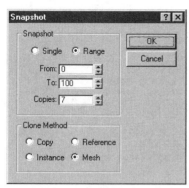

Figure 5.69 The Snapshot dialog box allows you to make clones of an object moving over time.

3. 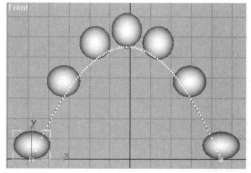 Choose Snapshot from the Array flyout in the Main Toolbar.

   The Snapshot dialog box appears (**Figure 5.69**).

4. Choose Range.

5. In the Copies field, enter the total number of clones you want to create.

6. Click OK.

   A snapshot array of the designated number of clones is created along the trajectory of the original object (**Figure 5.70**).

Figure 5.70 The resulting snapshot array positions the clones along the trajectory of the original object.

MAKING ARRAYS

Spacing Objects

Strictly speaking, the spacing tool is an array tool because it creates multiples, but practically we use it more to arrange objects between points or along the length of a spline or multiple splines.

The Spacing tool in the Array flyout allows you to distribute objects evenly between two points or along the length of a spline.

The Spacing tool has four basic parameters:

◆ Count sets the number of clones to be distributed.

◆ Spacing sets the distance between clones.

◆ Start Offset sets how far away from the starting point the set of clones appear.

◆ End Offset sets how far away from the end point the set of clones appear.

As you check and uncheck spacing parameters, different options automatically appear in the Spacing tool drop-down list. These options reflect the combination of parameters that have been checked. Selecting an option from the list also provides a convenient shortcut for enabling parameters (**Figure 5.71**).

When you change parameters in the rollout, the changes persist; you'll see the same settings the next time you open the rollout unless you click Reset to return to the default settings.

MAX does not actually use the spacing parameters until you click the parameter field or use a spinner; then the parameters take effect interactively. You can change the parameters until you click the Apply button.

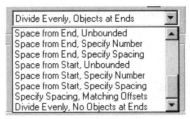

Figure 5.71 The Spacing tool drop-down list offers the parameters for distributing objects between points or along a spline.

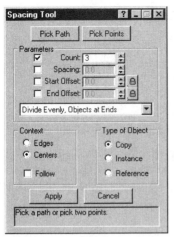

Figure 5.72 In the Spacing Tool dialog box you set the number of objects as well as their alignment and relationship to the ends.

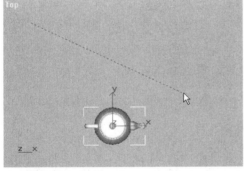

Figure 5.73 A dashed line appears as you drag to locate the second point for distributing the objects.

Figure 5.74 Enter a number of objects.

To distribute a series of clones between two points:

1. Select an object to clone.

2. Select the Spacing tool from the Align flyout.

   The Spacing Tool dialog box appears (**Figure 5.72**).

3. In the Spacing tool drop-down list, choose a distribution option.

   In the example, the choice is Divide Evenly, Objects at Ends.

4. Select a clone type in the Type of Object area.

5. Click Pick Points.

6. In a viewport, click to pick the start point.

7. Move the cursor to the location where you want the end point and then click to set the end point.

   A dotted line "rubber bands" from the cursor as you move it (**Figure 5.73**).

   A temporary spline is drawn between the two points.

8. Choose a number of clones to distribute by checking the Count box in the parameters area and then entering a number (**Figure 5.74**).

(continues on next page)

SPACING OBJECTS

The clones appear along the temporary spline interactively as you increase or decrease the value of Count (**Figure 5.75**).

9. If necessary, adjust the spacing of clones between two end points by unchecking Count, checking Spacing, and then entering a value for the spacing parameter.

   Note that the Count value is inversely affected by the change in Spacing, even though the Count value is grayed out.

10. Click Apply and then close the dialog box.

    The temporary spline disappears.

✔ Tips

- To extend clones in a straight line from the start point of a spline to the end point or beyond, check both Count and Spacing (**Figure 5.76**).

- To offset clones from the end point rather than the start point, check End Offset.

- Use the Context options in the Spacing Tool dialog box to choose how to align clones to a spline. To align clones by the edge of their bounding boxes, select Edges. To align clones by their pivot points, select Centers. To align the pivot points of the clones to the tangent of a spline, so as to affect their orientation, check Follow (**Figure 5.77**).

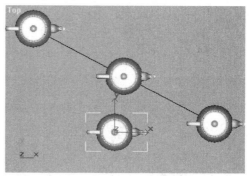

Figure 5.75 The objects appear along the temporary spline.

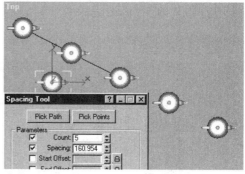

Figure 5.76 Check Count and Spacing to extend clones from the starting point of a spline.

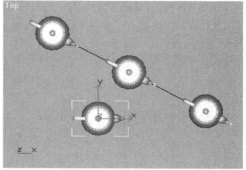

Figure 5.77 Use the Spacing tool's Context options to set alignment to the spline.

SPACING OBJECTS

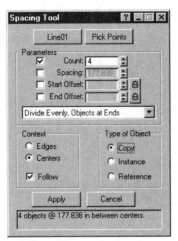

Figure 5.78 Set distribution of objects along a spline in the Spacing Tool dialog box.

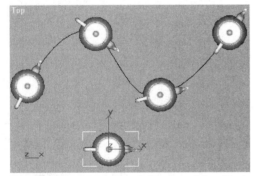

Figure 5.79 Enter a number of objects, and the object clones appear along the spline.

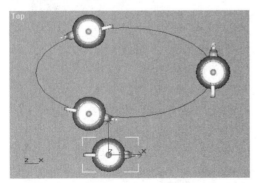

Figure 5.80 On closed splines, using the setting Divide Evenly, Object at Ends, it may appear as if some of the distributed objects are missing. In reality, the evenly spaced objects are just overlapping each other as they go around the spline.

To distribute a series of clones along a spline:

1. Select an object.

2. Select the Spacing tool from the Align flyout.

   The Spacing Tool dialog box appears (**Figure 5.78**).

3. In the Spacing tool drop-down menu, choose Divide Evenly, Objects at Ends.

4. Select a clone type in the Type of Object area.

5. Click Pick Path.

6. Click a spline object.

7. Check the Count parameter and specify a number of clones to distribute.

   The clones are distributed interactively along the spline as you change the count (**Figure 5.79**).

8. Click Apply and then close the dialog box.

✔ Tips

- MAX counts clones a little differently along an open spline (such as a line) as opposed to along a closed spline (such as an ellipse). When clones are counted along an open spline, they equal the value of the Count parameter. Along a closed spline, they might number one less than the count (**Figure 5.80**).

- The first vertex of a spline is always used to set the start point for spacing. *(For how to change the first vertex of a spline, see Chapter 8, "Editing Objects.")*

ANIMATION

According to Webster, the word *animation* is based on the Latin verb *animare,* which means "to give life to." This chapter tells you how to bring objects to life by changing their creation parameters and transforming them over time. Applying traditional animation principles such as anticipation, squash and stretch, overlapping action, exaggeration, and follow-through can infuse your scenes with humor and bring them to life. An excellent reference to get you started is *The Illusion of Life: Disney Animation,* revised edition, by Frank Thomas and Ollie Johnston (Hyperion, 1995).

About Animation

Animation is based on a physiological characteristic called *persistence of vision*. When you view a series of images in rapid succession, the mind creates the illusion of continuous motion because each image persists in your vision until the next image appears.

In animation, successive images are called *frames* (**Figure 6.1**). The faster the frames play, the smoother the motion appears to be. Common playback rates are 15, 24, and 30 frames per second, or *fps*. That adds up to 900, 1440, or 1800 frames for one minute of animation!

In traditional cel animation, the key poses, or *keyframes,* are drawn by a head animator to show the high point of an action (**Figure 6.2**). Junior animators draw the frames in between, or *tweens*. Drawing and painting the tweens by hand can be a long, laborious project when you consider that a 30-minute cartoon show on television requires up to 54,000 frames. MAX takes the tedium out of animation by calculating tweens automatically.

The Poetry of Animation

Animation introduces the concept of time. We recognize that time is passing by observing changes in our world: sunlight moving through the clouds, a beating heart, a ticking clock, bodies dancing to a beat, the steady rhythms of machines, rivers flowing to the sea, the turning cycles of the moon and stars. We also draw conclusions about the passage of time by comparing experience to memory: white hair, a wrinkled brow, an empty glass, an empty house. Time can make the world empty or full, high or low, light or dark, loud or soft, near or far, old or new.

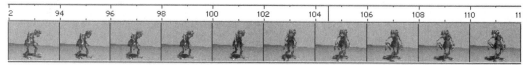

Figure 6.1 Frames in an animation segment show a character stopping and turning.

Figure 6.2 These two keyframes show the character at the maximum extent of two motions: stopping and turning.

Figure 6.3 Parametric animations change creation parameters, such as the radius, height, width, location, and so on.

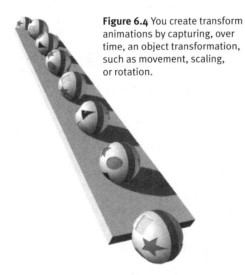

Figure 6.4 You create transform animations by capturing, over time, an object transformation, such as movement, scaling, or rotation.

Creating Animations

You create animations by changing objects over time. There are two basic ways to do this in MAX:

- **Parametric animations** change object parameters over time (**Figure 6.3**).

- **Transform animations** move, rotate, or scale objects over time (**Figure 6.4**).

When you animate an object in MAX, every frame in which you make changes becomes a keyframe. The value of a parameter or transform at a particular keyframe is called an animation *key*.

3D Studio MAX assigns *animation controllers* to every key. Animation controllers handle all of the computations involved in animating objects. This includes storing key values, interpolating values for tween frames, and calculating procedural (formula-based) animations.

To change an animation, you can either adjust the timing of keyframes, change their key values, or assign different controllers to the keys. Whether you change the keyframes, the keys, or the animation controllers, MAX updates all the tween frames automatically.

MAX has two interfaces for changing controllers: the Motion command panel for changing transform controllers, and the Track View for changing all types of controllers. This chapter explores some of the basic features of the Motion panel. The Track View is a much deeper interface worthy of a book in itself; in this chapter, it's discussed only briefly.

Animating an object

When you animate an object with keyframes, MAX creates animation keys in the track bar to mark the location of each keyframe in time. This process is known as *setting keyframes,* or *keyframing.*

To animate an object:

1. Select an object.

2. Drag the time slider all the way to the left.

   The time slider displays the first and last frame numbers of the active time segment (**Figure 6.5**).

3. Click the Animate button in the status bar controls.

   The Animate button and the boundary of the active viewport turn red (**Figure 6.6**).

4. Drag the time slider to the right to choose the next keyframe.

   The current frame number increases on the time slider display (**Figure 6.7**).

5. Change the parameters of the object or transform it in some way.

   A key appears in the track bar at frame 0 and at the current frame (**Figure 6.8**).

6. Click Play Animation to see the results. *(See the next section, "Playing Animations," for details.)*

7. Set additional keyframes by repeating steps 4 through 6.

8. Turn off the Animate button when you are through, or like the sorcerer's apprentice, you may create unforeseen effects.

✔ Tip

- Only animation keys for objects appear in the track bar. You access keys for animated *scene* parameters, such as Environment effects and sound keys, from the Track View.

Figure 6.5 The simplest of the MAX animation controls appear in the status bar and track bar under the viewports.

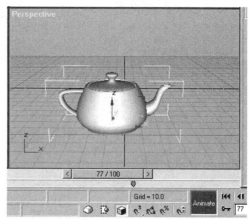

Figure 6.6 The Animate button and the boundary of the active viewport turn red when the Animate button is clicked.

Figure 6.7 The numbers on the time slider tell you the number of the current frame (on the left) and the length of the active time segment (on the right).

Figure 6.8 Drag the time slider all the way to the right to reach the last frame in the active segment.

CREATING ANIMATIONS

Figure 6.9 The object's animation keys appear in the track bar.

To adjust key settings:

1. ⬚ Select an animated object.
   The object's animation keys appear in the track bar (**Figure 6.9**).

2. ⬚ Click Animate.

3. ⬚ Click Key Mode Toggle.
   The Key mode is activated.

4. ⬚ Move to the key you want to adjust.
   (See "Working with Keys," later in this chapter.)

5. Adjust the transform or parameter settings of the keyframe.

6. ⬚ Click Play Animation.
   The animation plays back in the viewport, reflecting the adjustments you have made.

7. Repeat steps 4 through 6 until all the keyframes are adjusted the way you want.

✔ Tip

- Adjusting keyframes in a move animation causes the trajectory of the object to adjust as well. *(See "Controlling Motion," later in this chapter.)*

CREATING ANIMATIONS

Playing Animations

The animation playback controls play back the active time segment of an animation in the viewports using controls similar to those on a VCR (**Figure 6.10**). *(For information about how to change the active time segment, see "Configuring Time," later in this chapter.)*

To play back an animation:

1. Open or create an animated scene file.

2. ▶ Click Play Animation.

   The Play Animation button changes to the Stop Animation button. The animation plays back in the active viewport. After it reaches the final frame, it repeats from the beginning.

3. ■ Click Stop Animation.

   The animation stops playing.

✔ Tips

- Pressing the forward slash key (/) toggles animation playback.

- You can get a rough review of an animation by dragging the time slider back and forth. This is called *scrubbing the time slider.*

- To advance to a specific frame, highlight the current frame number in the animation playback controls and type in the desired frame number (**Figure 6.11**).

- ▮▶ Click Go to Next Frame to advance a single frame, or click the right arrow on the time slider. You can also press the period key (.) to advance one frame.

- ◀▮ Click Previous Frame to move back a single frame, or click the left arrow on the time slider. You can also press the comma key (,) to move back.

- Use ▮◀◀ Go to Start and ▶▶▮ Go to End to jump to the beginning or end frame of the active time segment.

Figure 6.10 Use the animation playback controls to play back the active time segment.

Figure 6.11 Enter a new frame number to advance the scene display to that frame.

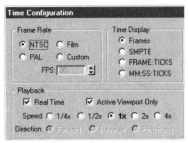

Figure 6.12 The Time Configuration dialog box allows you to change the way the scene is played back in the viewports.

Figure 6.13 Unchecking Active Viewport Only causes the animation to play back in all of the viewports at once.

Figure 6.14 Setting the viewport animation to play back at quarter speed.

Figure 6.15 Setting the viewport animation to ping-pong forward and backward.

To play back an animation in all of the viewports:

1. Open or create an animated scene file.

2. Click Time Configuration.
   The Time Configuration dialog box appears (**Figure 6.12**).

3. In the Playback group, uncheck Active Viewport Only (**Figure 6.13**).

4. Close the dialog box.

5. Click Play Animation.
   The animation plays back in all of the viewports, unless a viewport is disabled.

✔ Tips

- To play back an animation at quarter speed, half speed, double speed, or quadruple speed, check 1/4x, 1/2x, 2x, or 4x in the Playback group (**Figure 6.14**). Changing animation playback speed in the viewports does not affect playback in the rendered output file.

- To play back an animation in reverse, uncheck Real Time and select Reverse

- To play back an animation in alternating forward and reverse, uncheck Real Time and select Ping-Pong (**Figure 6.15**).

PLAYING ANIMATIONS

Animating Parameters

Virtually every parameter can be animated in MAX. A very simple way to animate an object is to change its creation parameters over time. Later, you can use the same approach to animate the parameters of modifiers, space warps, materials, and advanced object types.

First, learn the method for creating all parametric animations. Then try the example for practice.

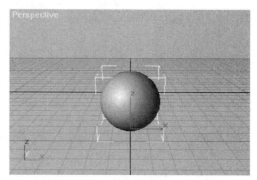

Figure 6.16 Selecting a small sphere.

To animate a parameter:

1. 🔲 Select an object, such as a sphere (**Figure 6.16**).

2. 🔳 Click Animate.

3. Drag the time slider to a new frame.

4. 🖉 Open the Modify panel and change one of the object's creation parameters, such as its radius (**Figure 6.17**).

   An animation key appears in the track bar below the time slider at the current frame.

5. Repeat steps 3 and 4 as needed until you reach the final frame.

6. ▶ Play the animation.

   The object changes smoothly from one keyframe to the next (**Figure 6.18**).

7. Make any adjustments necessary.

✔ Tips

■ For a striking effect, try animating the P and Q family parameters of a polyhedron.

■ Try animating the Hemisphere parameter of a sphere with Base to Pivot checked. See if you can make the sphere melt down to the grid (**Figure 6.19**).

Figure 6.17 Changing the radius parameter over time.

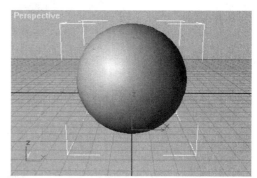

Figure 6.18 The enlarged sphere is rendered smoothly over time.

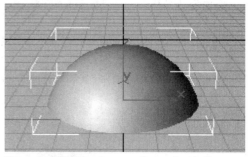

Figure 6.19 Melting down a sphere using the Base to Pivot and Hemisphere parameters.

Figure 6.20 Filtering the track bar to display only object parameter keys.

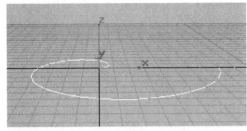

Figure 6.21 Creating a flat helix with Radius 1 = 80. Radius 2 and Height are both set to 0.

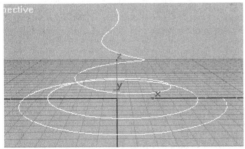

Figure 6.22 Animating the helix so that it rises from the grid like a coiling snake.

■ To filter keys in the track bar so that only parametric keys show, right-click the track bar and choose Filter > Object from the pop-up menu (**Figure 6.20**).

Animating the parameters of a helix

Splines can be used as animation paths and as components of compound objects. By animating a spline, you can indirectly—and very powerfully—animate the position or contours of the objects that depend on them. Splines can also be quite interesting to animate by themselves.

To animate the parameters of a helix:

1. Create a helix in the Perspective viewport using the keyboard-entry method. Set Radius 1 = 80 and leave Height and Radius 2 set to 0 (**Figure 6.21**).

2. ▬ Click Animate.

3. Drag the time slider to frame 100.

4. Set Height = 65, Turns = 4, and Bias = -.2.

5. ▶ Click Play Animation.
   The helix appears to rise from the grid like a coiling snake (**Figure 6.22**).

✔ Tips

■ If your graphics card has trouble keeping up with the changing viewport display, it degrades the display to bounding boxes. This effect is called *adaptive degradation*. To maintain the display in shaded mode, activate the 🔲 🔲 Degradation Override buttons in the status bar controls.

■ To alter the degradation level of active viewports, right-click the Degradation Override button and check a new level in the Active Degradation group of the Viewport Configuration dialog box.

ANIMATING PARAMETERS

Animating Transforms

One of the most effective ways to animate objects is to apply transforms over time. By combining move, rotate, and scale transforms, you can choreograph the motion of life.

To animate a transform:

1. ⬚ Select an object (**Figure 6.23**).

2. Drag the time slider to frame 0.

3. ⬚ Click Animate.

4. Drag the time slider to a new frame.

5. Transform the object using a move, rotate, and/or scale transform (**Figure 6.24**).

   An animation key appears in the track bar below the time slider at the current frame.

6. Repeat steps 4 and 5 until you reach the final frame.

7. ▶ Play the animation.

   The object transforms smoothly from one keyframe to the next.

8. Make any adjustments necessary.

✔ Tips

- To filter keys in the track bar so that only transform keys appear, right-click the track bar and choose Filter > All Transform Keys from the pop-up menu (**Figure 6.25**).

- Try animating a Mexican jumping bean using a move and squash transform!

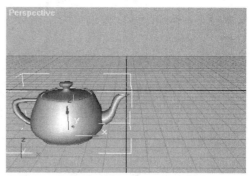

Figure 6.23 Selecting a teapot to begin the animation.

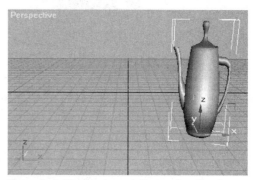

Figure 6.24 After moving, rotating, and scaling the teapot.

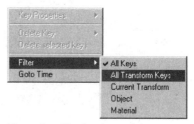

Figure 6.25 Filtering the track bar to display only object transform keys.

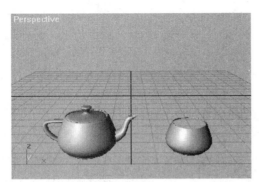

Figure 6.26 A teapot and "teacup." The teacup is created by turning off the handle, spout, and lid of a teapot primitive.

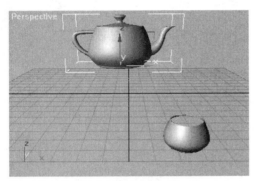

Figure 6.27 Positioning the teapot at frame 50.

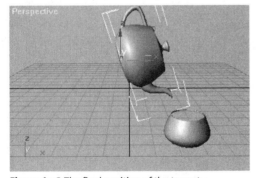

Figure 6.28 The final position of the teapot.

Animating movement

Animating move and rotate transforms is the most fundamental way to create motion.

To animate a teapot pouring:

1. ⬚ Create a teapot in the Perspective viewport.

2. ⬚ Create a second teapot just to the right. Uncheck the handle, spout, and lid, and reduce the radius to create a tea cup (**Figure 6.26**).

3. Drag the time slider to frame 0.

4. ⬚ Click Animate.

5. Drag the time slider to frame 50.

6. ⬚ Move the first teapot in X and Y so that its spout is positioned over the tea cup (**Figure 6.27**).

7. Drag the time slider to frame 100.

8. ⬚ Rotate the first teapot in Y so that the teapot appears to be pouring tea (**Figure 6.28**).

9. ⬚ Click Play Animation.

   The teapot lifts and rotates as if it were pouring tea. Notice that the rotation extends from frames 0 to 100, but the move transform applies only from frames 0 to 50.

Working with Keys

Once you have keyframed an animation and played it back in the viewports, you will probably need to adjust the animation keys. You can move, delete, and clone keys. You can even jump from one key to another as a way to navigate through an animation.

To select a key:

◆ 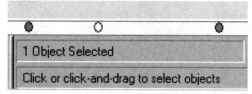 Click a key.

The key and the track bar turn white (**Figure 6.29**).

✔ Tips

■ To add to a selection of keys, use Ctrl-click.

■ To subtract from a selection of keys, use Alt-click.

To jump from key to key:

1. Select an animated object.

The object's animation keys appear in the track bar (**Figure 6.30**).

2. Click Key Mode Toggle.

The Key mode is activated.

3. Click Next Key in the animation play-back controls.

The time slider jumps to the next keyframe (**Figure 6.31**).

4. Continue clicking Next Key or Previous Key until you reach the keyframe you want.

Figure 6.29 Selecting a key in the track bar.

Figure 6.30 Selecting an animated object causes its animation keys to appear in the track bar.

Figure 6.31 Clicking Next Key causes the time slider to jump to the next key.

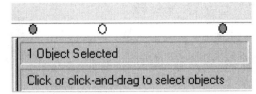

Figure 6.32 Select a key in the track bar.

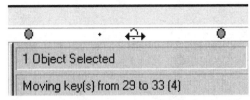

Figure 6.33 Dragging a key. A small dot appears at the old location of the key to provide a reference point.

Moving a key in the track bar

Moving keys in the track bar adjusts the timing of an animation. Moving keys closer together speeds up the animation. Moving keys farther apart makes the animation run slower.

To move a key in the track bar:

1. ▨ Select the key by clicking it.

   The key and the track bar turn white (**Figure 6.32**).

2. Drag the key to the left or right.

   As you drag the key, a small dot stays at the original location of the key until the mouse button is released. The prompt line provides a readout of the old frame number of the key, the new frame number, and the number of frames moved (**Figure 6.33**).

✔ Tip

- You can select multiple keys and move them by dragging a selection region across them.

To delete a key:

1. Select the key in the track bar.

2. Press the Delete key.

✔ Tip

- Deleting all the keys in the track bar eliminates all animation from the selected object. Settings for the current frame are applied globally to the scene.

Cloning keys

There are at least two reasons to clone keys. One is to make a moving object pause. If you drag the time slider with the Animate button on, the program does not generate a new Animation key unless you make a change to the object. But if you clone a key, the object will pause between the clone key and the original key. A second reason to clone keys is to return an object to a previous position or state. You may also need to straighten out the trajectory between the keys. *(See "Straightening a trajectory between keys," later in this chapter.)*

To clone a key in the track bar:

1. Select a key in the track bar (**Figure 6.34**).

2. Hold down the Shift key, and drag the key to a new location.

    A copy of the key is placed at the new location (**Figure 6.35**).

✔ Tips

■ To make the teapot in the example animation in Figures 6.26 through 6.28 pour more gracefully, try cloning the key at frame 50 to frame 75.

■ You can also clone keys by right-clicking the time slider to open the Create Key dialog box. There you can select a key from one position (the source time) and copy it to another position (the destination time) (**Figure 6.36**).

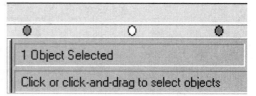

Figure 6.34 Selecting a key in the track bar.

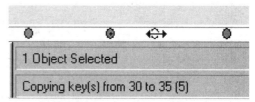

Figure 6.35 Copying the key to a new location.

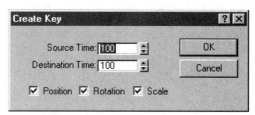

Figure 6.36 The Create Key dialog box allows you to copy keys from one position in time to another.

Display Properties
- ☐ Display as Box
- ☑ Backface Cull
- ☑ Edges Only
- ☐ Vertex Ticks
- ☑ Trajectory
- ☐ See-Through
- ☐ Ignore Extents
- ☐ Vertex Colors [Shaded]

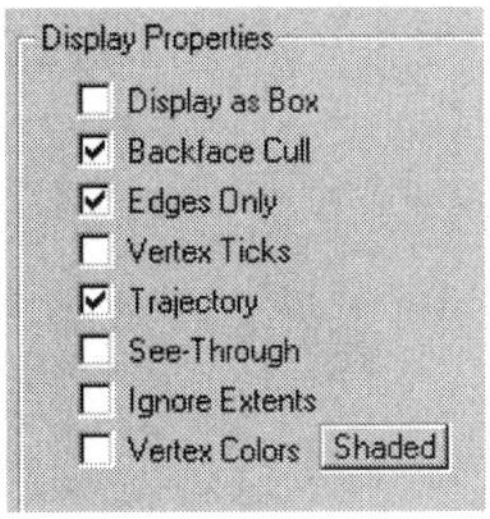

Figure 6.37 Checking Trajectory in the Object Properties dialog box.

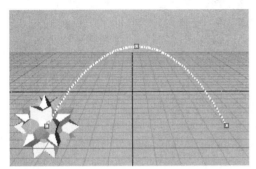

Figure 6.38 The trajectory of the object appears. It runs through the pivot point of an object.

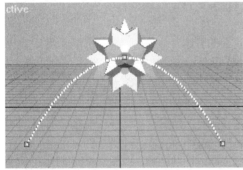

Figure 6.39 The hedra follows the trajectory during animation playback.

Controlling Motion

When you animate move, rotation, and scale transforms, MAX assigns separate animation controllers to each transform. Also known as *motion controllers, transform controllers* interpolate values between position, rotation, and scale keys. These interpolated values allow the program to calculate the in-between frames.

If you animate an object with a move transform, MAX automatically assigns a Bézier position controller to the transform. By applying a Bézier function to the key values, Bézier position controllers create motion paths that curve smoothly between keyframes.

You view the motion path of an object by displaying its trajectory.

To display a trajectory:

1. Select an object that changes position over time.

2. Right-click the object.
   The Object Properties dialog box appears.

3. In the Display Properties group, check Trajectory (**Figure 6.37**). Then click OK.
   The trajectory of the object appears in the viewports—a thick white line that runs through the pivot point of the object (**Figure 6.38**). Animation keys are represented as small squares along the trajectory's length. The keys turn red when the object is deselected and white when it is selected.

4. Play the animation.
   The object moves along the trajectory from one key to the next (**Figure 6.39**).

✔ Tip

■ You can display the trajectories of all the objects in the scene by checking Trajectory in the Display Properties rollout of the Display panel.

CONTROLLING MOTION

Moving a key in a trajectory

Moving keys in a trajectory adjusts both the timing and key settings of an animation. The advantage of this method is that you can see the shape of the trajectory change interactively as you change the position of each key.

To move a key in a trajectory:

1. [icon] Select an object that has been animated with a move transform..

2. [icon] Open the Motion command panel (**Figure 6.40**).

3. Click the Trajectories button.

   The Trajectories rollout appears (**Figure 6.41**). The trajectory of the object appears, if it was not already displayed.

4. Click the Sub-Object button.

   Keys become selected (**Figure 6.42**).

5. [icon] Choose Select and Move.

6. Select an animation key in the trajectory by clicking a key or dragging a region around it.

   The key turns from white to gray.

7. Drag the key to a new position.

   The trajectory deforms to follow the key (**Figure 6.43**).

8. [icon] Play the animation to check the results.

   The animation plays back in the viewports, following the new shape of the trajectory.

✔ Tip

■ You can select multiple keys, clone keys, and add and delete keys in a trajectory in much the same way you do in the track bar. Use whichever method seems most convenient for you.

Figure 6.40 The Motion command panel allows you to assign animation controllers and manipulate trajectories.

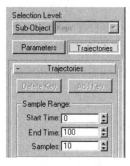

Figure 6.41 The Trajectories rollout allows you to choose keys as a sub-object of trajectories.

Figure 6.42 Selecting key sub-objects.

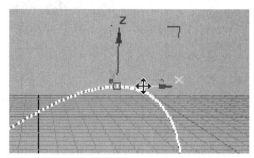

Figure 6.43 Moving a key causes the trajectory to deform interactively.

CONTROLLING MOTION

Figure 6.44
The Parameters rollout contains commands for transform controllers.

Figure 6.45 Selecting the position controller from the Assign Controller rollout.

Figure 6.46 The Assign Position Controller dialog box presents you with fifteen different position controllers.

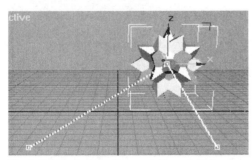

Figure 6.47 Assigning a linear position controller causes the trajectory to straighten out between all the keys.

Straightening a trajectory between keys

Another way to change the shape of a trajectory is to assign a new controller to the object's position. Some of the most important position controllers are Bézier, TCB, Noise, Audio, and Path. Assigning a Linear position controller straightens out a trajectory's curve into a series of line segments that connect each key.

To assign a position controller:

1. ⬉ Select an object that has been animated with a move transform.

2. Turn on its trajectory.

3. ⬚ Open the Motion command panel.
   The Parameters rollout appears (**Figure 6.44**).

4. Open the Assign Controller rollout.
   Four animation tracks appear. Each one is marked by a green triangle (**Figure 6.45**).

5. Select the Position track.
   The Assign Controller button becomes available.

6. ⬚ Click the Assign Controller button.
   The Assign Position Controller dialog box appears. In it, a list of all possible position controllers is displayed (**Figure 6.46**).

7. Select a position controller and click OK.
   The position controller is assigned to the transform.

To assign a linear position controller:

1. Follow steps 1 through 6 above.

2. Select Linear Position and click OK.
   The trajectory straightens out between the animation keys (**Figure 6.47**).

Accelerating motion

Acceleration gives important clues as to the subject and mood of your animation. Characters usually speed up or slow down gradually as they start, stop, or change the direction of motion. Abrupt acceleration or braking usually indicates extreme agitation, a collision, or mechanical motion.

Bézier controllers allow you to change the acceleration of an object as it approaches and moves beyond each key.

To change acceleration:

1. ⬛ Select an object that has a Bézier position controller assigned to it, and turn on its trajectory.

2. ⬛ Open the Motion command panel.

3. Open the Key Info [Basic] rollout (**Figure 6.48**).

4. Click the right arrow in the upper left-hand corner of the rollout.

   The time slider advances to the next keyframe. At the same time, the object moves to the next key on the trajectory.

5. Click the In button and choose the Step, Slow, or Fast tangent type from the In flyout (**Figure 6.49**).

   The trajectory of the object approaching the key changes shape (**Figure 6.50**).

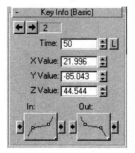

Figure 6.48 The Key Info [Basic] rollout allows you to adjust an object's rate of speed before and after each key.

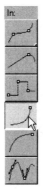

Figure 6.49 Choosing a fast tangent type from the In flyout.

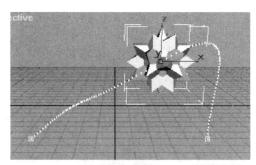

Figure 6.50 The trajectory of the object changes shape as it approaches the second key.

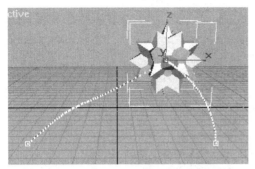

Figure 6.51 After choosing a Slow tangent type, the trajectory of the object changes shape to match.

6. Click the Out button and choose the Step, Slow, or Fast tangent type from the flyout.

The trajectory of the object after the key changes shape (**Figure 6.51**).

7. ▶ Play the animation to see the result.

8. Repeat steps 5 through 7 until you are satisfied with the object's acceleration.

Tangent Types

Tangent types are like mini-controllers that can be applied to trajectories before and after keys. They are available for any controller that uses a Bézier function.

Smooth: Smoothly curves the trajectory between keys.

Linear: Straightens the trajectory between keys.

Step: Creates a pause followed by an abrupt change between keys.

Slow: Decelerates motion between keys.

Fast: Accelerates motion between keys.

Custom: Places Bézier control handles at each key. These controls can be seen and manipulated only in the Function Curves mode of the track view.

Configuring Time

The Time Configuration dialog box allows you to set all the time parameters for an animation: the length of the active time segment, playback rate, the units of time measurement, and the configuration of the Key mode. It also allows you to rescale an animation as a whole.

The *active time segment* is a period of time in which an animation can be defined and played back in the viewports. The default active time segment for a MAX scene file is 0 to 100 frames. Time can also be displayed in terms of hours, minutes, seconds, and *ticks* (1/4800 of a second).

Adding frames to the active time segment increases its length without affecting the speed at which the animation plays back.

To add frames to the active time segment:

1. Open or create an animated scene file.

2. ◨ Click Time Configuration.
   The Time Configuration dialog box appears (**Figure 6.52**).

3. In the Animation group, increase the length (**Figure 6.53**).
   The number of frames in the active time segment increases. The distance between keys in the track bar shrinks to the left.

4. Close the dialog box.

5. ▶ Click Play Animation.
   The animation plays back at its usual speed and stops before the final frame.

✔ Tips

■ You can also subtract frames from the active time segment.

■ *(See "To change the time display," later in this chapter.)*

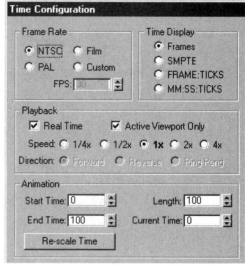

Figure 6.52 The Time Configuration dialog box allows you to set all the time parameters for an animation.

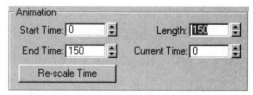

Figure 6.53 Increasing the length of the animation.

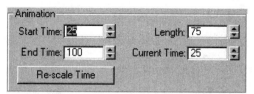

Figure 6.54 Entering a new start time for the active time segment.

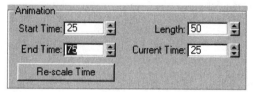

Figure 6.55 Entering a new end time for the active time segment.

Figure 6.56 The time slider adapts to the range of the active time segment.

Changing the range of the active time segment

Changing the range of the active time segment allows you to focus on the animation of specific frames without affecting the rest of the frames. Changing the range increases or decreases the length of the active time segment.

To change the range of the active time segment:

1. Open or create an animated scene file.

2. ⏱ Click Time Configuration to display the Time Configuration dialog box.

3. In the Animation group, enter a new start time (**Figure 6.54**).

   The new start time becomes the first frame of the active time segment. The length of the active time segment increases or decreases accordingly.

4. In the Animation group, enter a new end time (**Figure 6.55**).

   The new end time becomes the last frame of the active time segment. The length of the active time segment increases or decreases accordingly.

5. Click OK to close the Time Configuration dialog box.

   The range of the active time segment changes. The change is reflected in the time slider, which shows a different start frame and length (**Figure 6.56**).

6. ▶ Click Play Animation.

   The animation plays back at its usual speed, but it starts and ends at different frames than it did before.

Rescaling time

Rescaling time allows you to scale the active time segment. If time is scaled up, the timing of the animation slows down. If time is scaled down, the timing of the animation speeds up.

To rescale time:

1. Open or create an animated scene file.

2. ⬛ Click Time Configuration to display the Time Configuration dialog box.

3. In the Animation group, click the Re-scale Time button.

    The Re-scale Time dialog box appears (**Figure 6.57**).

4. Enter a new Length value.

    The active time segment scales up or down accordingly (**Figure 6.58**).

5. Click OK to close the Re-scale Time dialog box.

    The number of frames in the active time segment changes in the time slider display (**Figure 6.59**). The keys in the track bar stay in the same position, but the number of frames between them changes.

6. Click OK to close the Time Configuration dialog box.

7. ▶ Click Play Animation.

    The animation plays back at a different speed.

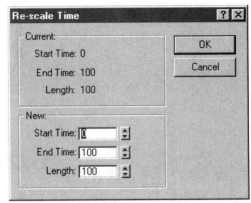

Figure 6.57 The Re-scale Time dialog box allows you to proportionally scale the length of the animation as well as its start and end times.

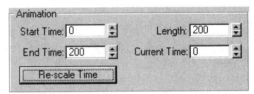

Figure 6.58 After rescaling the length of the animation, the end time rescales automatically.

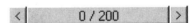

Figure 6.59 The time slider updates to show the new end time.

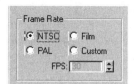

Figure 6.60 Choosing a frame rate.

Setting the Frame Rate

The *frame rate* is the number of frames that are played back per second by an animation after it has been rendered to an output file. It is measured in frames per second, or *fps*. Selecting a higher frame rate produces a smoother animation and creates a larger animation output file. Selecting a lower frame rate produces a choppier animation and creates a smaller animation output file.

To set the frame rate:

1. Click Time Configuration.

   The Time Configuration dialog box appears.

2. In the Frame Rate group, click one of the four choices for frame rates (**Figure 6.60**).

3. If you chose Custom, enter a frame rate in the now-active FPS entry field

4. Click OK.

Frame Rate Options

The Time Configuration dialog box provides the following choices of frame rates:

◆ **NTSC**, or National Television Standards Committee, is the standard used in the Americas and Japan. Choosing NTSC sets the frame rate to 30 fps.

◆ **PAL**, or Phase Alternation Line, is the standard used in Europe. Choosing PAL sets the frame rate to 25 fps.

◆ **Film** is the standard for the film industry. Choosing Film sets the standard to 24 fps.

◆ **Custom** is a standard that you create. If you are creating animation for a CD-ROM, you might set a custom frame rate of 15 fps because of the reduced number of frames that result in the final animation output file.

Setting the Time Code

A *time code* is a system of measuring and displaying time. In MAX, time is internally measured in a unit called a *tick,* which is 1/4800 of a second. Although a tick is an extremely accurate measure of time, it is rather awkward to use for displaying longer intervals such as minutes or seconds.

To change the time display:

1. 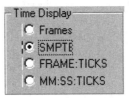 Click Time Configuration to display the Time Configuration dialog box.

2. In the Time Display group, click one of the four time code choices (**Figure 6.61**).

   The time code changes in the Animation group, in the animation playback controls, and in the time slider (**Figure 6.62**).

3. Click OK.

Figure 6.61 Choosing a time code.

Figure 6.62 The new time code is displayed on the time slider.

Time Code Types

The Time Configuration dialog box allows you to select from the following time codes for displaying time in the user interface:

- **Frames**, the default, measures time by frame number. The time slider displays both the current frame and the last frame of the active time segment.

- **SMPTE** (Society of Motion Picture Technical Engineers) measures time in minutes, seconds, and frames. The number of frames per second is determined by the frame rate.

- **FRAME:TICKS** measures time in frames and ticks.

- **MM:SS:TICKS** measures time in minutes, seconds, and ticks. At 30 frames per second, one frame equals 160 ticks, and one minute of animation equals 1800 frames.

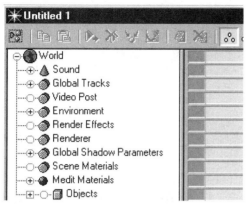

Figure 6.63 The Track View module displays animation tracks as a hierarchical tree.

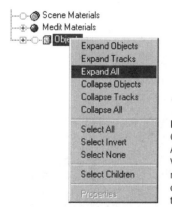

Figure 6.64 Choosing Expand All from the Track View right-click menu to make all of the Object tracks appear.

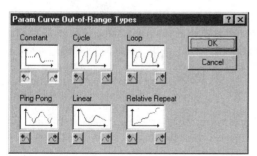

Figure 6.65 The Param Curves Out-of-Range dialog box allows you to cycle animations.

Figure 6.66 Cycle causes an animation to repeat the same sequence over and over.

Cycling Animations

If you are creating an animation that repeats, you can save a lot of effort by making a short animation sequence repeat in a cycle. Animation cycles must be created in the Track View, which is one of the more complex animation staging areas in MAX.

To cycle an animation:

1. Create a short and simple animation, such as a ball bouncing once over the course of 10 frames. (Hint: You can do this in three keyframes using the move and scale transforms. Try using squash for scaling.)

2. Click Open Track View in the main toolbar.

   The Track View module appears (**Figure 6.63**).

3. Maximize the Track View window.

4. On the left side of the Track View module, right-click the word Objects and choose Expand All from the pop-up menu (**Figure 6.64**).

5. Click Position.

   The word Position is highlighted. Buttons that were dimmed now become available in the Track View toolbar.

6. Click Parameter Curve Out-of-Range Types in the Track View toolbar.

   The Param Curves Out-of-Range Types dialog box appears. Constant is selected by default (**Figure 6.65**).

7. Choose Cycle by clicking its graph.

   The two buttons under the graph indent indicate that the position transform will cycle both before the first keyframe and after the last keyframe (**Figure 6.66**).

(continues on next page)

8. Click OK to close the dialog box.

9. Close the Track View window.

10. ▶ Play the animation.

    The ball bounces along in the viewport. The cycling action can now be rendered to an animation file.

✔ Tips

■ Try the other parameter curve out-of-range types. *(See the following sidebar, "Parameter Curve Out-of-Range Types," for a description of each.)*

Parameter Curve Out-of-Range Types

◆ **Constant:** Holds the value of the end key of the range for all frames. Use Constant when you do not want any animated effect to appear before the first key of the range or after the last key. It is the default out-of-range type.

◆ **Cycle:** Repeats the same animation as within the range. If the first and last keys in the range have different values, the animation will show an abrupt jump from the last key to the first. Use Cycle when you want an animation to repeat but do not need the ends to match.

◆ **Loop:** Repeats the same animation as within the range, but interpolates between the last key and first key in the range to create a smooth loop. If the first and last keys are both at the extreme ends of the range, Loop will behave exactly like Cycle. If you use Position Ranges to extend the range bar beyond the keys, the added length determines the amount of time used to interpolate between the last key and the first key. Use Loop with an extended range bar to produce smoothly repeating animation.

◆ **Ping Pong:** Alternates between a forward and backward repeat of the animation within the range. Use Ping Pong when you want your animation to alternate back and forth.

◆ **Linear:** Projects the animation value along a line tangent to the function curve at the end of the range. Use Linear when you want the animation to enter and leave the range at a constant velocity.

◆ **Relative Repeat:** Repeats the same animation as within the range but offsets each repetition by the value at the end of the range. Use Relative Repeat to create animations that build on each other as they repeat.

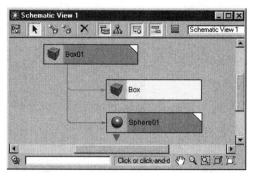

Figure 6.67 The Schematic View allows you to view and affect hierarchical structures.

Family Linking

Here are descriptions of each object's role in the hierarchy:

◆ **Child:** An object that has been linked to another object.

◆ **Parent:** The object to which a child object is linked. Each child can have only one parent, but a parent object can have multiple children.

◆ **Grandparent:** The parent of a parent.

◆ **Ancestor:** The parent and all of a parent's parents.

◆ **Grandchild:** The child of a child.

◆ **Descendant:** The child and all of a child's children.

◆ **Root:** An object at the top of a hierarchy.

◆ **Scene:** The root of an object that is not linked to a parent.

◆ **Leaf:** An object at the end of a hierarchy.

◆ **Branch:** The path through a hierarchy from an ancestor to a leaf.

Using Hierarchical Linking

To multiply the possibilities of transform animation, objects can be *linked* together to form a branching tree structure called a *hierarchy*. In a hierarchy, a *parent* object passes its transforms on to a *child* object. *(See the sidebar, "Family Linking.")* When a child inherits a parent's transforms, it follows the position, rotation, and scale of the parent. This allows you to create sophisticated animation sequences involving multiple objects and complex motions.

Another trick comes into play with linking. You can create dummy objects to aid in efficient production. A *dummy object* is a nonrendering helper object that you can use as an additional pivot point in a hierarchical linkage. Linking to a dummy object allows you to animate the dummy and pass the dummy's transforms further down the hierarchy. This is especially useful if you are animating objects that have a high polygon count or need an additional point of rotation. For example, you can place a dummy object at the center of some objects and link them; when you rotate the dummy, all the linked objects rotate as well. Dummies also work well for helping to animate cameras and lights. Dummies can link to other dummies. *(See "To create a dummy object," later in this chapter, for details.)*

The Schematic View allows you to view hierarchical structures of linked objects as well as hierarchies of modifiers, materials, maps, animation controllers, and bones (**Figure 6.67**). You can modify the links in the Schematic View as well.

The Select and Link tool links the pivot point of a child object to the pivot point of a parent object. When linked, the child follows the parent as it is moved, rotated, or scaled.

To link objects:

1. ⬚ Select an object.

   This object will be the child.

2. ⬚ Choose Select and Link from the main toolbar.

3. ⬚ Drag the Link cursor from the selected object to a second object. When the upper box in the cursor turns white, release the mouse button (**Figure 6.68**).

   The second object (the parent) flashes momentarily, indicating that the objects are linked.

4. Test the link by transforming the parent object in some way.

   The child object follows the parent (**Figure 6.69**).

5. Leave the Link mode by clicking the Select Object button in the toolbar.

✔ Tips

- Here's a shortcut: Select an object, press the H key, and choose a parent from the Select Parent dialog box (**Figure 6.70**).

- A great way to check links is in the Schematic View. *(See "To view a hierarchy in the Schematic View" later in this chapter.)*

- You cannot link a parent to its child.

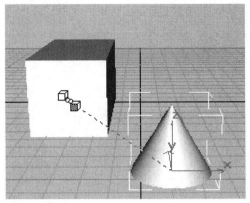

Figure 6.68 Linking a cone to a box with the Select and Link tool.

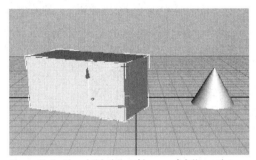

Figure 6.69 The child object (the cone) follows the parent object (the box) because it inherits the box's transforms.

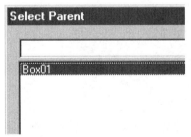

Figure 6.70 Choosing a parent from the Select Parent dialog box. This dialog box can be reached by clicking the Select by Name tool or by pressing the H key.

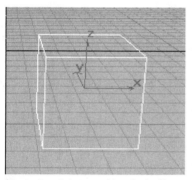

Figure 6.71 The Helpers menu with Dummy selected. There are no parameters for dummy objects.

Figure 6.72 A dummy object looks like wireframe box.

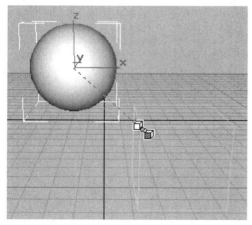

Figure 6.73 Linking a sphere to a dummy object.

To create a dummy object:

1. Click the Helpers toolbar.

2. Click Dummy.

   The Helpers menu appears in the Create command panel. The Dummy object type is selected (**Figure 6.71**).

3. Drag in the viewport to create a dummy object (**Figure 6.72**).

To link an object to a dummy object:

1. Select an object.

2. Link the object to a dummy object (**Figure 6.73**).

   The object is now a child of the dummy and will follow all of the dummy's movement, rotation, and scaling actions.

✔ Tip

- Click the edge of the dummy to select it, just as you would any wireframe mesh.

Unlinking objects

Unlinking stops the flow of transforms from parent to child.

To unlink objects:

1. Select a child object.

2. Choose Unlink Selection from the main toolbar.

3. Click the child object.

   The object unlinks from its parent.

To view a hierarchy in the Schematic View:

1. Open a scene that has a hierarchical linkage in it.

2. ▣ Choose New Schematic View from the main toolbar.

   A Schematic View of the scene appears (**Figure 6.74**).

3. ▣ ▲ Choose a mode of display from the Schematic View toolbar.

   The Schematic View changes the display (**Figure 6.75**).

4. Click the red triangle underneath any object to view its subtree, or right-click on the object and then choose Show/Hide > Show Downstream (**Figure 6.76**).

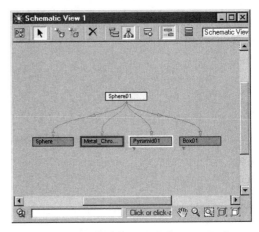

Figure 6.74 A Schematic View in References mode showing objects and materials linked to a parent object.

Figure 6.75 The same Schematic View in Hierarchy mode.

Figure 6.76 The Schematic View right-click menu allows you to show and hide an object's subtree.

USING HIERARCHICAL LINKING

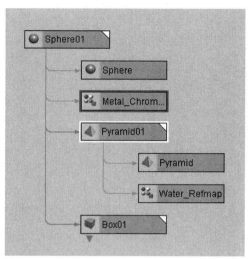

Figure 6.77 Displaying the subtree of the pyramid.

Figure 6.78 Viewport controls for the Schematic View appear in the lower-right corner of the window.

Figure 6.79 The Schematic View filter allows you to select the types of hierarchies that are displayed.

The subtree of the object appears in the Schematic View (**Figure 6.77**).

5. To hide a subtree, right-click the object and choose Show/Hide > Hide Downstream.

✔ Tips

■ Viewport controls for the Schematic View appear in the lower-right corner of the window (**Figure 6.78**).

■ 🔲 Use the Schematic View filter to select the type of hierarchies to display (**Figure 6.79**).

■ 🔲 🔲 Link and Unlink Selection allow you to link and unlink objects from the Schematic View.

■ ✕ Delete Objects allows you to delete objects from the Schematic View.

MODIFYING OBJECTS

Modifiers are parametric modeling tools that change the structure and surface appearance of objects. With modifiers, you can bend, twist, taper, ripple, wave, lathe, and extrude objects. Objects can be squeezed, sliced, stretched, or smoothed. You can even turn them inside out.

Modifiers are specific to different types of objects. Some modifiers work only with splines. Other modifiers work with meshes, patches, and NURBS (Non-Uniform Rational B-Splines), as well as splines.

Unlike transforms, which are calculated in an updating matrix, modifiers are tracked in an ordered list that stays with the definition of the object. This list, or history, of modifiers is called the *modifier stack*. The advantage of the modifier stack is that you can apply multiple modifiers to an object and later go back and adjust their parameters. You can also turn off, rearrange, or remove modifiers from the stack. This is because the modifier stack takes the basic definition of the object and passes that data up the stack. Every time a modifier is applied or adjusted, the object data is modified and then passed along. This flexibility is what gives the modifier stack its tremendous power for modeling, mapping, and animating objects.

About Modifiers

When certain modifiers are applied to an object, a gold wireframe box called a *gizmo* surrounds the object (**Figure 7.1**). You can think of a gizmo as a force field that transfers a modifier command to an object. When the modifier's parameter settings are adjusted, the gizmo changes shape. This, in turn, alters the shape of the modified object.

A gizmo is defined as a *sub-object* of a modifier. A modifier sub-object is the part of a modifier that transfers the modifier's effect to an object. Other modifier sub-objects include centers, lattices, and control points (**Figure 7.2**). Each of these sub-objects can be selected and transformed. Like changing the parameter settings of a modifier, transforming a modifier sub-object affects the object to which the modifier has been applied.

Like transforms, multiple modifiers can be applied in succession to obtain cumulative results. They can also be animated. You animate modifiers by changing parameter settings or by transforming sub-objects of modifiers over time. Modifier animation keys appear in the track bar as parameter keys.

More than 60 modifiers ship with 3D Studio MAX 3. Commands for applying modifiers are found in the Modifiers command panel (**Figure 7.3**). If a modifier cannot be applied to a selected object, it is dimmed in the Modifiers panel. Shortcuts for the most commonly used modifier commands are found in the Modifiers Toolbar (**Figure 7.4**).

Figure 7.1 A gizmo is a wireframe box that transfers the parameters of a modifier to an object.

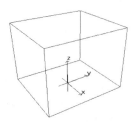

Figure 7.2 Modifier sub-objects include a gizmo with a center (top) and a lattice with control points (bottom).

Figure 7.3 The Modifiers command panel contains more than 60 modifiers. Many are hidden under the More button.

Figure 7.4 The Modifiers Toolbar contains shortcuts for the most commonly used modifiers.

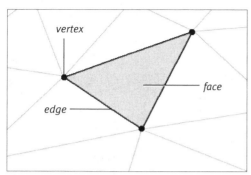

Figure 7.5 The sub-object components of a Mesh object are the vertex, face, and edge.

Figure 7.6 The first five modifiers on the Modifiers Toolbar—Bend, Taper, Skew, Twist, and Stretch—perform simple deformations of the selected object.

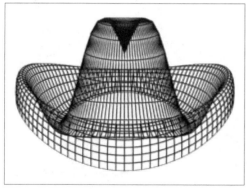

Figure 7.7 A Mesh object with a high degree of surface complexity, or mesh density.

Applying Geometric Modifiers

In this chapter, you'll start by applying some simple geometric modifiers, so you get the hang of modifiers in general. Then you will apply multiple modifiers to an object and manipulate them in the modifier stack. But first, before you plunge in, a little technical background about Mesh objects is in order.

Mesh objects have a continuous surface of triangular polygons known as *faces*. Each face is composed of three vertex points and three straight edges that connect them. Together, the vertex, face, and edge components are known as the *sub-objects* of a Mesh object (**Figure 7.5**).

Geometric modifiers deform objects by moving vertices with respect to the axes of a gizmo. The first five modifiers on the Modifiers Toolbar (**Figure 7.6**) are basic geometric modifiers: Bend, Taper, Skew Twist, and Stretch. Because these modifiers work in essentially the same way, only Bend, Twist, and Taper are covered in this section. Be sure to try Skew and Stretch as well before you go on to the next section.

For a mesh to deform smoothly, it must have a high degree of *surface complexity,* meaning many faces make up the mesh relative to its surface area. This is also known as *mesh density.* Extra faces make mesh deformations appear smooth because the mesh surface can bend at its vertices in many small increments (**Figure 7.7**).

To increase the complexity of a mesh primitive:

1. ⬚ Select a mesh primitive (**Figure 7.8**).

2. ⬚ Open the Modify panel.

3. If the mesh primitive has already been modified, click the Modifier Stack drop-down menu and select the primitive from the bottom of the stack.

   The object's creation parameters rollout appears in the Modify panel (**Figure 7.9**).

4. Increase the Segments parameters.

   A good rule of thumb for making an object smoothly deformable is to create one segment division for every 10 units of length, width, height, or radius. In the example in the figure, I'd enter 4, 6, and 5 for Segments Length, Width, and Height parameters, respectively.

   The mesh surface increases complexity in the Segment dimensions you have chosen (**Figure 7.10**).

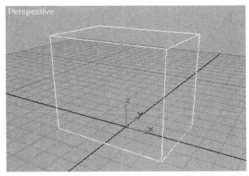

Figure 7.8 Selecting a box primitive.

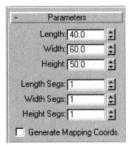

Figure 7.9 The creation parameters for a box. You increase the complexity of the box by increasing the number of length, width, and height segments.

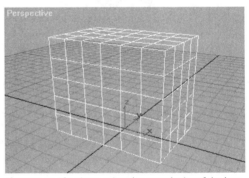

Figure 7.10 After increasing the complexity of the box.

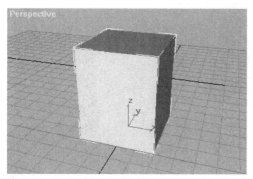

Figure 7.11 Selecting a box to bend.

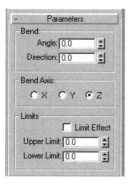

Figure 7.12 The Bend rollout appears in the Modify panel.

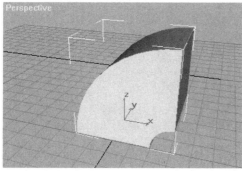

Figure 7.13 Bending the box in its Z-axis. Notice that the gizmo and box bend together.

Bending an object

The Bend modifier bends an object uniformly throughout its geometry.

To bend an object:

1. Select an object (**Figure 7.11**).

2. Click the Modifiers Toolbar.

3. Click Bend in the Modifiers Toolbar. The Modify command panel opens, and the Bend rollout appears. (**Figure 7.12**).

4. Select the Bend axis.

   The Bend axis refers to the orientation of the Modifier gizmo, which is not always the same as the orientation of the object.

5. Enter an Angle value in degrees or drag the Angle spinner.

   The gizmo and the object bend together (**Figure 7.13**).

✔ Tips

■ Changing the Direction parameter causes the object to bend perpendicular to the Bend axis.

■ Check Limit Effect and enter a value to constrain the modifier to the upper or lower part of the object.

■ If an object seems to lean or buckle or otherwise resists your attempts to deform it, try increasing the complexity of the mesh.

APPLYING GEOMETRIC MODIFIERS

Twisting an object

The Twist modifier causes an object to corkscrew (twist) along a central axis.

To twist an object:

1. Increase the complexity of the object surface.

   You need to add plenty of segments to your object before using this modifier.

2. ▨ Select an object (**Figure 7.14**).

3. Click the Modifiers Toolbar.

4. ▨ Click Twist in the Modifiers Toolbar.

   The Modify command panel opens, and the Twist rollout appears (**Figure 7.15**).

5. Select a Twist axis.

   The axis refers to orientation of the Modifier gizmo, rather than that of the object.

6. Enter an Angle value in degrees or drag the Angle spinner.

   The gizmo and the object twist together. (**Figure 7.16**).

✔ Tips

- Bias causes the object to twist more at one end of an axis than the other.

- Check Limit Effect and enter a value to constrain the modifier to the upper or lower part of the object.

APPLYING GEOMETRIC MODIFIERS

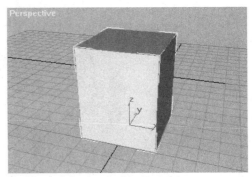

Figure 7.14 Selecting an object to twist.

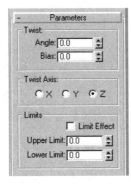

Figure 7.15 The Twist rollout appears in the Modify panel.

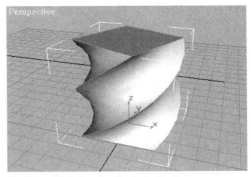

Figure 7.16 Twisting the box in its Z-axis.

Figure 7.17 Selecting a box to taper.

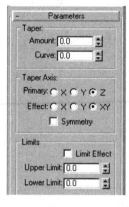

Figure 7.18 The Taper rollout appears in the Modify panel.

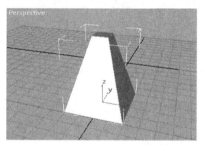

Figure 7.19 Tapering the box in its Z-axis.

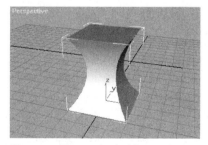

Figure 7.20 The result of adding a curve to the Taper modifier.

Tapering an object

The Taper modifier tapers the sides of an object towards or away from a central axis. It can also be used to curve the sides of an object.

To taper an object:

1. Select an object (**Figure 7.17**).

2. Click the Modifiers Toolbar.

3. Click Taper on the Modifiers Toolbar. The Modify command panel opens, and the Taper rollout appears (**Figure 7.18**).

4. Select a primary axis.

   This sets the central axis of tapering in the Taper gizmo.

5. Select an effect axis of deformation for the Taper gizmo.

   This determines which sides of the gizmo and object taper. Tapering is always symmetrical in the effect axis.

6. Enter an amount between -10 and 10, or drag the Amount spinner.

   The gizmo and the object taper together (**Figure 7.19**).

✔ Tip

- Enter a Curve value if you want to make the sides of the object curve as they taper (**Figure 7.20**).

- Check Symmetry if you want the taper to be symmetrical on both sides of the primary axis.

- Remember that you can animate nearly any parameter in MAX. For practice, animate each of these basic geometric modifiers by changing their parameters over time.

APPLYING GEOMETRIC MODIFIERS

Using the Modifier Stack

Modifier stack commands allows you to add, remove, adjust, and rearrange modifiers (**Table 7.1**). You can also turn modifiers on and off at will. Commands for manipulating the modifier stack are located in the Modifier Stack rollout, underneath and next to the modifier stack (**Figure 7.21**).

Figure 7.21 Modifier stack commands are located in the Modifier Stack rollout (top). They are temporarily obscured when the modifier stack drop-down menu is open (bottom).

USING THE MODIFIER STACK

Table 7.1

Modifier Stack Commands

BUTTON	NAME	
	Pin Stack	Pins the entire stack to the currently selected object. If another object is selected, the stack for the pinned object continues to be displayed.
	Active/Inactive Modifier Toggle	Turns on/off the effect of the currently displayed modifier in the viewports and during rendering.
	Active/Inactive in Viewport	Turns on/off the effect of the currently displayed modifier in the viewports only.
	Show End Result On/Off Toggle	Previews the way the object will look when the entire stack of modifiers has been evaluated.
	Make Unique	Converts instanced modifiers into copies. *(See "Clone Types" in Chapter 5, "Object Transforms," for more about instances.)*
	Remove Modifier from the Stack	Deletes the currently displayed modifier from the stack.
	Edit Stack	Converts primitive objects from one type to another. Allows you to cut, copy, and paste modifiers and to collapse the modifier stack.
Sub-Object	Sub-Object	Allows you to select the sub-object of a modifier or to select sub-object components of an object.

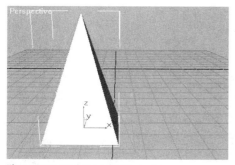

Figure 7.22 Applying a taper to a box.

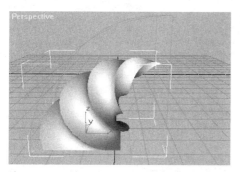

Figure 7.23 Adding the Twist and Bend modifiers to the tapered box.

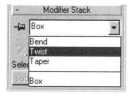

Figure 7.24 Selecting the Twist modifier from the Modifier Stack drop-down list.

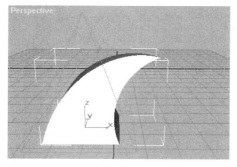

Figure 7.25 After removing the Twist modifier from the stack.

To apply multiple modifiers to an object:

1. ⬚ Select an object.

2. Apply a simple geometric modifier, such as a Bend, Twist, or Taper modifier (**Figure 7.22**).

3. Adjust the parameters of the modifier.

4. Repeat steps 2 and 3 as many times as you need (**Figure 7.23**).

To select a modifier:

1. ⬚ Select an object that has had multiple modifiers applied to it.

2. ⬚ Open the Modify panel.

3. Select the modifier from the Modifier Stack drop-down list (**Figure 7.24**).

To remove a modifier from the stack:

1. Select the modifier you want to remove.

2. ⬚ Click Remove Modifier from the stack. The modifier is removed from the stack, and the modifier's effect upon the object ceases (**Figure 7.25**).

✔ Tips

- Clicking Undo restores a modifier that was removed from the stack.

- To select a modifier sub-object, such as a gizmo or center, click the Sub-Object button. You can then transform the modifier sub-object and animate the transform over time.

- You cannot select another object by clicking or region selection when the Sub-Object button is active.

USING THE MODIFIER STACK

To turn a modifier off or on:

1. Select the modifier you want to turn off. (**Figure 7.26**).

2. 💡 Click the Active/Inactive Modifier Toggle.

   The effect of the modifier on the object is turned off (**Figure 7.27**).

3. Turn the modifier back on by clicking the Active/Inactive Modifier Toggle again.

To turn the modifier stack off or on:

1. Select the base object by name at the bottom of the modifier stack (**Figure 7.28**).

2. ∥ Click the Show End Result On/Off Toggle.

   All the modifiers in the stack are turned off (**Figure 7.29**).

3. Turn the stack back on by clicking Show End Result again.

✔ Tips

■ Show End Result turns off all the modifiers above the current stack level. If you select a modifier instead of the base object, Show End Result turns off just the modifiers above it in the stack.

■ Because Show End Result affects modifiers only above the current modifier, turning off Show End Result when the top modifier in the stack is selected has no effect.

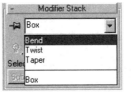

Figure 7.26 Selecting the Bend modifier from the Modifier Stack drop-down list.

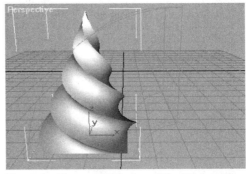

Figure 7.27 The result of turning off the Bend modifier.

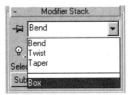

Figure 7.28 Selecting the Box primitive at the bottom of the Modifier Stack drop-down list.

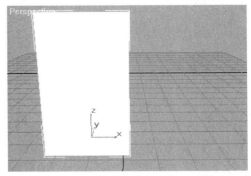

Figure 7.29 The result of turning off the modifier stack: the original Box object is revealed.

Editing the Modifier Stack

The effect that modifiers have on an object depends upon the order in which they are applied. To rearrange the order of modifiers, you edit the modifier stack using the Cut, Copy, and Paste commands. When you are satisfied with your modifications, you collapse the modifier stack.

Collapsing the modifier stack condenses all the modifiers and creation parameters of an object and converts it to an *editable object*. An editable object is an explicit description of vertices, faces, and edges that you can manipulate at the sub-object level. *(Chapter 8, "Editing Objects," discusses mesh sub-object editing.)*

Why would you want to get rid of any modifier and creation parameters? After all, isn't the power of the modifier stack in manipulating these parameters after the fact? Collapsing the stack has a stabilizing effect on an object because it preserves the effects of all the modifiers and creation parameters. Collapsing the stack also saves memory because the program doesn't need to evaluate parameters every time it works with an object.

Even if objects have no modifiers applied, you can use the Edit Stack button to convert them to other types of objects. You can convert standard primitives to editable meshes, editable patches, or NURBS surfaces. You can also convert spline shapes to editable meshes, editable splines, or NURBS surfaces.

To edit the modifier stack:

1. 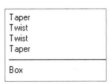 Select an object that has modifiers applied to it.

2. Open the Modify panel.

3. Click the Edit Stack button.

   The Edit Modifier Stack dialog box appears (**Figure 7.30**).

4. Select the modifiers you want to edit.

5. Use the Cut, Copy, and Paste commands to remove, copy, or rearrange modifiers (**Figure 7.31**).

   The object updates in the viewport as the modifiers are rearranged (**Figure 7.32**).

6. Click OK to accept these changes, or click Cancel.

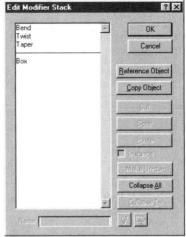

Figure 7.30 The Edit Modifier Stack dialog box allows you to cut, copy, and paste modifiers.

Taper
Twist
Twist
Taper
Box

Figure 7.31 The modifier stack looks like this after cutting the Bend modifier and copying and pasting the Twist and Taper modifiers back into the stack.

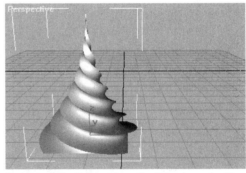

Figure 7.32 The finished box after it has been doubly twisted and tapered. Adding extra height segments smoothes out the effect of the added modifiers.

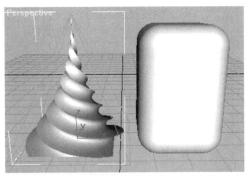

Figure 7.33 Selecting the doubly twisted and tapered box.

Figure 7.34 Selecting the modifiers in the stack to copy.

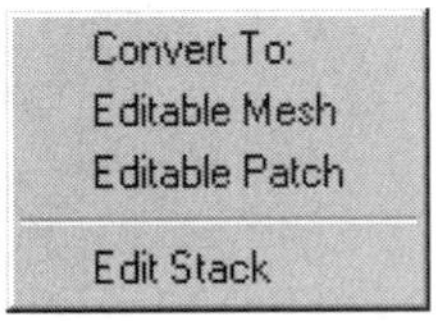

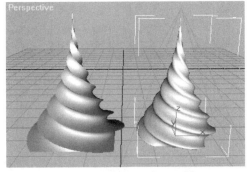

Figure 7.35 Choose Edit Stack in the Convert To menu to open the Edit Stack dialog box for an unmodified primitive.

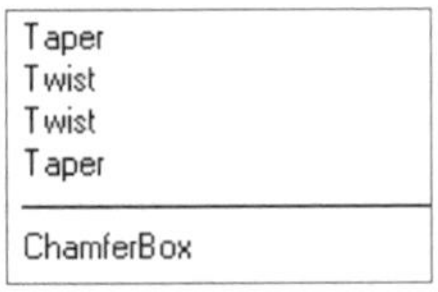

Figure 7.36 Pasting the modifiers onto a ChamferBox.

Figure 7.37 The result of pasting the modifiers onto the ChamferBox. Note that the ChamferBox has been set to a high face density.

To copy and paste modifiers:

1. Open a scene that has two or more mesh objects in it.

2. Modify one of the objects.

3. With the object still selected, click the Edit Stack button.

4. Select an object that has modifiers applied to it (**Figure 7.33**).

5. Open the Modify panel.

6. Click the Edit Stack button.

7. Select the modifiers you want to copy from the object (**Figure 7.34**).

8. Click Copy and then click OK.

9. Select another object.

10. Click the Edit Stack button.
    The Edit Stack dialog box appears.
    If you are modifying a primitive object that does not have any modifiers applied to it, the Convert To pop-up menu appears instead (**Figure 7.35**). If this happens, choose Edit Stack to bring up the Edit Modifier Stack dialog box.

11. Select the modifier below the position where you want to paste the modifier.

12. Click Paste.
    Pasted modifiers are inserted above the currently selected modifier or object (**Figure 7.36**).

13. Click OK.
    The modifiers are applied to the object (**Figure 7.37**).

✔ Tip

■ If you paste a modifier onto an incompatible object type, the modifier has no effect on the object.

EDITING THE MODIFIER STACK

183

To collapse the modifier stack:

1. Select an object that has modifiers applied to it.

2. Open the Modify panel.

3. Click the Edit Stack button.

   The Edit Modifier Stack dialog box appears (**Figure 7.38**).

4. Click Collapse All.

   The Warning dialog box appears (**Figure 7.39**) to let you know that you can't uncollapse the stack and retrieve the specific modifiers and creation parameters.

5. Click Yes to collapse everything.

   or

   Click Hold/Yes if you want to have a way to return to the uncollapsed state for a short while.

   If you click Hold/Yes, the object in its uncollapsed state goes into the Hold buffer, where it will remain until something else replaces it in the Hold buffer. If you want to retrieve the scene in its original state, choose Edit > Fetch. Everything returns just as it was before you collapsed the stack.

6. Click OK to go ahead and collapse the stack.

   Objects are converted to editable objects, and the modifiers disappear from the stack (**Figure 7.40**).

✔ Tip

■ Use the Convert To pop-up menu to convert unmodified objects that do not have a modifier stack (**Figure 7.41**).

Figure 7.38 The Edit Modifier Stack dialog box allows you to collapse the modifier stack and freeze all the modifier parameters at their current state.

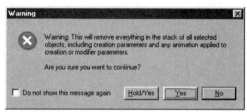

Figure 7.39 The Warning dialog box warns you of the consequences of collapsing the stack and gives you the option of holding the scene.

Figure 7.40 The modifiers and creation parameters are replaced by an editable mesh.

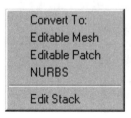

Figure 7.41 Use the Convert To menu to convert unmodified objects.

Figure 7.42 The second five modifiers on the Modifiers Toolbar—Noise, Wave, Melt, Spherify, and Ripple—displace the surfaces of objects.

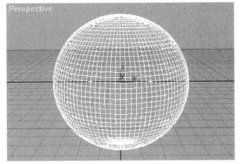

Figure 7.43 Selecting a Plane object that has a lot of segments.

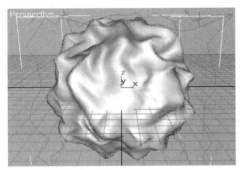

Figure 7.44 The Noise rollout appears in the Modify panel.

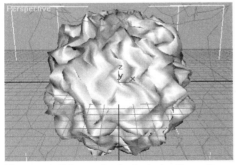

Figure 7.45 Noise randomly displacing the surface of the plane.

Displacing Surfaces

The next five modifiers on the Modifiers Toolbar (**Figure 7.42**) deform objects by displacing vertices in random or regular patterns. Especially useful are Noise, Wave, and Ripple, which displace vertices in a direction perpendicular to an object's surface.

The random effect of Noise is very important because most surfaces in nature are irregular. On a small scale, Noise introduces surface texture to pristine, perfect surfaces, which makes them seem much more real. On a larger scale, Noise creates great surface contours for landscapes. Use it for rocks, hills, mountains, oceans, moons, asteroids, and alien planets.

To apply noise to a surface:

1. Select a Mesh object with a very dense mesh (**Figure 7.43**).

2. Click Noise in the Modifiers Toolbar. The Noise rollout appears (**Figure 7.44**).

3. Set Scale to a number between 10 and 20 for starters.

4. Gradually increase the Strength parameters. For flat surfaces, you need only increase the one parameter that is perpendicular to the surface—usually the Z-axis.

   The vertices of the mesh are increasingly displaced above and below the mesh surface in a random pattern (**Figure 7.45**).

   (continues on next page)

5. For a rougher surface, check Fractal and increase the amount of roughness and the number of iterations (**Figure 7.46**).

✔ Tip

■ Checking Animate Noise automatically animates noise using the Frequency and Phase settings.

Rippling an object

Ripple and Wave create regular patterns on surfaces. Use them for creating ripples on water and shock waves in outer space. Because Ripple and Wave have identical parameters, learning one teaches you how to use the other.

To ripple an object:

1. Select a Mesh object with a very dense mesh (**Figure 7.47**).

2. Click Ripple in the Modifiers Toolbar. The Ripple rollout appears (**Figure 7.48**).

3. Adjust Amplitude 1 to affect rippling in one direction, and adjust Amplitude 2 to affect rippling in the other direction (**Figure 7.49**).

4. Change the wave length as needed.

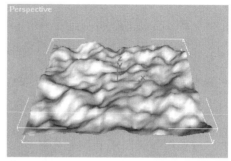

Figure 7.46 Fractal settings increase the roughness of the noise.

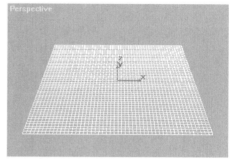

Figure 7.47 Selecting a Plane object with a very dense mesh.

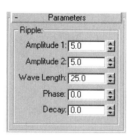

Figure 7.48 The Ripple rollout has effective default settings.

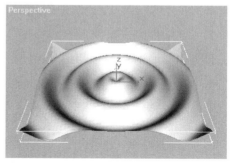

Figure 7.49 Rippling the Plane object with both amplitude settings.

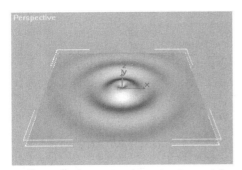

Figure 7.50 Decay causes the ripple effect to fall off from the center.

5. Drag the Phase spinner to make the surface ripple interactively. Use the Animate button to animate this effect.

6. Use Decay if you want the ripple to fall off as it moves away from the modifier center (**Figure 7.50**).

✔ Tip

■ You can animate a Ripple or Wave modifier by selecting and transforming its gizmo or center.

DISPLACING SURFACES

Using Free-Form Deformation Modifiers

The next two modifiers on the Modifiers Toolbar are called free-form deformation modifiers. ⬚ FFD Box and ⬚ FFD Cyl deform objects using a lattice of control points instead of a gizmo to better articulate details of surface displacement.

To freely deform an object:

1. ⬚ Select a Mesh object.

2. ⬚ ⬚ Click FFD Box or FFD Cyl in the Modifiers Toolbar.

    The FFD rollout appears (**Figure 7.51**).

    A lattice of control points surrounds the object (**Figure 7.52**).

3. Click the Sub-Object button in the Modifier Stack rollout.

    The Sub-Object button turns yellow, and Control Points is activated, indicating that lattice control points can be selected.

4. ⬚ ⬚ ⬚ Select and transform some control points.

    The control points deform the proximal surface of the object (**Figure 7.53**).

✔ Tips

- Click Set Number of Points to increase or decrease the number of points in the lattice (**Figure 7.54**).

- ⬚ Locking the control points makes them easier to transform and prevents them from being accidentally deselected. Remember to unlock them when you want to choose different control points.

Figure 7.51 The upper part of the FFD Cyl rollout.

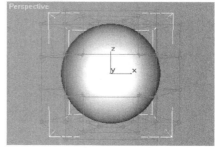

Figure 7.52 An FFD Cyl lattice of control points surrounding a sphere.

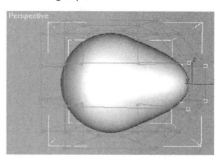

Figure 7.53 Moving control points deforms the sphere.

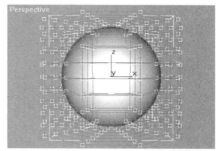

Figure 7.54 Increasing the number of control points allows you to model smaller details.

USING FREE-FORM DEFORMATION MODIFIERS

Applying XForm Modifiers

Of special note is the XForm modifier. When you transform the gizmo of an XForm modifier, the transform is applied to the object it modifies in what appears to be a completely normal transformation. The difference is that XForm modifiers provide a container for transforms and places them in the modifier stack. You can add as many transforms as you want, or you can remove the modifier from the stack. When you remove the XForm modifier, the object transforms that it contains are removed as well.

This ability of XForm modifiers to place transforms in the modifier stack is important for both modeling and animation. Normally, MAX evaluates transforms after modifiers, even though transforms may have been applied first. This can lead to unexpected results, particularly when you scale an object before modifying it. Generally speaking, if you are going to modify an object after scaling it, you should either place the scale transform in the stack with an XForm modifier or, if possible, skip scaling the object altogether and adjust the creation parameters of the object instead.

Using XForm modifiers for animation allows you to transform objects and their sub-object components using the power of the modifier stack. *(For more information, see Chapter 8, "Editing Sub-Objects," and see the "Lofting" section of Chapter 9, "Compound Objects.")*

APPLYING XFORM MODIFIERS

To place a transform in the modifier stack:

1. Select an object (**Figure 7.55**).

2. Click the XForm modifier in the Modifiers Toolbar.

   The XForm rollout appears. The Sub-Object button is turned on, and the sub-object selection level is set to Gizmo. The XForm modifier has no parameters (**Figure 7.56**).

3. Move, rotate, and/or scale the object.

   The object is transformed, and the object transforms are placed in the modifier stack (**Figure 7.57**).

✔ Tips

- Right-clicking an object or the viewport background brings up a menu that allows you to change and constrain transforms without having to switch back to the Main Toolbar (**Figure 7.58**).

- Choosing Center from the sub-object drop-down menu allows you move the center of rotation and scaling.

- You cannot Shift-clone an object when you are using the XForm modifier.

- A Linked XForm modifier causes an object to inherit the transforms of the object to which it is linked.

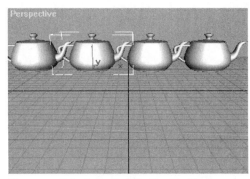

Figure 7.55 Selecting one of the Teapot objects.

Figure 7.56 The XForm rollout has no parameters.

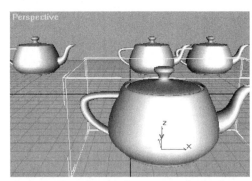

Figure 7.57 Transforming the teapot on the XY plane. The transform will be stored in the XForm container in the modifier stack.

Figure 7.58 This context-sensitive menu allows you to change and constrain transforms.

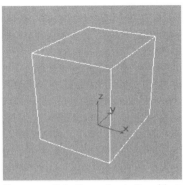

Figure 7.59 Selecting a simple Box object.

Figure 7.60 The Tessellate rollout offers two ways to increase mesh density.

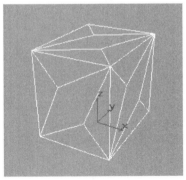

Figure 7.61 The Box object after one iteration of tessellation.

Altering Surface Complexity

You control the complexity of a primitive by adjusting the segment-creation parameters. Once a primitive has been converted to an editable object, however, its creation parameters disappear.

Tessellate increases the complexity of a Mesh object by dividing edges and faces. Optimize intelligently reduces mesh complexity by eliminating coplanar faces. The Tessellate and Optimize modifiers do not have sub-objects.

MeshSmooth adds an extra face for every vertex and edge in a mesh surface. It can be used as a modeling tool because it rounds off corners and edges at the same time. Starting with rough, block forms, you can quickly create birds, fish, monsters, and spaceships. Try combining MeshSmooth with the Extrude modifier to convert splines to rounded forms.

To tessellate a mesh:

1. Select a Mesh object (**Figure 7.59**).

2. Open the Modify panel and click More.

   The Modifiers dialog box appears.

3. Select Tessellate and click OK.

   The Tessellate rollout appears (**Figure 7.60**).

   The complexity of the object is increased (**Figure 7.61**).

   (continues on next page)

4. In the Parameters rollout, try both the Edge and Face-Center options to see which one makes the object look better.

5. Increase the Iterations value to further increase the complexity of the mesh (**Figure 7.62**).

✔ Tips

■ Face-center divisions work better on objects with planar surfaces, such as boxes.

■ To tessellate a limited surface area, select the faces using Mesh Select before applying the Tessellate modifier. *(Mesh Select is explained in Chapter 8, "Editing Sub-Objects.")*

To optimize a mesh:

1. 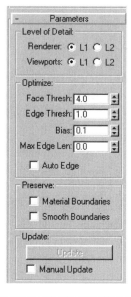 Select a Mesh object (**Figure 7.63**).

2. Click Optimize in the Modifiers Toolbar.

The Modify panel opens, and the Optimize rollout appears (**Figure 7.64**).

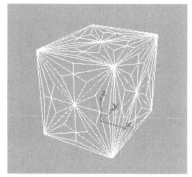

Figure 7.62 The tessellated Box object after a second iteration.

Figure 7.63 Selecting a Mesh object to optimize.

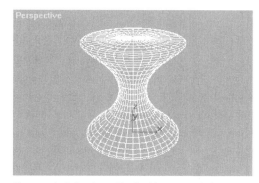

Figure 7.64 The Optimize rollout has different settings for viewport display and rendered output.

ALTERING SURFACE COMPLEXITY

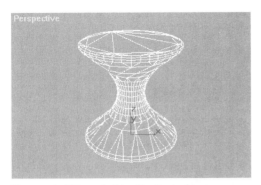

Figure 7.65 After optimizing the Mesh object.

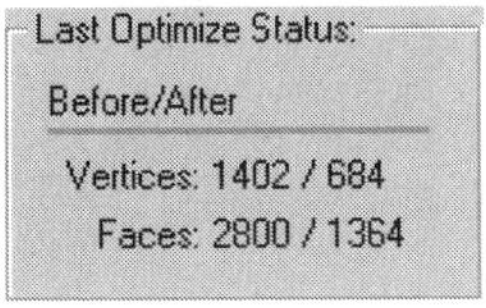

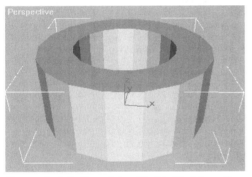

Figure 7.66 This counter shows you the number of faces and vertices before and after the mesh is optimized.

Figure 7.67 Selecting a Tube object to MeshSmooth.

3. Slowly increase the Face Threshold while keeping an eye on the viewports. Stop when curved surfaces begin to lose their smoothness.

The number of faces decreases, reducing the complexity of the mesh (**Figure 7.65**).

✔ Tips

■ Level of Detail has two settings: one for viewports and one for rendered output.

■ To see how many vertices and faces have been eliminated, check the Before/After counter at the bottom of the rollout (**Figure 7.66**).

■ For a complete description of Optimize parameters, see the online help files.

To MeshSmooth a mesh:

1. Select a Mesh object (**Figure 7.67**).

2. Click MeshSmooth in the Modifiers Toolbar.

(continues on next page)

ALTERING SURFACE COMPLEXITY

3. The MeshSmooth rollout appears (**Figure 7.68**).

The object is automatically smoothed using the default parameters (**Figure 7.69**).

4. Adjust the Subdivision Amount parameters.

Slowly increase the Iterations value to increase the overall number of divisions in the mesh.

5. Reduce the Smoothness value to optimize the mesh.

✔ Tips

- The MeshSmooth type is set to NURMS by default. *NURMS* stands for *Non-Uniform Rational MeshSmooth*, a humorous play on the term NURBS. For complete instructions on how to use the weighted control mesh and the other MeshSmooth types, see the online help files.

- To avoid severely deforming objects with planar surfaces, make sure that the mesh has a reasonable number of divisions on each side before you apply MeshSmooth.

Figure 7.68 The MeshSmooth rollout. As with Tessellate and Optimize, you increase the MeshSmooth effect by increasing the number of iterations.

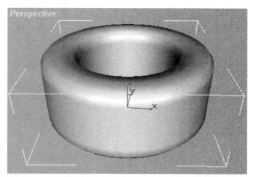

Figure 7.69 After MeshSmoothing the Tube. Note the rounded edges.

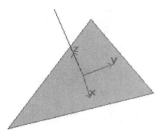

Figure 7.70 A surface normal projects from a face in the direction of the face's local *Z*-axis.

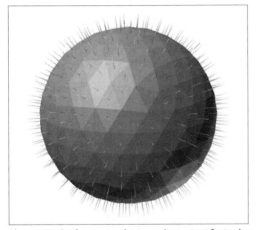

Figure 7.71 Surface normals are an important factor in determining shading.

Figure 7.72 This Teapot object has two smoothing groups. One group has been smoothed; the other has not.

Controlling Face Rendering

To speed up rendering, MAX shades only the outside surfaces of objects by default. This means that each face is shaded on only one side. To indicate which side of a face should be shaded, a vector called a *surface normal* projects at a right angle from the center of each face (**Figure 7.70**). Also called a *face normal*, or a *normal* for short, surface normals tell the program which direction a face is facing. By comparing a normal to the direction of a light, the program can determine how brightly to shade the normal's face. Faces that point toward a light receive brighter shading. As faces turn away from the light, they are assigned darker shading values (**Figure 7.71**).

In faceted shading modes, MAX shades the entire area of each face uniformly. This allows you to see each face on a curved surface distinctly. In smooth shading modes, MAX averages the intensity values between normals. This creates a gradient across curved surfaces that obscures the edge boundaries between faces. Such faces are said to be *smoothed*.

You already know how to control smoothing in the viewports by choosing between faceted and smooth modes of display. But when you render a scene to an image, objects that appear faceted in the viewports are smoothed automatically. To control smoothing during rendering, you apply a Smooth modifier. By specifying a threshold value, you determine the angle between face normals for smoothing to be applied. In Chapter 8, when you learn to select sets of contiguous faces, you can assign them to *smoothing groups* to control smoothing and edge boundaries between different areas of a surface (**Figure 7.72**). If you are working with curved primitives, checking and unchecking the Smooth parameter has the same effect as applying a Smooth modifier to an entire object.

To smooth faces:

1. [cursor icon] Select a Mesh object that is not smoothed. For example, you might select a GeoSphere object and uncheck Smooth in its creation parameters (**Figure 7.73**).

2. [icon] Click Smooth in the Modifiers Toolbar. The Smooth rollout appears (**Figure 7.74**).

3. Check Auto Smooth.

   The faces of the object become smoothed (**Figure 7.75**).

✔ Tip

- The Threshold parameter sets the minimum angle at which smoothing is applied. By dragging the Threshold spinner, you can see smoothing applied interactively. Try applying a Smooth modifier to a teapot and observe which faces get smoothed first as you drag the Threshold spinner up from 0.

- The Normal modifier changes the direction of surface normals so that they project from the opposite side of each face. When applied to an object, a Normal modifier can have the effect of turning the object inside out. This comes in handy when you want to create a sky inside a sphere or a the walls of a room inside of a box.

- When you import a 3D object into MAX from another program, it sometimes appears as if certain parts of the surface are missing. Chances are, the surface normals of those faces were flipped during the import process so that they cannot be seen. The Normal modifier can fix this problem by restoring surface normals to their original orientation. This causes the "missing" parts of an object to reappear.

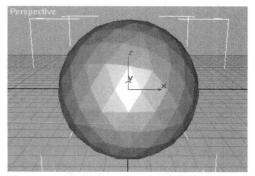

Figure 7.73 Selecting an unsmoothed GeoSphere object.

Figure 7.74
The Smoothing Groups rollout parameters perform automatic smoothing past a certain threshold.

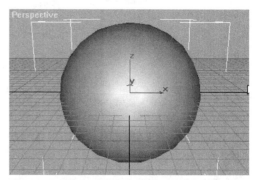

Figure 7.75 The GeoSphere object after it has been smoothed.

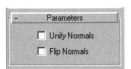

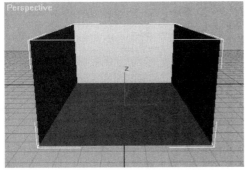

Figure 7.76 The Normal rollout has just two parameters.

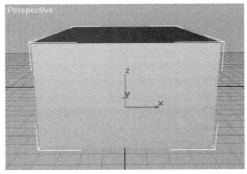

Figure 7.77 The result of flipping the normals of a box.

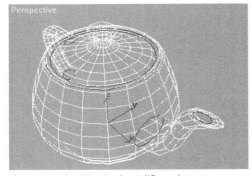

Figure 7.78 Unifying normals restores their original orientation.

To flip normals:

1. ▨ Select a Mesh object, such as a box.

2. ▨ Open the Modify panel and click More.

3. Double-click Normal.

   The Normal rollout appears (**Figure 7.76**).

4. Check Flip Normals.

   The surface normals of the faces are flipped so that the surface of the object is rendered inside out (or outside in, to be exact) (**Figure 7.77**).

To unify normals:

1. ▨ Select a Mesh object that you suspect has flipped normals.

2. Apply a Normal modifier.

3. Check Unify Normals.

   The flipped surface normals of the object are restored to their original orientation (**Figure 7.78**).

✔ Tip

■ The STL-Check and Cap Holes modifiers can find and fix actual holes in your mesh. Try setting the viewport display to wireframe and applying the STL-Check modifier to a teapot. Use Select Edges and check Check. This causes open edges to become selected and turn red (**Figure 7.79**). Then apply the Cap Holes modifier. To get a really good look at how well this works, go back to the teapot creation parameters and uncheck Lid. Then change the viewport to a smooth mode of display. I find that this combination of modifiers works great for preparing objects for Boolean operations. *(For more information on Boolean operations, see Chapter 9, "Compound Objects.")*

Figure 7.79 The STL-Check modifier selects open edges, which turn red. Here we see that the teapot has open edges around the lid, rim, spout, and handle.

Modifying Splines

A spline, you may recall, is a line or surface that uses a series of points to control curvature. MAX has three types of splines:

- **Shapes** use Corner, Smooth, and Bézier controls to define angled and curved lines.

- **Patches** use Bézier controls to define curved surfaces.

- **NURBS** use Non-Uniform Rational B-Splines to approximate highly complex curves and surfaces.

Shapes, the most basic type of spline in MAX, are commonly referred to simply as splines. Spline shapes are made up of vertex and segment sub-objects (**Figure 7.80**). Although patches and NURBS are simple enough to create from primitives, modifying them is too complex to explain in a book of this scope.

You use modifiers to create custom 3D objects by extruding, lathing, or beveling splines. The Extrude modifier generates a Mesh object by extruding a spline in a straight line along its Z-axis. The Lathe modifier generates a Mesh object by revolving a spline on one of its axes. The Bevel modifier extrudes a spline using different widths to bevel the edges. When you extrude, lathe, or bevel a spline, the result is a Mesh object, a patch, or a NURBS surface. The complexity of the resulting object is determined by the number of vertex points on the original spline and settings in each modifier.

The Extrude and Bevel modifiers do not have sub-objects. The Lathe modifier sub-object is its axis of revolution.

(To extrude a spline along the path of another spline, see "Loft Objects" in Chapter 9, "Compound Objects.")

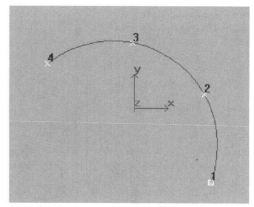

Figure 7.80 A spline with vertex numbering displayed. This spline has four vertices and three segments. Note that the first vertex is bounded by a square.

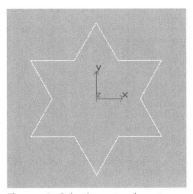

Figure 7.81 Selecting a star shape to extrude.

Figure 7.82 The Extrude rollout has settings for the amount of extrusion as well as the number of segments that will be built on the sides.

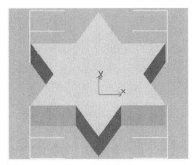

Figure 7.83 The extruded star.

To extrude a spline:

1. Select a Spline object (**Figure 7.81**).

2. Click the Modeling Toolbar.

3. Click Extrude in the Modeling Toolbar.

   The Extrude rollout appears (**Figure 7.82**).

4. Enter a value for Amount.

   The spline is extruded. If the spline is a closed shape, then a surface, or cap, is built on the enclosed area (**Figure 7.83**).

✔ Tips

- To increase the complexity of a mesh or patch, increase the Segments parameter.

- To create patches or NURBS objects, choose Patch or NURBS in the Output area.

To lathe a spline:

1. ![icon] Select a Spline object (**Figure 7.84**).

2. ![icon] Click Lathe in the Modeling Toolbar. The Modify panel opens, and the Lathe rollout appears (**Figure 7.85**).

   The spline is lathed along its central Y-axis (**Figure 7.86**).

3. Adjust the axis of revolution as needed.

   To use a different axis of revolution, change the Direction parameter.

   To align the axis of revolution to the minimum, center, or maximum extents of the object, change the Align parameter.

   To freely move the axis of revolution, click the Sub-Object button and move the axis (**Figure 7.87**).

✔ Tips

- To lathe an object less than 360 degrees, decrease the Degrees parameter.

- Enabling Weld Core causes coincident vertices along the axis of revolution to be welded together. Uncheck this box if you are creating morph targets to control the number of vertices that are generated. *(See Chapter 9, "Compound Objects," for more information on morphing. See Chapter 8, "Editing Sub-Objects," for more information on welding.)*

- Check Flip Normals to shade the object on the reverse side.

- To increase the complexity of the lathed object, increase the Segments parameter.

Figure 7.84 Selecting an arc to lathe.

Figure 7.85 The Lathe rollout can be set for different object axes.

Figure 7.86 The lathed arc.

Figure 7.87 Moving the axis of revolution created these three vases out of the same spline profile.

MODIFYING SPLINES

Figure 7.88 A Text Spline object can be extruded and beveled.

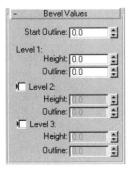

Figure 7.89 The lower half of the Bevel rollout.

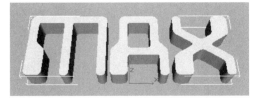

Figure 7.90 After setting the initial extrusion and bevel amounts.

Figure 7.91 Rendered output of a two-level bevel.

To bevel text:

1. Select a Text Spline object (**Figure 7.88**).

2. Click Bevel in the Modeling Toolbar. The Modify panel opens, and the Bevel rollout appears (**Figure 7.89**). The text is capped.

3. In the Bevel Values rollout, enter a value for the Start Outline, or leave the value at 0. The starting width of the outline is set.

4. Set the Height and Outline values for Level 1. Height sets the initial extrusion amount, and Outline sets the bevel amount (**Figure 7.90**).

5. Set the Height and Outline values for Level 2 and, if needed, Level 3. Setting values for each level causes additional extrusion and beveling to be added to the text (**Figure 7.91**).

✔ Tips

- In the Parameters rollout, check Smooth Across Levels to smooth the edges of the levels.

- Bevel Profile is a related modifier that extrudes a shape using a second shape to define the outline of the beveled edge.

MODIFYING SPLINES

EDITING OBJECTS

Editing allows you to model and animate objects at the smallest level of detail. This is essential for character animation, medical illustration, or any other application that requires detailed visual information.

You edit objects by applying modifiers, transforms, or edit commands to a sub-object selection. Mesh objects can be edited at the vertex, edge, or face level. Spline objects can be edited at the vertex, segment, or spline level.

Before you begin, it is important to evaluate whether sub-object editing is needed. Will the work be visible when you play the animation? Will it be obscured by shadow? Lost in the distance? Hidden behind other objects? Proportionally insignificant? If so, you might want to concentrate on the larger issues of scene composition, materials, lighting, and timing, or on editing just those objects that appear prominently in the scene.

Tools for Editing Objects

The following will help you decide which editing tools to use:

◆ 🖲 🖳 🖳 **Select modifiers** such as Mesh Select, Spline Select, and Volume Select allow you to make a sub-object selection and pass it up the modifier stack. If the Sub-Object button is active, the next modifier that you place in the stack will be applied to just the sub-object selection. Select modifiers are simple to use and allow you to import selections from other sub-object levels. Because transforms are disabled in Select modifiers, you must apply an XForm or Edit modifier or convert the object to an editable object to apply a transform to your sub-object selection.

◆ 🖳 🖳 **Edit modifiers** such as Edit Mesh and Edit Spline allow you to make a sub-object selection, transform it, and pass it up the modifier stack. You can also apply sub-object editing commands. Edit modifiers are flexible and nondestructive. With an Edit modifier you can transform and edit an object while preserving its creation parameters. If you don't like the results, you can remove the Edit modifier from the stack. On the other hand, Edit modifiers add memory and calculation overhead to your scene because they must constantly be evaluated in the modifier stack.

◆ **Editable objects** such as editable meshes and editable splines give you access to the same selection, transformation, and editing commands as Edit modifiers. Editable objects are more stable and have less overhead because they do not create a modifier stack. However, previously applied modifiers and creation parameters are lost and cannot be adjusted because the modifier stack has been collapsed.

Creating Sub-Object Selections

To edit an object, you must first make a sub-object selection. In many ways, selecting sub-objects is like selecting objects:

◆ You select sub-objects by clicking them, dragging a selection region around them, or choosing a named sub-object selection set.

◆ You add to a sub-object selection by holding down the Ctrl key while making a selection.

◆ You subtract from a selection by holding down the Alt key while selecting.

◆ Deselect a sub-object selection by clicking the background.

◆ You can lock a selection. This is especially useful for applying sub-object transforms.

The main differences between object and sub-object selection are these:

◆ You create sub-object selections in the Modify panel.

◆ You apply a Select modifier or Edit modifier or convert an object to an editable object to access sub-object levels.

◆ You choose a sub-object level of selection before you make a selection.

◆ Different sub-object selections can exist simultaneously at different selection levels.

◆ When you are in a sub-object selection mode, object selection by clicking or dragging is disabled.

◆ Sub-object selections are preserved in the modifier stack even when the object is not in sub-object mode.

Use the Mesh Select modifier to create sub-object selections of mesh objects.

Mesh Sub-Object Selection

The mesh sub-object modifiers offer five levels of selection:

◆ ▫ **Vertex:** For selecting vertices.

◆ ◁ **Edge:** For selecting edges.

◆ ◀ **Face:** For selecting faces.

◆ ▩ **Polygon:** For selecting (more or less) coplanar pairs of faces, such as the sides of a box.

◆ ▨ **Element:** For selecting sets of contiguous faces, such as the body and lid of a teapot.

Spline Sub-Object Selection

The spline sub-object modifiers offer three levels of selection:

◆ ▫ **Vertex:** For selecting vertices.

◆ ◢ **Segment:** For selecting segments.

◆ ◇ **Spline:** For selecting splines in multi-spline objects, such as donuts and text objects.

To make a sub-object selection with Mesh Select:

1.  Select an object.

2. Set the viewport display to Wireframe.

3. Open the Modify panel.

   The Mesh Select rollout appears. Most of the commands are dimmed.

4. Click a Sub-Object button to choose a selection level.

   The Sub-Object button turns yellow, and an asterisk appears in the modifier stack to indicate that the object is in a sub-object selection mode. Commands for that selection level become enabled (**Figure 8.1**). At the vertex level, vertices appear as blue dots.

5. Click a sub-object or drag a selection region around the set of sub-objects you want to select (**Figure 8.2**).

   The selection extends all the way through the volume of the object. The sub-object selection turns red (**Figure 8.3**).

6. To return to object selection mode, click the Sub-Object button to deactivate it.

✔ Tips

- Ignore Backfaces prevents face and edge selection on the far side of a mesh object.

- To toggle between object and sub-object modes from the keyboard, press Ctrl+B.

- To cycle through sub-object levels from the keyboard, press the Insert key.

- To import a selection from another sub-object selection level, click the appropriate button in the Get from Other Levels group.

- Use Select Open Edges to verify the continuity of a mesh surface before performing a 3D Boolean operation.

Figure 8.1 The Modify panel shows commands specific to the Mesh Select modifier at the Edge sub-object level.

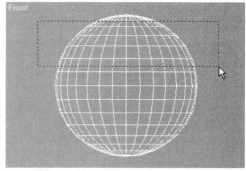

Figure 8.2 Dragging a selection region around part of the sphere.

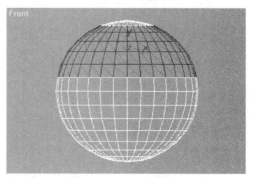

Figure 8.3 The sphere with a region of edges selected.

Figure 8.4
Default parameters for the Volume Select modifier.

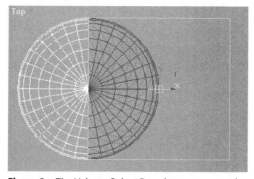

Figure 8.5 The Volume Select Box gizmo was moved to the right side of the sphere.

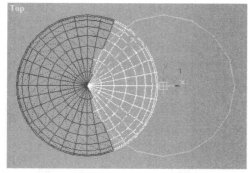

Figure 8.6 The Volume Select Sphere gizmo with Invert turned on.

Making a sub-object selection with Volume Select

Use the Volume Select modifier to create sub-object selections from the volume of an object that is enclosed by the Volume Select gizmo. Gizmos include a wireframe box, sphere, cylinder, and any mesh object that you select.

To make a sub-object selection with Volume Select:

1. Select an object.

2. Set the viewport display to Wireframe.

3. Click the Modifiers Toolbar.

4. Apply a Volume Select modifier.
   The Volume Select rollout appears (**Figure 8.4**), and a gizmo surrounds the object.

5. In the Stack Selection Level group, choose Object, Vertex, or Face selection.

6. Click the Sub-Object button.

7. Move, rotate, or scale the gizmo until it surrounds the part of the object that you want to select.
   The sub-object components that are enclosed by the gizmo are selected and turn red (**Figure 8.5**).

✔ Tips

- Take advantage of these Volume Select options: select by window or crossing; use different gizmos; or add, subtract, or invert your selection (**Figure 8.6**).

- Applying a Mesh Select, Volume Select, or Edit Mesh modifier to a spline object converts the spline object to a mesh object. Converting a closed spline shape to an editable mesh automatically creates faces and edges in the enclosed area. Converting an open spline shape to an editable mesh creates a series of vertices without any connecting edges or faces.

Soft-selecting a mesh

The falloff from a selection area to the rest of a mesh object can be rather abrupt. The Soft Selection feature creates a selection that has a gradual falloff when commands are applied.

To soft-select a mesh:

1. 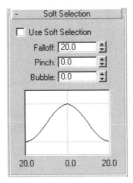 Select an object.

2. Create a vertex selection using Mesh Select, Volume Select, or Edit Mesh, or by selecting vertices in an editable mesh.

3. Open the Soft Selection rollout (**Figure 8.7**).

4. Turn on Soft Selection.

5. Drag the Falloff spinner upward to increase the falloff and downward to decrease it.

   The sub-object selection falls off. Vertices change colors from red to yellow to green to blue as they fall off (**Figure 8.8**).

6. Adjust the Pinch and Bubble parameters, using the graph shown here as a guide (**Figure 8.9**). To see the effect of these parameters on a move transform, see the last figure under "To transform sub-objects" later in this chapter.

✔ Tip

■ You can see falloff only at the vertex level. To get around this, soft-select at the vertex level and use Get Vertex Selection to import the selection to another level. You can also soft-select sub-objects at another level and import them to the vertex level to see the selection falloff.

Figure 8.7 The Soft Selection rollout depicts falloff with a graph.

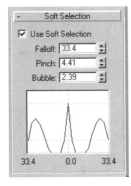

Figure 8.8 Soft selection falloff colors vertices with a gradient.

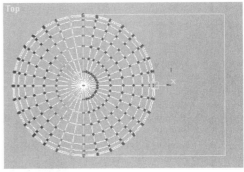

Figure 8.9 Pinch and Bubble are adjusted to create an unusual-shaped falloff.

Figure 8.10 Choosing the Vertex sub-object level from the drop-down list.

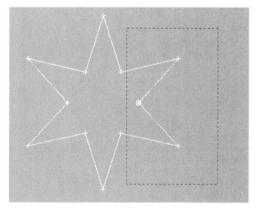

Figure 8.11 Dragging a selection region around part of the spline.

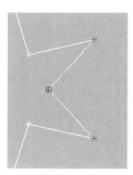

Figure 8.12 The spline's first vertex is indicated by a small box.

Making a sub-object selection with Spline Select

Use the Spline modifier to create sub-object selections of spline objects. You select sub-objects in an editable spline or with an Edit Spline modifier in the same way, except that you choose a selection level by clicking an icon instead of choosing from a drop-down list.

To make a sub-object selection with Spline Select:

1. Select an editable spline.

2. Open the Modify panel.
   The Spline Select rollout appears.

3. Click Sub-Object and choose a selection level from the drop-down list (**Figure 8.10**).
   The Sub-Object button turns yellow. Vertices appear as X marks on the spline.

4. Click a sub-object or drag a selection region around the sub-objects you want to select (**Figure 8.11**).
   The sub-object selection turns red. The first vertex of a spline always appears with a box around it at the vertex level (**Figure 8.12**).

✔ Tips

- To switch between object and sub-object modes from the keyboard, press Ctrl+B.

- To cycle through sub-object levels from the keyboard, press the Insert key.

- Get Vertex Selection, Get Segment Selection, and Get Spline Selection create a selection based on adjacent sub-objects that are selected on other levels.

- There is no Soft Selection option available for splines.

Modifying Sub-Objects

One way to edit an object is to make a sub-object selection and apply a modifier to it. So long as the Sub-Object button is active when you apply the modifier, the sub-object selection is passed up the modifier stack. If you deactivate the Sub-Object button, the entire object is passed up the stack until you click the Sub-Object button again. If you want to modify a different selection while preserving the old one, simply add another selection modifier to the stack and make a new selection.

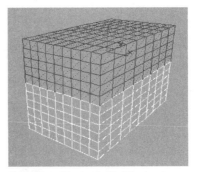

Figure 8.13 The top half of the box is selected.

To modify a sub-object selection:

1. Make a sub-object selection by any method (**Figure 8.13**).

2. Optional: Lock the selection.

3. Apply a modifier.

    The modifier is applied to the sub-object selection. If the modifier has a gizmo or lattice, the gizmo or lattice surrounds just the sub-object selection (**Figure 8.14**).

4. If you use a soft selection, the effect of the modifier will fall off gradually toward the unselected portion of the object (**Figure 8.15**).

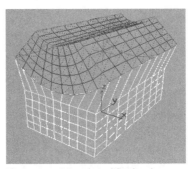

Figure 8.14 A Bend modifier has been applied to the selection.

✔ Tip

■ If you change the creation parameters of an object after selecting or modifying the object at a sub-object level, you may get unwanted results. The Warning dialog box reminds you of this before you make your changes (**Figure 8.16**).

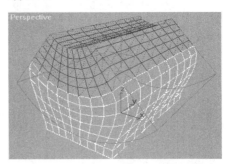

Figure 8.15 The Bend modifier is modulated via soft-selection falloff.

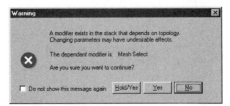

Figure 8.16 Changing creation parameters after sub-object editing can cause unexpected results. Choose Hold/Yes to go back if necessary.

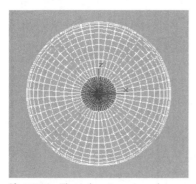

Figure 8.17 The sphere's center edges are selected.

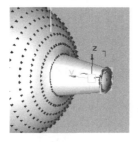

Figure 8.18 Applying a move transform to a sub-object selection with an XForm modifier.

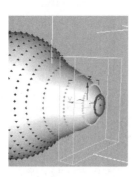

Figure 8.19 Using soft selection causes gradual falloff.

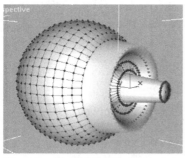

Figure 8.20 The result of the Pinch and Bubble settings shown in Figure 8.9.

Transforming Sub-Objects

You transform sub-object selections exclusively in the Modify panel. Typically, there are three ways that this is done:

◆ Make a sub-object selection with a selection modifier and then apply an XForm modifier.

◆ Make a sub-object selection with an edit modifier and then apply a transform.

◆ Make a sub-object selection within an editable object and then transform the sub-object directly.

The last option uses the term *directly* because with an editable object, you work directly on sub-objects, whereas with the Select and Edit modifiers, you work with the modifier stack and can remove the modifiers at any time.

To transform sub-objects:

1. Make a sub-object selection using a Select modifier or Edit modifier, or by converting the object to an editable object and then making your selection (**Figure 8.17**).

2. Optional: Lock the selection.

3. Apply an XForm modifier if you used a Select modifier to create the selection.

4. Move, rotate, or scale the selection.

   The transform is applied to the sub-object selection (**Figure 8.18**).

✔ Tip

■ If you used a soft selection on a mesh, the effect of the transform will fall off gradually toward the unselected portion of the object (**Figure 8.19**). Adjusting the Pinch and Bubble parameters in the Mesh Select modifier changes the shape of the transformed selection (**Figure 8.20**).

TRANSFORMING SUB-OBJECTS

211

Editing Mesh Objects

Mesh objects can be edited at the vertex, edge, face, polygon, object, and element sub-object levels. Converting a mesh object to an editable mesh causes editing tools to become available in the Modify panel for each level. You can also apply an Edit Mesh modifier to gain access to the same set of tools. *For instructions on how to convert a mesh object to an editable mesh, see Chapter 7, "Modifying Objects."*

When you choose a sub-object level, different sets of editing commands become available. Some commands are available at every level. Other commands are specific to certain sub-object types.

The Attach command appends objects and turns them into a single object with one name and one set of object properties. Each of the attached objects becomes sub-object elements. Detach turns elements back into objects.

Welding simplifies a mesh structure by eliminating vertices within a certain distance of each other and closing attachment seams.

Extruding faces or polygons is a quick way to build geometry. Use Extrude to add details to an existing model or to build a low polygon (low-poly) model from scratch.

The Delete command erases any sub-objects that you select. Sometimes, parts of an object are deleted by accident, leaving holes in your mesh. The Create command creates new vertices and faces and patches these holes.

Editable meshes and the Edit Mesh modifier have identical command rollouts. For the sake of general explanation, both options are given here. In subsequent exercises, I will just use the example of editable meshes, with the understanding that you can apply an Edit Mesh modifier to any mesh object, including an editable mesh, if you prefer to do so.

Mesh Sub-Object Editing

- **Vertex** editing manipulates a mesh at its most profound level. Because vertex locations determine the actual coordinates of a mesh surface, vertex commands affect the smallest details of an object.

- **Edge** editing affects the interstices of a mesh. Because edges form boundaries between faces and connections between vertices, edge commands influence both vertices and faces.

- **Face** editing changes the surface of a mesh. Because faces determine rendering properties, face commands affect shading, smoothing, visibility, and material assignments, as well as structure.

- **Polygon** editing affects coplanar pairs of faces. Polygon commands are essentially the same as face editing commands. The difference is polygon commands enable you to select faces as coplanar pairs.

- **Element** editing alters collections of faces that form discrete elements within objects. Element commands are essentially the same as face and polygon commands.

- **Object** editing acts upon the entire mesh. It is used primarily to attach other objects to the mesh and to improve displacement maps.

Figure 8.21 The Modify panel enables only commands applicable to the current sub-object level.

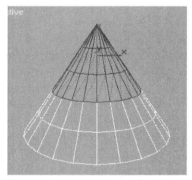

Figure 8.22 The cone's upper faces are selected.

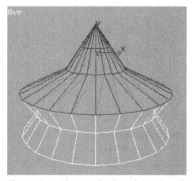

Figure 8.23 The result of applying Bevel to the selection.

To edit a mesh object:

1. Select an editable mesh object.

   or

   Select a mesh object and apply an Edit Mesh modifier.

   The editable mesh or Edit Mesh rollout appears in the Modify panel. It is set to Object level by default. Most of the commands at this level are dimmed.

2. Set the viewport to Wireframe display.

3. In the Selection rollout, choose a sub-object level.

   All the commands that are available for the sub-object level you chose become enabled (**Figure 8.21**).

4. Make a sub-object selection.

   The selection turns red (**Figure 8.22**).

5. Optional: Adjust the selection falloff in the Soft Selection rollout.

6. Apply an available editing command or a transform to your selection.

   The mesh object updates interactively (**Figure 8.23**).

✔ Tips

- As a beginner, you may find the Edit Mesh modifier to be more forgiving. As you develop your skills and begin making more complex models, you will probably want to switch to editable meshes.

- Pressing the Insert key cycles through sub-object selection levels. Pressing Ctrl+B switches between object and sub-object modes.

- Use Hide and Unhide All to toggle the display of vertex, face, polygon, and element selections.

To attach an object:

1. 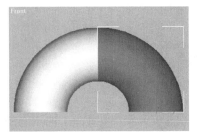 Select an editable mesh object (**Figure 8.24**).

2. Open the Modify panel.

3. In the Edit Geometry rollout, click Attach (**Figure 8.25**).

4. Click the object you want to attach.

   The second object attaches to the first.

   If the objects are different colors, the attached objects will inherit the color of the current object (**Figure 8.26**).

5. If the attached object has a different material, you will be given a choice as to how to incorporate it into the material of the current object (**Figure 8.27**). Click OK to keep the current material assignments.

✔ Tip

- Clicking Attach List in the Edit Geometry rollout brings up a list of attachable objects so that you can attach multiple objects at one time.

To detach an element:

1. Select an editable mesh object and choose Wireframe display.

2. Open the Modify panel.

3. Click Element.

4. Select an element by clicking it.

5. In the Edit Geometry rollout, click Detach.

6. Name the new object in the Detach dialog box (**Figure 8.28**).

✔ Tip

- You can detach selections of vertices, faces, and polygons using the same tool.

Figure 8.24 Two objects ready for attaching; the object on the right is selected.

Figure 8.25 Click Attach before attaching objects.

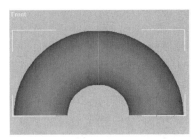

Figure 8.26 With Attach on, clicking the second object appends it to the first and applies the first object's color.

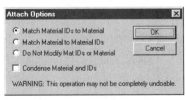

Figure 8.27 The Attach Options dialog box lets you choose how materials are combined.

Figure 8.28 The Detach dialog box lets you rename detached objects.

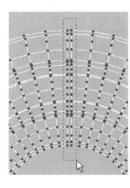

Figure 8.29 Selecting a group of vertices to weld.

Figure 8.30 The Weld group gives you options for welding vertices.

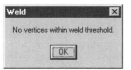

Figure 8.31 The Weld dialog box may warn you that the weld didn't work.

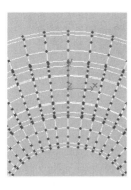

Figure 8.32 The selected vertices in Figure 8.29 have been welded.

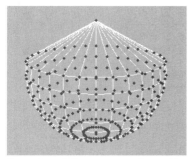

Figure 8.33 Collapse was used to weld all of a sphere's upper vertices into a single point.

To weld vertices:

1. Select an editable mesh object and choose Wireframe display.

2. Open the Modify panel.

3. Click Vertex.

   Vertex dots appear in the mesh.

4. Select a set of adjacent vertices by dragging a selection region (**Figure 8.29**).

5. In the Weld group, click Selected (**Figure 8.30**).

   If there are no vertices within the threshold value, the Weld dialog box appears (**Figure 8.31**). Vertices that are within the threshold value to the right of the Selected button weld together (**Figure 8.32**).

6. If the vertices you selected were too far apart to weld, increase the threshold value and click Selected again.

   or

   Scale down the vertices so they draw tightly together and then click Selected.

✔ Tip

- At the bottom of the Edit Geometry rollout are five commands that affect all levels:

  - **Remove Isolated Vertices** deletes vertices that are not connected to faces with edges.

  - **View Align** and **Grid Align** line up a selection with the plane of the view or the plane of the grid, respectively.

  - **Make Planar** flattens the selection onto a plane whose normal is the average of all the normals of the faces attached to the vertices.

  - **Collapse** is like a super-powerful weld command. At the vertex level, Collapse welds all the vertices into one vertex at the center of the selection (**Figure 8.33**).

EDITING MESH OBJECTS

215

To extrude polygons:

1. 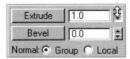 Select an editable mesh object and choose Wireframe display.

2. Open the Modify panel.

3. Click Polygon.

4. Click a polygon to select it.

5. Drag the Extrude spinner or type a value (**Figure 8.34**).

   The polygon extrudes from the surface of the mesh (**Figure 8.35**). The extrude amount is reset to zero. The polygon remains selected in case you want to extrude it again.

✔ Tips

- You can also extrude faces to create triangular-shaped extrusions. Extruding edges creates planar extrusions.

- Applying move, rotate, and scale each time you extrude can be an elegant way to create a low-poly model (**Figure 8.36**).

- Applying a MeshSmooth modifier is a great way to convert your low-poly model into a curvy, organic form (**Figure 8.37**).

Figure 8.34 Drag the Extrude spinner to extrude polygons.

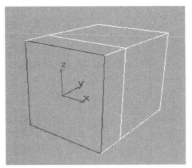

Figure 8.35 The box's front polygon has been extruded.

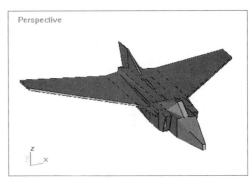

Figure 8.36 This low-poly jet fighter was created with Extrude.

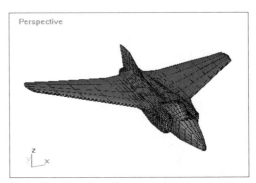

Figure 8.37 MeshSmooth was used to add curves to the fighter.

Figure 8.38 Use Slice Plane to subdivide an object along a plane.

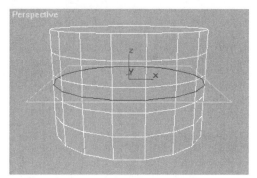

Figure 8.39 A new set of edges has been created using Slice Plane.

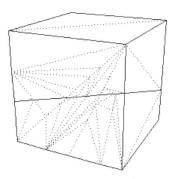

Figure 8.40 Newly divided edges with dotted lines on the left and a cut going across the whole cube in a solid line.

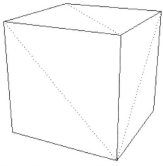

Figure 8.41 Two turned edges: the dotted centerline on the left and the dotted center line at the top.

To slice edges:

1. Select an editable mesh object and choose Wireframe display.

2. Open the Modify panel.

3. Click Edge.

4. In the Edit Geometry rollout, click Slice Plane (**Figure 8.38**).

   The Slice plane appears in the middle of the object. Like the Section object, it appears limited but it actually extends infinitely into space.

5. Place the plane where you want it to slice the object.

6. Click Slice.

   All faces intersected by the Slice plane are subdivided (**Figure 8.39**).

✔ Tips

- While slicing an object, if you use the Split option, you can then select and detach one of the two elements that result.

- Create Shape from Open Edges selects all the open edges in a mesh object and clones them into a new shape. Used with the Slice command, it sections an object.

- To subdivide a selected edge or face, use Divide and Cut. The Divide command divides one edge at a time. The Cut command divides all edges on the visible surface that you drag across (**Figure 8.40**).

- The Turn command rotates an edge and connects it to the other vertices of the two faces it divides (**Figure 8.41**). Try playing with this one for a while and then view the object in shaded mode.

EDITING MESH OBJECTS

To delete any part of a mesh:

1. ⬚ Select an editable mesh object.

2. ✎ Open the Modify panel.

3. ⬚ ⬚ ⬚ ⬚ ⬚ Click a sub-object button.

4. ⬚ Select the part of the mesh that you want to delete (**Figure 8.42**).

5. Click Delete or press the Delete key.

   If you are working at the Edge, Face, Polygon, or Element level, the Delete Face dialog box appears (**Figure 8.43**).

6. Click Yes.

   The selected part of the mesh is deleted (**Figure 8.44**).

✔ Tips

- ■ Isolated vertices are usually considered junk. They don't render, but they add unnecessary overhead and confusion to your model. The only time you don't delete them is when you want to build new faces off of them.

- ■ If you have attached two objects that intersect one another, deleting the faces in the intersecting region will improve rendering performance.

- ■ You use the Create command to rebuild faces and vertices that have accidentally been deleted.

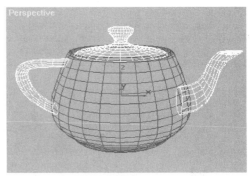

Figure 8.42 The body of the teapot has been selected for deletion.

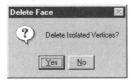

Figure 8.43 The Delete Face dialog box asks if you want to delete isolated vertices.

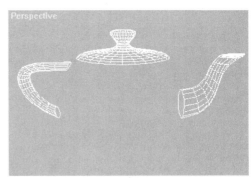

Figure 8.44 The teapot body has been deleted, leaving behind the cover, handle, and spout.

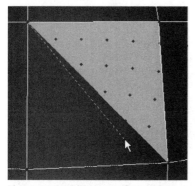

Figure 8.45
Create lets you add faces by clicking points.

Figure 8.46 Adding a new face with Create.

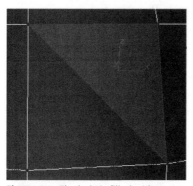

Figure 8.47 The hole is filled with a new face.

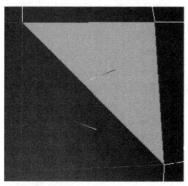

Figure 8.48 Two normals on two selected faces. The face on the right is flipped; its normal points inward.

Creating faces

Imported models from other programs sometimes lose faces during translation. Creating new faces patches the holes.

To create faces:

1. Select an editable mesh that is missing a face and zoom in on the face.

2. Open the Modify panel.

3. Click Face.

4. Click Create (**Figure 8.45**).
   The vertex points of the object appear.

5. Move the cursor over one of the vertices that border the missing face.

6. Click the vertex to start the face.

7. Move the cursor to the next vertex, proceeding counterclockwise.
   A dashed line stretches from the first point to the second point (**Figure 8.46**).

8. Click the vertex to set the second corner of the face.

9. Move the cursor to the final vertex and click to anchor the last point of the face.
   The new face fills the hole in the mesh (**Figure 8.47**).

10. Click Auto Smooth in the Surface Properties rollout to smooth the face.

✔ Tips

- Picking points in a clockwise order builds a face whose normal points away from you.

- If the face does not appear when you build it, the normal is probably flipped. Click Show in the Surface Properties rollout to display the surface normal of a selected face. Click Flip or Unify to flip the face (**Figure 8.48**).

Editing Splines

You edit splines at the vertex, segment, and spline sub-object levels. Converting a spline to an editable spline and selecting a sub-object level causes the appropriate editing tools to become available in the Modify panel. Applying an Edit Spline modifier gives you access to the same set of tools. *For instructions on how to convert a spline object to an editable spline, see Chapter 7, "Modifying Objects."*

Each spline, or shape, has a first vertex. The first vertex determines the starting point of a motion path or the beginning point of a loft path. The Make First feature allows you to choose which vertex of a spline is first.

Attaching splines creates a single shape with multiple spline sub-objects. The Detach command reverses this process by detaching segments and splines into separate shapes.

Welding combines the end points of attached splines into a single vertex. It is especially useful for putting together motion paths and cleaning up 2D drawings that are imported from CAD programs. Related commands include Fuse, which brings vertices together without welding them; Connect, which builds a segment between two end points of a spline; and Break, which snips a spline in two, creating new end points at either end.

Sometimes a spline requires more vertices to get the shape you want. Refine, Insert, and Divide all add vertices to a spline or segment. Chamfer and Fillet split a vertex into two vertices and spread them apart evenly. If the vertex is on the corner of a shape, these commands flatten or round off the corner.

The Outline command offsets a spline a specified distance from the original spline. More complex spline operations include Trim, Extend, and 2D Boolean operations.

Spline Sub-Object Editing

When we speak of editing splines, we usually mean editing spline *shape objects* rather than editing spline *sub-objects*. Never mind that patches and NURBs are technically spline objects as well.

◆   **Vertex** editing manipulates the basic building blocks of a spline or shape. Each vertex is a control point that can be moved or scaled. If a vertex is a Bezier or Bezier Corner type, you can adjust a spline by moving control handles that are attached to the vertex.

◆   **Segment** editing affects the section of a spline that is between vertices. You can move, rotate or scale segments, but there are only a few editing commands that affect them.

◆   **Spline** editing alters an entire spline. In this case, we are speaking of a spline that is a sub-object of a shape object. Note that shape objects can be made up of more than one spline. In addition to being able to move, scale, and rotate at a spline level, you can perform more complex functions such as Boolean operations.

Figure 8.49 The Edit Spline modifier is set to the object level by default.

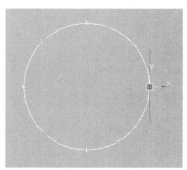

Figure 8.50 You can adjust Bezier vertices with their handles.

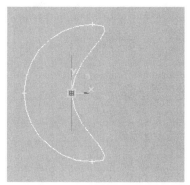

Figure 8.51 Moving a vertex reshapes the spline.

Editing a spline object

Lines, editable splines, and the Edit Spline modifier have identical command rollouts. For the sake of general explanation, both options are given here. In subsequent exercises, I will just use the example of editable splines, with the understanding that you can apply an Edit Spline modifier to any spline object, including an editable spline, if you prefer to do so.

To edit a spline object:

1. Select an editable spline object.

   or

   Select a spline object and apply an Edit Spline modifier.

   The editable spline or Edit Spline rollout appears in the Modify panel. It is set to the Object level by default (**Figure 8.49**).

2. In the Selection rollout, choose a sub-object type.

   All the commands that are available for the chosen sub-object type become enabled.

3. Make a sub-object selection.

   The selection turns red. At the vertex level, handles appear on selected Bezier points (**Figure 8.50**).

4. Apply an available editing command or a transform to your selection.

   The spline object updates interactively (**Figure 8.51**).

To attach splines:

1. Select an editable spline shape (**Figure 8.52**).

2. Open the Modify panel.

3. Click Attach in the Geometry rollout (**Figure 8.53**).

4. Click the spline you want to attach.

   The splines are attached (**Figure 8.54**). The attached spline takes on the color of the originally selected spline.

5. Continue clicking splines to attach them, or click Attach again to end the command.

✔ Tips

- Clicking Attach Mult brings up a list of attachable shape objects so that you can attach multiple shapes at one time.

- To create multiple splines that are already attached, uncheck the Start New Shape checkbox on the Spline creation menu before creating the splines (**Figure 8.55**).

To detach splines:

1. Select an editable spline shape that is made up of more than one spline.

2. Open the Modify panel.

3. In the Selection rollout, choose the spline sub-object type.

4. Select the spline you want to detach.

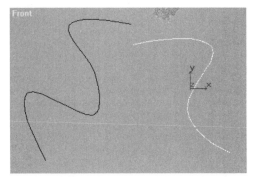

Figure 8.52 Selecting a spline shape in preparation for attaching another.

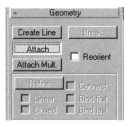

Figure 8.53 Click Attach before clicking the spline to append.

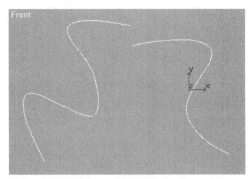

Figure 8.54 After the second spline is attached, the two are combined into a single shape.

Figure 8.55 Unchecking Start New Shape lets you attach splines as you create them.

EDITING SPLINES

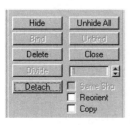

Figure 8.56 Click Detach to separate a selected spline from the shape.

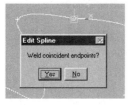

Figure 8.57 3D MAX provides automatic welding when you drop one spline end point on top of another.

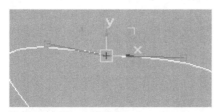

Figure 8.58 The two vertices have become one, thanks to welding.

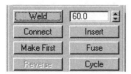

Figure 8.59 You can weld selected vertices within a set distance of each other.

5. Click Detach in the Geometry rollout (**Figure 8.56**).

6. Click OK to accept the default name for the detached spline.

   The spline is detached.

To weld vertices:

1. Select a shape that has at least one open spline.

2. Open the Modify panel.

3. Click Vertex.

4. Move one of the end points onto the other so that they coincide.

   When you release the mouse button, the Edit Spline dialog box appears (**Figure 8.57**).

5. Click Yes.

   The vertices weld and become one vertex. One of their vertex numbers disappears, and you cannot drag the vertices apart (**Figure 8.58**).

✔ Tips

- You can also use the Weld command to weld selected vertices (**Figure 8.59**).

- A quick way to tell if coincident vertices in a spline are welded is to click Show Vertex Numbers and make sure there's only one number at the vertex.

- Use the Break command to break open a spline at a vertex or segment. Breaking a spline at a vertex or segment creates coincident end points at the break point.

- Connect builds a segment between two end points when you drag from one end point to the other.

- The Fuse command moves selected vertices together to their averaged center. Fused vertices coincide but are not welded.

To convert vertices:

1. ⬚ Select a line or editable spline shape.
2. ⬚ Open the Modify panel.
3. ⬚ Click Vertex.
4. ⬚ Select the vertex points you want to convert (**Figure 8.60**).
5. Right-click your selection.
   The vertex right-click menu appears.
6. Choose a vertex type: Smooth, Corner, Bezier, or Bezier Corner (**Figure 8.61**).
   The vertices are converted to the selected vertex type (**Figure 8.62**).

To adjust a vertex:

1. ⬚ Select a line or editable spline shape.
2. ⬚ Open the Modify panel.
3. ⬚ Click Vertex.
4. ⬚ Select a vertex.
5. ⬚ Move the vertex.
6. ⬚ ⬚ ⬚ If the vertex is a Bezier type, you adjust its Bezier handles by moving, rotating, or scaling them (**Figure 8.63**).

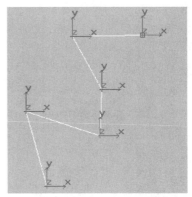

Figure 8.60 Selecting Corner vertices before converting them.

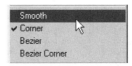

Figure 8.61 Choose Smooth to add some curves.

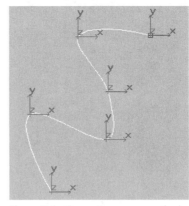

Figure 8.62 The vertices are smoothed.

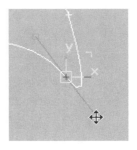

Figure 8.63 You can adjust the curves with Bezier vertices.

Figure 8.64 Turn on Show Vertex Numbers to see the vertex sequence.

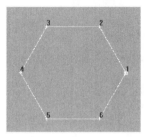

Figure 8.65 The NGon's first vertex is at the right.

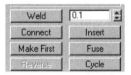

Figure 8.66 Use Make First to reorder the vertices.

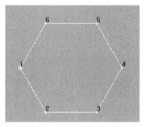

Figure 8.67 Now the NGon's first vertex is at the left. The numbering still proceeds counter-clockwise.

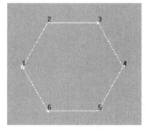

Figure 8.68 Thanks to the Reverse command, the numbering now proceeds clockwise.

To set a first vertex:

1. ⬚ Select an editable spline shape.

2. ✐ Open the Modify panel.

3. ⠿ Click Vertex.

4. Check Show Vertex Numbers in the Selection rollout (**Figure 8.64**).

   Vertex numbers appear by each vertex, numbering the vertices in order from beginning to end. The first vertex has a square around it (**Figure 8.65**).

5. ⬚ Select a vertex.

6. Click Make First in the Geometry rollout (**Figure 8.66**).

   The selected vertex becomes the first vertex. The vertex number changes to 1, and the square moves to enclose the vertex mark (**Figure 8.67**).

✔ Tips

- You can make any vertex on a closed spline the first vertex.

- In an open spline, such as an arc or line, you can make only one of the end points the first vertex.

- Clicking the Cycle button advances a vertex selection to the next vertex in a spline. If the shape contains more than one spline, the selection will cycle from one spline to the next and then back to the beginning.

- The Reverse command reverses the direction, or vertex order, of a spline. The Reverse command is available only at the Spline selection level (**Figure 8.68**).

EDITING SPLINES

Chamfering a vertex

Chamfer files down the corner of a spline to a 45-degree angle.

To chamfer a vertex:

1. ⬛ Select an editable spline shape that has a distinct corner (**Figure 8.69**).

2. ⬛ Open the Modify panel.

3. ⬛ Click Vertex.

4. ⬛ Select a vertex on a corner.

5. Drag the Chamfer spinner or enter a value to set the chamfer distance (**Figure 8.70**).

   The vertex splits into two vertices, which spread apart and chamfer the corner (**Figure 8.71**).

✔ Tips

- Fillet is a related command that rounds a corner to an arc (**Figure 8.72**).

- If the segments on either side of the selected vertex do not form a corner or curve, the vertices will spread apart evenly until they run into their nearest neighbors.

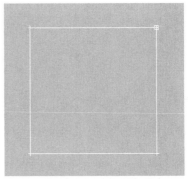

Figure 8.69 A rectangle is a good shape to use to learn about Chamfer and Fillet.

Figure 8.70 Use the Chamfer spinner to set the chamfer distance.

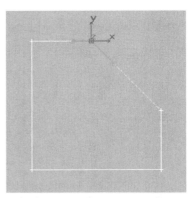

Figure 8.71 The rectangle corner after chamfering.

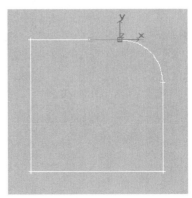

Figure 8.72 Fillet produces a rounded corner.

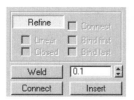

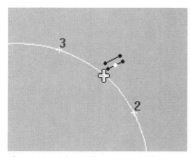

Figure 8.73 Use Refine to add new vertices to a spline.

Figure 8.74 The Refine cursor tells you that you can click to add a vertex.

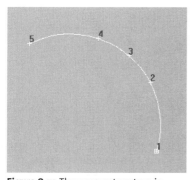

Figure 8.75 The new vertex stays in numeric sequence with the rest.

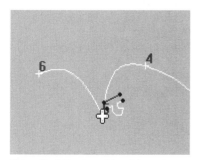

Figure 8.76 Use Insert to add a vertex and move it at the same time.

To add a vertex to a spline:

1. Select an editable spline.

2. Open the Modify panel.

3. Click Vertex.

4. Optional: Check Show Vertex Numbers. The vertex numbers of the spline appear.

5. Click Refine in the Geometry rollout (**Figure 8.73**).

6. Position the cursor over the spline. The cursor changes to the Refine cursor (**Figure 8.74**).

7. Click to place the vertex. A new vertex is added to the spline. The vertex numbers update accordingly (**Figure 8.75**).

✔ Tips

- You can add as many vertices as you wish so long as the Refine button is active.

- You cannot create a stand-alone vertex. Vertices must always be on a spline and must be connected to another vertex by a segment.

- The Insert command adds vertices and moves them as well (**Figure 8.76**).

To delete any part of a spline:

1. Select an editable spline object.

2. Click a sub-object button.

3. Select the part of the spline that you want to delete.

4. Press the Delete key or click the Delete button in the Geometry rollout.

Outlining a spline

Use Outline in architectural modeling to add thickness to walls or to create a profile for lathing a two-sided vase.

To outline a spline:

1. ⬚ Select an editable spline shape.

2. ✏ Open the Modify panel.

3. ⌁ Click Spline.

4. Choose the spline.

5. Drag the Outline spinner or enter a value to specify the distance between the original spline and the outline (**Figure 8.77**).

   An outline of the spline is created (**Figure 8.78**).

✔ Tips

- If you want to offset the spline and its outline an equal distance on either side of the original, activate the Center checkbox.

- Outline the profile of a vase to add thickness to the vase when it is lathed (**Figure 8.79**).

- The Mirror command flips splines vertically, horizontally, or both. It also gives you the option of cloning your spline (**Figure 8.80**).

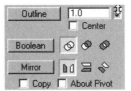

Figure 8.77 Dragging the Outline spinner. A positive number offsets to the inside of the spline; a negative number offsets to the outside.

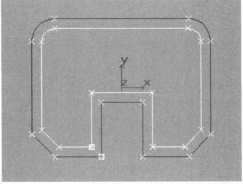

Figure 8.78 An outline has been added to the spline.

Figure 8.79 Because the profile was enhanced using Outline, the vase will have thickness when lathed.

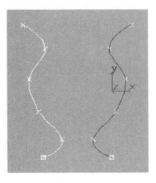

Figure 8.80 Use Mirror to flip or clone a spline.

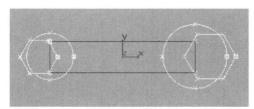

Figure 8.81 This is a single shape made up of a rectangle, two circles, and two NGons.

Figure 8.82 The Boolean button is active and is set to the Union mode.

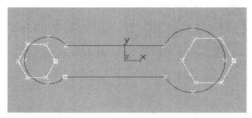

Figure 8.83 The two circles are attached to the rectangle with Union, and the intersecting lines have been removed.

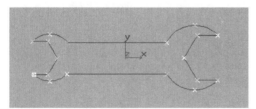

Figure 8.84 After the NGons are subtracted, the final product is a wrench template.

Performing a Boolean operation on a shape

Spline Boolean operations combine two or more splines using the Boolean operations of union, subtraction, and intersection. Boolean commands can be applied only to splines that are already attached as part of a single shape.

◆ **Union:** Combines two splines into one and deletes the part of the splines that intersect.

◆ **Subtraction:** Combines two splines into one and deletes the part of the first spline that intersects the second, and the part of the second spline that does not intersect the first.

◆ **Intersection:** Combines two splines into one and deletes the part of the splines that do not intersect.

To perform a Boolean operation on a shape:

1. Select an editable spline shape that is made up of several overlapping splines.

2. Open the Modify panel.

3. Click Spline.

4. Select one of the splines (**Figure 8.81**).

5. Click Boolean in the Geometry rollout. Make sure this option is set to Union (**Figure 8.82**).

6. Click the splines you want to which you want to apply a union operation.

   As you click each spline, the overlapping parts of each one disappears (**Figure 8.83**).

7. Click Subtraction.

8. Click the splines you want to subtract.

   The splines are subtracted from the shape (**Figure 8.84**).

Trimming a spline

The Trim command has the same requirement as Boolean operations in that the splines you are working with must be part of the same shape. Whereas the Boolean operation combines different splines into one, Trim simply cuts them and leaves them as separate splines.

To trim a spline:

1. ▶ Select an editable spline shape with overlapping splines (**Figure 8.85**).

2. ✏ Open the Modify panel.

3. ⌇ Click Spline.

4. Click the Trim button (**Figure 8.86**).

5. Click the lines that you want deleted (**Figure 8.87**).

   The lines are trimmed up to where they intersect the nearest spline.

✔ Tips

■ Click the Extend button and see what happens when you click the lines that you just trimmed (**Figure 8.88**).

■ Note that you do not have to select one of the splines to use Trim or Extend. You simply activate the button and start picking lines you want trimmed or extended.

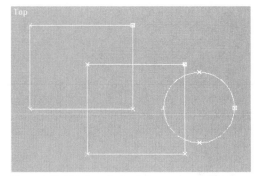

Figure 8.85 This is a single shape made up of two rectangles and a circle.

Figure 8.86 The Trim button turns green when it is active.

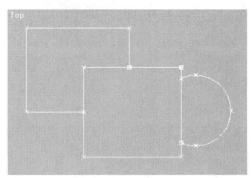

Figure 8.87 The lines inside the center spline are trimmed away.

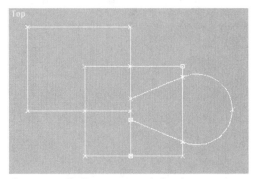

Figure 8.88 The lines are extended to the center spline.

COMPOUND OBJECTS

Compound objects combine two or more objects into one. They greatly assist complex modeling operations and facilitate certain types of animation solutions. 3D Studio MAX 3 ships with eight types of compound objects: Boolean, Connect, Scatter, ShapeMerge, Terrain, Conform, Loft, and Morph.

Compound objects combine some of the best characteristics of modifiers and arrays. With compound objects, you can deform, cut, join, remove, and extrude surfaces. You can also create ordered or random arrays of clones.

When you apply a compound object command to individual objects, the objects become *operands* of the compound object operation—meaning that they are operated upon. Because compound object commands cannot be used to select the first object, you must first select an object before choosing a compound object command. Commands for creating compound objects are found in the drop-down menu of the Create/Geometry branch. Shortcuts to these commands are found in the Compounds tab panel.

Creating Boolean Objects

Boolean algebra is a branch of mathematics that was developed in the 1800s to combine and manipulate sets of mathematical symbols. Named for its inventor, Charles Boole, Boolean algebra is used today to create Boolean compound objects in 3D graphics.

Boolean operations can use additive or subtractive modeling techniques, just like in traditional sculpture. In sculpture, you can add to a form by applying additional mass, or you can subtract from a form by carving away mass. In Boolean operations, adding mass to and subtracting mass from a form is accomplished by combining two objects. The type of Boolean operation and the position of the objects determine the final result.

Boolean operations are used mostly on meshes, but they can be applied to spline objects as well. By performing a Boolean operation on a spline, you can shape complex profiles for lathing or extrusion, as well as for lofting. *(For instructions on applying Boolean operations to splines, see Chapter 8, "Editing Objects.")*

When a Boolean command is applied to a selected object, that object is assigned as operand A. Operand B is assigned by picking a second object that is cloned and then assigned. When both operands have been assigned, the Boolean operation takes place. The object that results from combining operands A and B inherits the name and color of operand A.

If a material was previously assigned to operand A, that material will be passed on to the resulting Boolean object. If a material was assigned to operand B, you will be given the opportunity to incorporate B's material into the final object in several ways. *(For information on multi/sub-object materials, see Chapter 12, "Maps and Materials.")*

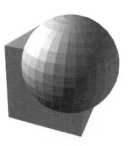

Figure 9.1 A Boolean Union compound object combines both operands into a unified object.

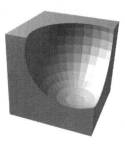

Figure 9.2 A Boolean Subtraction (A-B) compound object carves operand B out of operand A.

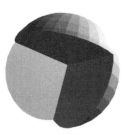

Figure 9.3 A Boolean Subtraction (B-A) compound object carves operand A out of operand B.

Figure 9.4 A Boolean Intersection compound object results in the overlapping volume of both operands.

Figure 9.5 A Boolean Cut Remove Inside compound object carves operand B out of operand A without leaving any faces from operand B.

Boolean operations for mesh objects are a bit more involved than Boolean operations for spline objects. This is because sets of faces are added or subtracted to build new surfaces based on the position of the operands. The five types of Boolean operations are as follows:

◆ **Union** combines operands A and B into one object and removes intersecting faces. If the operands do not intersect, they are combined into a single object made of separate elements in space (**Figure 9.1**).

◆ **Subtraction (A-B)** subtracts the volume of operand B from the volume of operand A. This operation builds an interior surface on operand A by adding the enclosed faces of operand B to it. It deletes the rest of operand B's faces (**Figure 9.2**).

◆ **Subtraction (B-A)** subtracts the volume of operand A from the volume of operand B. This operation uses faces from operand B to cover the hole that would otherwise remain (**Figure 9.3**).

◆ **Intersection** takes the overlapping volume of the two operands and deletes any nonintersecting volume. This operation uses the faces of the interpenetrating surfaces to build the new object. This, in effect, creates the piece you drilled out in a Boolean subtraction. If the operands do not intersect, both will disappear (**Figure 9.4**).

◆ **Cut** cuts open the surface of operand A with the volume of operand B. No faces from operand B are added to operand A. Instead, faces are refined, split, or deleted in operand A along the intersection of its surface with operand B (**Figure 9.5**).

CREATING BOOLEAN OBJECTS

Performing a Boolean operation

Boolean operations sometimes fail to work properly, although they have improved significantly since MAX was first released. *(See the sidebar "Tips for Performing Successful Boolean Operations" later in this chapter.)* However, it is still a good idea to save your scene often and to hold it (using Edit > Hold) before performing a Boolean operation. That way, if the operation fails, you can retrieve the scene from the hold file using Edit > Fetch.

To perform a Boolean operation:

1. ▨ Create two objects, such as a box and a sphere.

2. ✛ Position the objects so that they intersect (**Figure 9.6**).

3. ▨ Select the object you want to assign to operand A.

4. 🖳 Click the Compounds tab and click Boolean Compound Object.

   The Compound Object category appears in the Create command panel. The Boolean panel appears below, showing that the selected object has already been assigned to operand A (**Figure 9.7**).

5. In the Operation group, choose a Boolean operation. The default is Subtraction (A-B) (**Figure 9.8**).

6. Click Pick Operand B and select a clone option. The first time, use Move, the default setting, which uses the original object and then deletes it. This makes it easy to see the result.

7. Click the sphere.

   If Subtract (A-B) was chosen and you used the Move clone option, the sphere takes a bite out of the box and disappears (**Figure 9.9**).

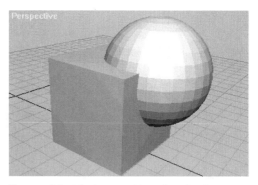

Figure 9.6 Positioning two objects for a Boolean operation.

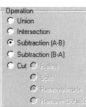

Figure 9.7 The Create panel shows the selected object assigned to operand A.

Figure 9.8 Subtraction (A-B) is the default Boolean operation.

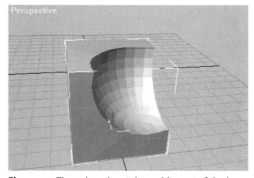

Figure 9.9 The sphere has taken a bite out of the box.

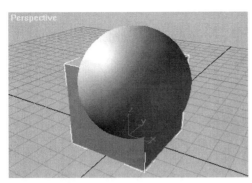

Figure 9.10 Position the two objects and then select the one you want to cut.

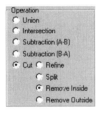

Figure 9.11 Choose the Cut > Remove Inside operation.

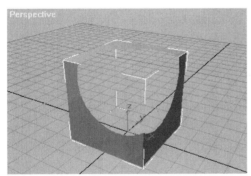

Figure 9.12 The sphere cuts a hole in the box without leaving any faces.

8. To interactively perform other Boolean operations, click Union, Subtraction (B-A), and Intersection in the Operation group box.

   The Boolean object updates to show the effect of each operation.

Performing a cut

The Cut operation allows you to cut open an object. There are four options for cutting:

◆ **Refine** adds new faces to operand A where it intersects the surface of operand B.

◆ **Split** adds two sets of new faces to operand A where it intersects the surface of operand B. Each of these sets of faces is used to define a separate element in the mesh so that the mesh can easily be split apart.

◆ **Remove Inside** deletes faces from operand A that are enclosed by the volume of operand B. This option works like Subtraction, except that it does not add faces to operand A.

◆ **Remove Outside** deletes faces from operand A that are not enclosed by the volume of operand B. This option works like Intersect, except that it does not add faces to operand A.

To perform a Cut:

1. Create two intersecting objects.

2. Select the object you want to cut (**Figure 9.10**).

3. Apply a Boolean command.

4. Choose Cut and a cutting option in the Operation group box (**Figure 9.11**).

5. Click Pick Operand B and click the intersecting object.

   The first object is cut by the second one (**Figure 9.12**).

Tips for Performing Successful Boolean Operations

Boolean objects can sometimes become unstable or fail, which may cause them to disappear or perform operations incorrectly. In this event, undo the operation and try these tips:

◆ Increase the number of faces on the simpler operand and try again. Boolean operations work best when the density of each mesh is roughly equal.

◆ Reposition the operands slightly.

◆ Collapse the operands' modifier stacks before using them.

◆ Make sure the operands are not too complex. Complexity can cause Boolean operations to take hours, and then fail. Decrease the number of segments or apply an Optimize modifier and collapse the stack before trying again.

◆ To escape from a Boolean operation, press the Esc key to end the operation.

◆ Good operands should have a closed, continuous surface that is not self-intersecting. Use the STL-Check modifier to check for open edges, double edges, double faces, internal faces, or unwelded vertices. *(See the tip after "To unify normals" in Chapter 7.)*

◆ Another way to check a mesh object for holes is to apply a Mesh Select modifier and choose Edge level selection. Then click Select Open Edges. Edges that do not have a face on both sides will turn red.

◆ Teapots and Hedra are poor Boolean operands because of their internal self-intersecting faces. To overcome this obstacle, perform a Union operation between two clones.

◆ Avoid using operands that have long, skinny faces. To shorten faces in objects, try adding extra height segments to primitives and adding extra steps when you are lofting, extruding, or lathing objects.

◆ When performing a series of Boolean operations, deselect the object between operations.

◆ If you are performing multiple Boolean operations on a model, collapse the stack and convert the model to an editable mesh between operations. This changes the object to an explicitly defined model, rather than a parametrically defined one, which is far more stable.

◆ If the Boolean operation is so unstable that it disappears when you convert it, try exporting it as a .3ds object and then importing it back into your scene.

◆ Another way to stabilize a Boolean operation is to apply a Snapshot command of it using the Mesh setting. This produces an editable mesh that you can use instead.

◆ Applying an Optimize modifier with a low (0.1) face threshold can sometimes help.

◆ If you are not planning to animate the Boolean operation, try using the Collapse utility in the Utility panel instead. The Collapse command outputs an editable mesh. By holding down the Ctrl key, you can pick and operate with multiple operands in succession.

Figure 9.13 In the Modify panel, check Result + Hidden Ops.

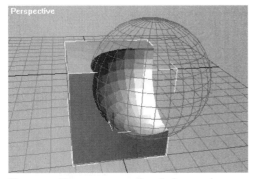

Figure 9.14 You can now see the wireframe sphere that was subtracted from the box.

Figure 9.15 Turning on Sub-Object lets you manipulate and animate Boolean operands.

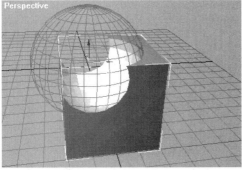

Figure 9.16 The space created by the subtracted operand seems to move through the solid operand.

Animating Boolean Operands

Boolean operands can be animated after a Boolean operation has been performed. The results can be elegant and magical to watch and have a wide variety of applications.

To animate a Boolean:

1. Select a Boolean object. For this example, use an object that has been created by subtraction.

2. Open the Modify panel.

3. In the Display area, check Result + Hidden Ops (**Figure 9.13**).

    The hidden operand appears in wireframe (**Figure 9.14**).

4. Click the Sub-Object button.

    Operands becomes highlighted in the Sub-Object drop-down menu (**Figure 9.15**).

5. Click the Animate button.

6. Drag the time slider to a new position.

7. Drag the wireframe operand all the way through the solid operand.

8. Turn off Show Hidden Operand.

9. Click Play Animation.

    The hole created by the hidden operand moves smoothly through the solid operand (**Figure 9.16**).

ANIMATING BOOLEAN OPERANDS

Creating Connect Objects

Connect objects connect two or more mesh objects by building bridges between holes in their surfaces. Use Connect objects to create architectural structures, furniture, handles, tools, and other manufactured objects. You can also use Connect objects to connect fingers to a hand or to connect appendages to a torso.

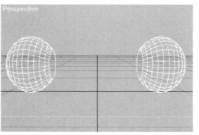

Figure 9.17 Positioning the objects so the holes face each other.

To create a Connect object:

1. ![ ] Create two mesh objects.

2. ![ ] Make a hole in the surface of each object by deleting a vertex.

   (Hint: For symmetrical output, create one object with a hole and then mirror it.)

3. ![ ] Position the objects so that the holes face each other (within a 90-degree angle) (**Figure 9.17**).

4. ![ ] Select one of the objects.

5. ![ ] Choose Connect Compound Object from the Compounds Toolbar.

   The Connect panel appears. The selected object is assigned as operand 0 (**Figure 9.18**).

6. Choose a clone type for your next operand, just as you would with a Boolean operand.

7. Click Pick Operand and click the second mesh object.

   A mesh structure bridges the gap between holes in the operands (**Figure 9.19**).

8. Smooth the bridge in the middle and at either end by checking Bridge and Ends.

9. Increase the number of segments and adjust the tension to make the bridge bulge or shrink (**Figure 9.20**).

Figure 9.18 The selected object is assigned as operand 0.

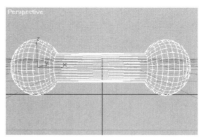

Figure 9.19 The result of connecting two spheres.

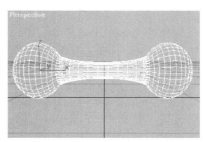

Figure 9.20 The result of adjusting the number of segments and tension setting.

Figure 9.21
The Scatter panel shows the selected object assigned as the source.

Figure 9.22 The result of scattering teapots on a planar surface.

Figure 9.23 Setting All Edge Midpoints in the Scatter panel.

Figure 9.24 The result of scattering teapots on a planar surface using the All Edge Midpoints option.

Creating Scatter Objects

Scatter objects distribute clones of a *source object* over the surface or within the volume of a *distribution object*.

To create a Scatter object:

1. Select or create a mesh object to scatter.

2. Choose Scatter Compound Object from the Compounds Toolbar.

   The Scatter panel appears. The selected object is assigned as the source object (**Figure 9.21**).

3. Choose a clone type for your next operand.

4. Click Pick Operand and click a mesh object on which to distribute the scatter objects.

   The source object positions itself on the surface of the mesh object.

5. In the Source Object Parameters group, enter a value for the number of duplicates.

   Duplicates of the source object distribute themselves evenly over the surface of the distribution object (**Figure 9.22**).

6. Try each of the distribution methods by clicking the radio buttons in the Distribution Object Parameters group (**Figure 9.23**).

   All Vertices, All Edge Midpoints, and All Face Centers ignore the Duplicates value and create regular arrays (**Figure 9.24**).

✔ Tip

■ To create a random distribution of objects within a volume, use a mesh object that encloses volume as the distribution object and check Volume in the Distribution Object Parameters group.

239

Using ShapeMerge

You use the ShapeMerge command to embed shapes in a mesh surface or to cut shapes out of it. The faces, vertices, and edges created by embedded shapes are automatically selected at the sub-object level so that you can easily extrude, bevel, or assign materials to them.

To perform a ShapeMerge operation:

1. Position a shape over the surface of a mesh object (**Figure 9.25**).

2. Select the mesh object.

3. Choose ShapeMerge Compound Object from the Compounds Toolbar.

   The ShapeMerge panel appears. The mesh object is assigned as the Mesh operand (**Figure 9.26**).

4. Choose a clone type and click Pick Shape. Then click the shape.

   The shape is embedded in the surface of the mesh (**Figure 9.27**).

5. Choose Cookie Cutter to cut the area enclosed by the shape out of the mesh surface. Check Invert to cut the surface away from the embedded shape area (**Figure 9.28**).

✔ Tip

■ To learn how to assign different colors to embedded shapes, see *"Creating a Multi/ Sub-Object Materials"* in Chapter 12, *"Maps and Materials."*

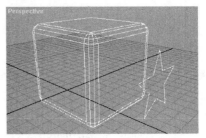

Figure 9.25 Getting a star shape ready to merge into a ChamferBox.

Figure 9.26 The ShapeMerge panel shows the ChamferBox assigned as the Mesh operand.

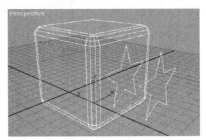

Figure 9.27 The star shape has been embedded into the ChamferBox surface.

Figure 9.28 Using Cookie Cutter to cut shapes out of a mesh.

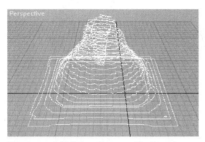

Figure 9.29 Using splines as the terrain contour lines.

Figure 9.30 The shape is assigned as Op 0 in the Terrain panel.

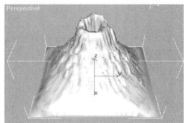

Figure 9.31 The Terrain compound object forms a volcano from the splines.

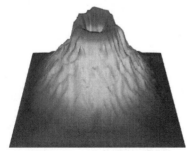

Figure 9.32 Using Color by Elevation to assign realistic shades to the volcano surface.

Creating Terrains

Terrains are 3D models that you make from contour line data. Terrains create landscapes for building sites, shadow studies, grading plans, and games. If you don't have any contour line models of landscapes, you can make one up using an array of closed splines, with each level being slightly smaller than the previous one.

1. Import a contour line data set or create your own set of splines (**Figure 9.29**).

2. Make sure the splines are all attached as one object. If they are not, select a single spline and convert it to an editable spline. Then apply an Attach Multiple command and select the rest of the splines in the set.

3. Click Terrain Compound Object in the Compound Object Toolbar.

   The Terrain panel appears (**Figure 9.30**). The contour lines are "skinned" and turned into a terrain (**Figure 9.31**). Note that complex contour lines may take a while to skin.

4. If any contour lines were skipped, click Pick Operand and click the contour line.

5. You can assign colors to each level of the terrain in the Color by Elevation rollout (**Figure 9.32**).

✔ Tip

■ To reduce the complexity of the mesh, choose Use 1/2 of Lines or Use 1/4 of Lines for vertical simplification or Use 1/2 of Points or Use 1/4 of Points for horizontal simplification in the Simplification rollout.

Creating Conform Objects

Conform objects are compound objects created by "wrapping" the vertices of one object around the vertices of another. This causes the surface of the first object, called a *Wrapper object,* to conform to the surface of the second, the W*rap-To object.* By placing the Wrapper object around the Wrap-To object, you can roughly duplicate the form of the Wrap-To object as if you were creating a very thin mold.

To create a Conform object:

1. 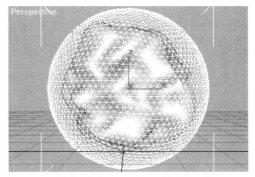 Create an object. This will be your Wrap-To object.

2. Create a GeoSphere that's slightly larger than the Wrap-To object and position it so it surrounds the first object. This will be your Wrapper object (**Figure 9.33**).

3. Choose Conform Compound Object from the Compounds Toolbar.

   The Conform Object panel appears. The selected outer object is assigned as the Wrapper object (**Figure 9.34**).

Figure 9.33 A GeoSphere encloses the Wrap-To object in preparation for creation of a Conform compound object.

Figure 9.34
The Conform panel shows the GeoSphere assigned as the Wrapper object.

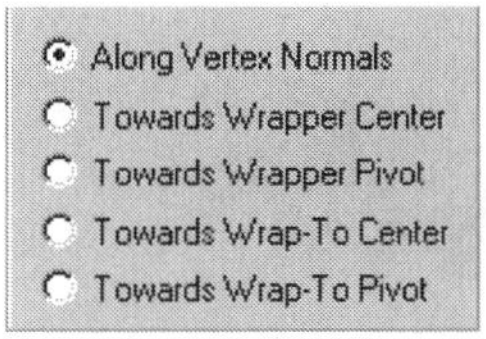

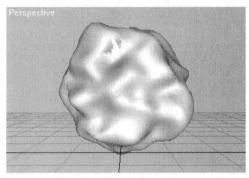

Figure 9.35 Choosing Along Vertex Normals causes the wrapper vertices to move inward perpendicular to the object surface.

Figure 9.36 The GeoSphere is wrapped around the Wrap-To object and conforms to its surface.

4. In the Vertex Projection Direction group, choose Along Vertex Normals (**Figure 9.35**).

5. In the Update group (near the bottom of the Parameters rollout), check Hide Wrap-To Object.

6. Click Pick Wrap-To Object and choose a clone option.

7. In a wireframe view, click the inner object.

The Wrapper object wraps around the Wrap-To object (**Figure 9.36**).

✔ Tip

■ Use Conform objects to make text lie on the surface of a mesh object (**Figure 9.37**).

Figure 9.37 Using Conform to make text lie on a teapot surface.

Lofting Objects

Lofting is an incredibly versatile means of modeling and animating 3D forms. The term *lofting* comes from early methods of ship-building in which the hull of a ship was constructed from a series of cross-sections, or ribs, placed along its length. A structure called a loft supported the hull while the ribs were hoisted into place. The process of hoisting the ribs into the loft gave rise to the term *lofting*.

As in the shipbuilding days of yore, lofting creates a 3D object by placing cross-section shapes along a path. But instead of hoisting wooden ribs into a hull, lofting places shapes along a spline path. As each shape is added to the path, the loft builds a surface, or *skin*, to accommodate the different outlines of each (**Figure 9.38**).

A loft path can be angular or curved, open or closed, flat or three-dimensional, but it must be a single continuous spline. Shapes made up of more than one spline, such as a donut, cannot be used as a path. In contrast, shapes that you use as cross-sections of the loft can be made up of single or multiple splines. If splines are nested inside of each other, then each nested layer will be lofted together (**Figure 9.39**).

To loft an object, you start with either a path or a shape. If you start with a path and then get the cross-section shapes, the shapes will be arranged perpendicularly along the length of the path. If you start with a shape and then get a path, the path will be positioned along the local Z axis of the shape. For this reason, starting with the path and then getting the shapes is usually preferred because it is easier to predict where the loft will be built.

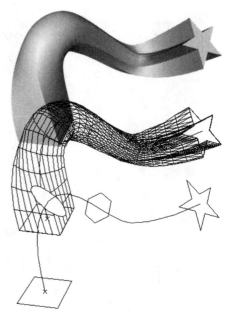

Figure 9.38 Using four shapes on a curved path to create an unusual lofted object.

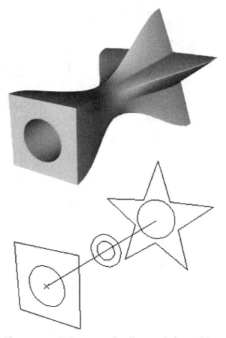

Figure 9.39 Using nested splines to loft an object with a hole through it.

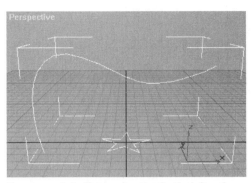

Figure 9.40 Selecting a spline line for the loft path.

Figure 9.41 The Loft panel provides Get Path and Get Shape functions.

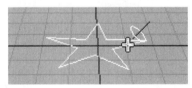

Figure 9.42 The mouse cursor is over a valid shape for lofting.

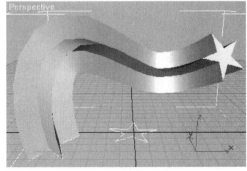

Figure 9.43 When you get the first shape, it's used along the entire path.

To loft an object with Get Shape:

1. ⬚ Select a valid shape for a path (**Figure 9.40**).

2. ⬚ Click Loft Compound Object in the Compounds Toolbar.

   The Loft Compound Object panel appears (**Figure 9.41**). If the selected spline shape is not a valid path, the Get Shape button will be dimmed.

3. Click Get Shape and choose a clone option. Accept the default option, Instance, if you plan to edit or animate the loft later.

4. Move the cursor over a shape.

   If the shape is valid, the cursor changes to a loft cursor (**Figure 9.42**). If the shape is invalid, the reason the shape is invalid is displayed in the prompt line.

5. Click the shape.

   The loft object appears. The shape, or a clone of it, is placed at the first vertex of the path and extruded along its length (**Figure 9.43**).

✔ Tips

- If you want to try lofting a different shape, click a new shape immediately after step 5. The new shape replaces the last shape you picked.

- Lofting a short line along a curved line creates a ribbon. Applying a two-sided material shades the ribbon on both sides.

- If you use shape objects that are made up of more than one spline, all shapes in the loft must contain the same number of splines, and the shapes must have the same nesting order, or levels of splines nesting within them.

LOFTING OBJECTS

To loft an object with Get Path:

1. [icon] Select a valid cross-section shape (**Figure 9.44**).

2. [icon] Click Loft Compound Object in the Compounds Toolbar.

   The Loft Compound Object panel appears (**Figure 9.45**). If the selected spline shape is not a valid shape, the Get Path button will be dimmed.

3. Click Get Path and choose a clone option.

4. Place the cursor over a shape you want to use as a path. Accept the default option, Instance, if you plan to edit or animate the loft later.

   If the shape is valid as a path, the cursor changes to a loft icon.

5. Click the shape.

   The loft appears, aligned to the local Z axis of the shape. The first vertex of the path is positioned at the pivot point of the shape (**Figure 9.46**).

✔ Tips

- If you want to try lofting a different path, click Get Path and click a new path. The new path replaces the last path you picked.

- To flip the orientation of the path, so that it follows the negative Z axis of the shape, hold down the Ctrl key when you click Get Path.

- Lines that are created by dragging Bézier end points generate uneven segment divisions, or steps, when used as paths (**Figure 9.47**). Converting the end points of the line to another vertex type and relofting the object corrects this problem.

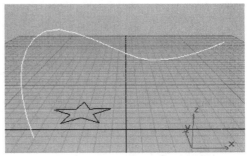

Figure 9.44 Selecting a valid shape for lofting.

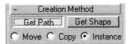

Figure 9.45 The Loft panel's Get Path button is active.

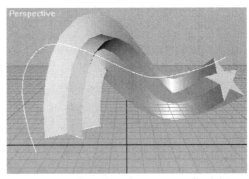

Figure 9.46 A loft generated using Get Path originates at the first shape.

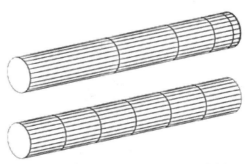

Figure 9.47 A loft path with uneven segment divisions uses Bézier end points (top); the problem is corrected by using Corner end points (bottom).

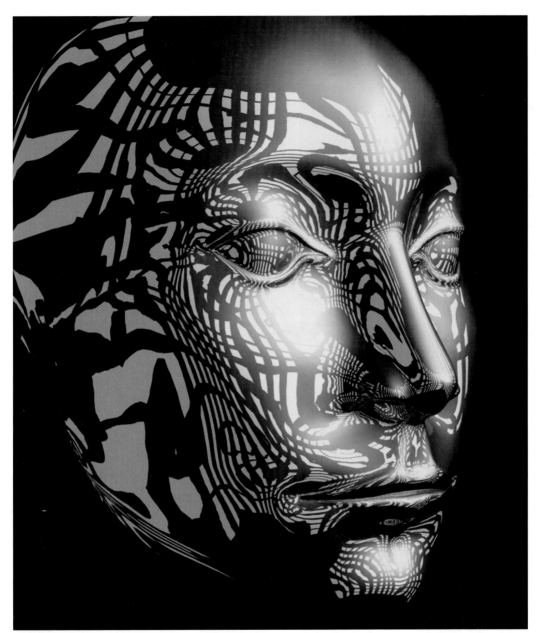

RayFlection
Bradford Stuart, 1999

Image courtesy of Autodesk, Inc.
brad.stuart@autodesk.com

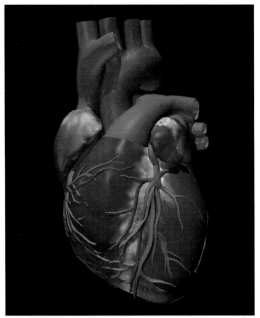

HEART
Sean Curtis, 1998

Image courtesy of Viewpoint Digital
sean.curtis@viewpoint.com

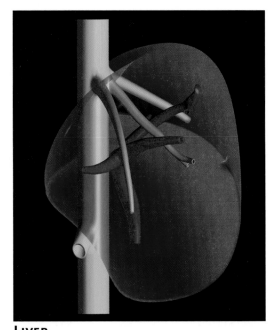

LIVER
Michele Matossian, 1996

Image courtesy of UCSF School of Medicine, Department of Radiology
3d@lightweaver.com

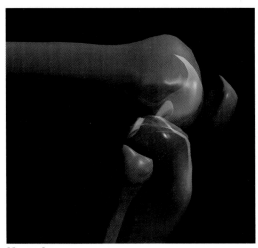

KNEE INJURY
Michele Matossian, 1997

Image courtesy of UCSF School of Medicine, Department of Radiology
3d@lightweaver.com

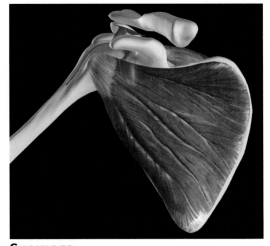

SHOULDER
Michele Matossian, 1998

Image courtesy of UCSF School of Medicine, Department of Radiology
3d@lightweaver.com

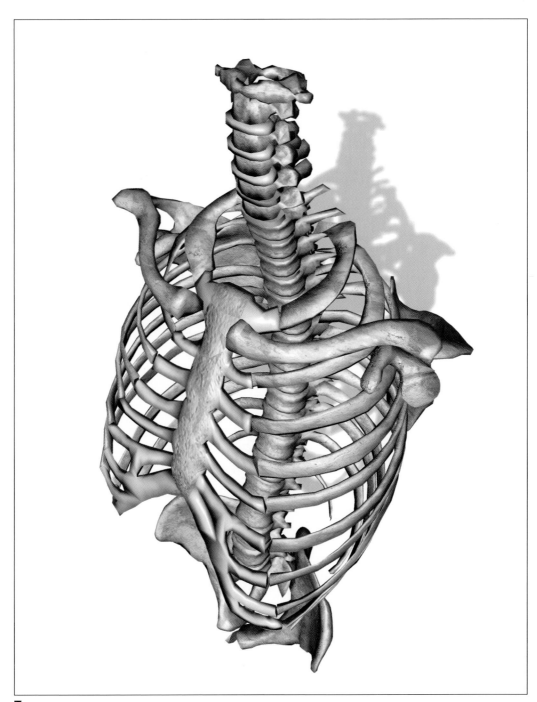

Torso

Tom Angus, 1998

Image courtesy of Viewpoint Digital
tom.angus@viewpoint.com

MAY THE BLESSINGS BE

Clark Heist, 1998

Image courtesy of Clark Heist
clark.heist@autodesk.com

GOD IS GREAT. GOD IS GOOD.
Clark Heist, 1998

Image courtesy of Clark Heist
clark.heist@autodesk.com

TAJ MAHAL Michele Matossian, 1997

SNOWSCAPE Brandon Davis, 1998

PRAIRIE Bob Prokopp, 1997

GALLERY Michele Matossian, 1999

THE U.S.S. JOHN SHAFT Karl Raade, 1997

IMAGE FROM THE GAME, "THE LONGEST JOURNEY" Didrik Tollefsen, 1999

MANIFESTATION Michele Matossian, 1998

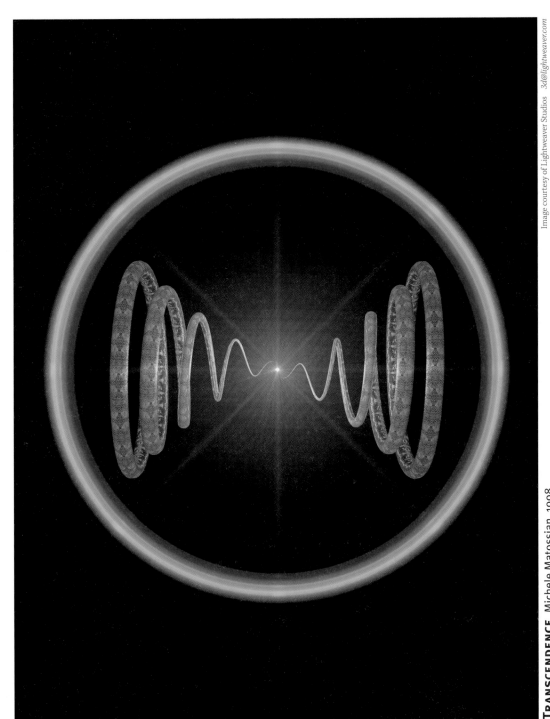

TRANSCENDENCE Michele Matossian, 1998

MANDALA Michele Matossian, 1998

EYECATCHER Michele Matossian, 1996

CHAMELEON Jared Trulock, 1998

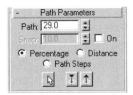

Figure 9.48 The Path Parameters rollout lets you adjust the loft path settings.

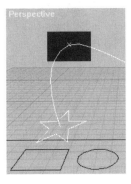

Figure 9.49 A small yellow X marks the point on the path where a new shape will be added.

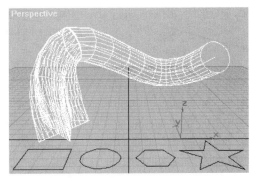

Figure 9.50 A circle shape has been added part way along the loft path.

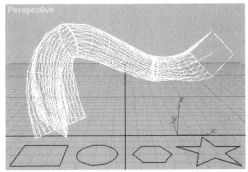

Figure 9.51 The loft object now uses four different shapes.

Adjusting Lofts

You adjust the shapes, path, skin, and surface rendering of a loft in the Modify panel. In addition to the creation parameters of the loft, the Modify panel includes a rollout called Deformations. Loft deformations scale, twist, teeter, bevel, and fit loft shapes along the path using function curves. This is an advanced topic, not covered in this book; however, most deformation effects can be achieved by editing individual shape sub-objects. *(See "Editing Lofts" later in this chapter for instructions.)*

To add shapes to a loft:

1. Select a loft object and set the viewport display to Wireframe.

2. Open the Modify panel.

3. Open the Path Parameters rollout (**Figure 9.48**).

4. Drag the Path spinner. Click Percentage or Distance to view the Path setting as a percentage along the path or as a distance in current units. Enable Snap if you want to snap to even intervals along the path.

   As you change the Path value, a yellow X moves along the path from the first shape to a new position, or level, on the path. This marks where the next shape will be added (**Figure 9.49**).

5. Click Get Shape and choose a clone option.

6. Click a shape.

   The shape, or a clone of it, is placed on the path at the current path level (**Figure 9.50**). The skin of the loft updates to incorporate the new shape.

7. Repeat steps 4 through 6 until you are done (**Figure 9.51**).

To replace shapes:

1.  Select a loft object and set the viewport display to Wireframe (**Figure 9.52**).

2. Open the Modify panel.

3. Open the Skin Parameters rollout and uncheck Skin at the bottom of the rollout (**Figure 9.53**).

4. Open the Path Parameters rollout and navigate the path level to the shape you want to replace. Click one of the following:

   ◆ **Next Shape**, to move up a level to the next shape in the path

   ◆ **Previous Shape**, to move back a level to the previous shape in the path

   ◆ **Pick Shape**, to pick a shape by clicking it in the loft (the mouse cursor changes its appearance when over a shape).

5. Click Get Shape and click the shape you want to insert at that level.

   The new shape replaces the old shape in the loft (**Figure 9.54**).

6. Repeat steps 4 and 5 until you have replaced all the shapes you want to replace. Turn Skin back on to see the results (**Figure 9.55**).

✔ Tip

■ You replace a path in the same way, except you use Get Path to select the new path.

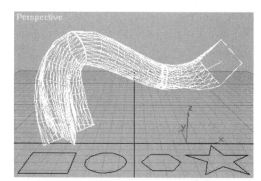

Figure 9.52 Selecting a loft object before replacing its shapes.

Figure 9.53 Turn off the Skin feature to easily see the shapes.

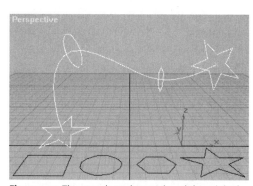

Figure 9.54 The star shape has replaced the original square at the end of the loft.

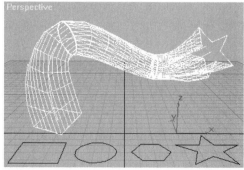

Figure 9.55 The square now replaces the star shape at the beginning of the path.

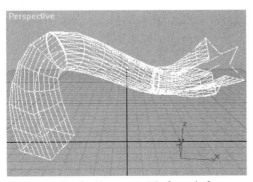

Figure 9.56 Set the viewport to Wireframe before adjusting skin complexity.

Figure 9.57
The Skin Parameters rollout lets you adjust skin complexity.

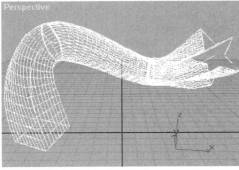

Figure 9.58 Increasing Shape Steps and Path Steps yields a better-looking, more complex loft object.

Adjusting skin complexity

Two factors govern the complexity of a loft:

◆ *Shape steps* are the number of segment divisions in the skin between each vertex of a cross-section shape. The number of shape steps determines the radial complexity of the loft.

◆ *Path steps* are the number of segment divisions in the skin between each cross-section shape on the path. The number of path steps determines the longitudinal complexity of the loft.

To adjust skin complexity:

1. Select a loft object and set the viewport display to Wireframe (**Figure 9.56**).

2. Open the Modify panel.

3. Open the Skin Parameters rollout (**Figure 9.57**). By default, the Shape Steps and Path Steps are each set to 5.

4. Increase or decrease Shape Steps or Path Steps to increase or decrease the complexity of the loft (**Figure 9.58**).

✔ Tips

■ To optimize the number of path steps automatically, check Optimize Path. This checkbox is available only when Path Steps is selected in the Path Parameters rollout.

■ To automatically generate the best-looking skin, check Adaptive Path Steps. This checkbox is available only when Percentage or Distance is selected in the Path Parameters rollout.

■ Contour and Banking cause path steps to turn with the path in a flat plane and in 3D. Constant Cross Section causes corners to be mitered correctly. These are all good options to leave checked (the default).

ADJUSTING LOFTS

249

Editing Lofts

The sub-object components of a loft are the path of the loft and its cross-section shapes. You edit loft objects by editing cross-section shapes and paths at the sub-object level or by manipulating originals or instances of the sub-object shapes used to create the loft.

Manipulating original or instanced shapes is usually the easiest solution. Just select a shape, open the Modify panel, and edit, modify, or adjust the shape's creation parameters. Transforms are not passed on from original shape objects to instanced loft sub-objects unless you place them in an XForm modifier.

Loft sub-object editing commands are limited to aligning and cloning loft components, but once you are in sub-object mode, you can move, rotate, and scale cross-section shapes. You can also rotate paths along their Z axes. Because loft sub-object selections are not passed up the modifier stack, any modifiers that are applied at the sub-object level will have the unexpected result of modifying the entire loft.

The following exercises explain how to edit cross-section shapes at the sub-object level. You edit paths in much the same way, but you are limited to rotating and cloning them. Deleting a path deletes the entire loft object.

Figure 9.59 At the Shape sub-object selection level, you can manipulate the loft object's shapes interactively.

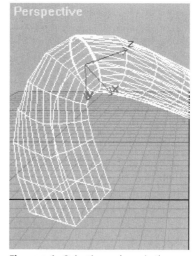

Figure 9.60 Selecting a shape in the loft object.

To select a shape at the sub-object level:

1. Select a loft object and set the viewport display to Wireframe.

2. Open the Modify panel.

3. Click Sub-Object and choose Shape from the Selection Level drop-down list.

   The Shape Commands rollout appears (**Figure 9.59**).

4. Click a cross-section shape to select it (**Figure 9.60**).

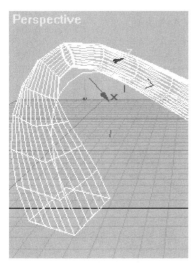

Figure 9.61 The shape is scaled down, reducing the loft object's diameter in that section.

Figure 9.62 The Put To Scene dialog box lets you specify a name for the cloned shape.

Figure 9.63 The Shape Commands rollout provides access to the Compare functions.

To remove a shape:

1. Select a shape at the sub-object level.

2. Click the Delete button or press the Delete key.

   The shape is removed from the loft object.

To transform a shape:

1. Select a shape at the sub-object level.

2. Move, rotate, or scale the shape.

   The shape is transformed in its local coordinate system. The skin updates to match the new position, orientation, or scale of the shape (**Figure 9.61**).

To clone a shape:

1. Select a shape at the sub-object level.

2. Click Put in the Shapes Commands rollout.

   The Put To Scene dialog box appears (**Figure 9.62**).

3. Name the new shape and then click OK.

   The copy or instance appears in the viewport at the origin of the home grid.

To align shapes to the path:

1. Open the Modify panel.

2. Select a loft and select the Shape sub-object level.

   The Shape Commands rollout appears (**Figure 9.63**).

   (continues on next page)

(continues on next page)

3. Click the Compare button.

The Compare window appears (**Figure 9.64**). In it, a cross marks the position of the path in relation to the shapes. A small box marks the first vertex of each shape.

Click **Pick Shape** and click a shape to bring it into the Compare window.

Click **Reset** to clear the window.

The first vertex of each shape in the window is marked by a small square (**Figure 9.65**).

4. In the viewport, select the shape or shapes you want to align.

5. In the Shape Commands rollout, click the align buttons that best approximate the alignment you want. Click Default to return to the original alignment.

The selected shapes change alignment to the path. The new alignment is shown in the Compare window and in the viewports (**Figure 9.66**).

✔ Tips

- Lofting typically aligns the first vertex of each shape, but if the shapes vary widely in shape or complexity, these vertices may get out of alignment. The result is a loft that twists or stretches unpredictably. Use the Compare window to check and realign the first vertex of each shape.

- Fine-tune your shape alignment by moving or rotating shapes at the sub-object level.

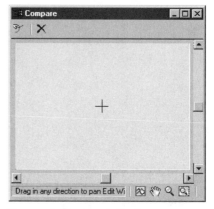

Figure 9.64 The cross in the Compare window represents the path, as seen looking down the length of the path.

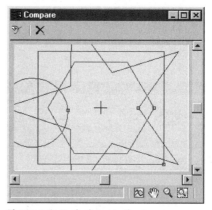

Figure 9.65 Each shape in the Compare window has a small square at its first vertex.

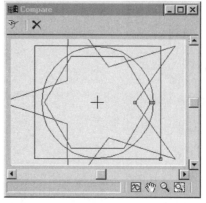

Figure 9.66 The Compare window lets you see how shapes line up in the loft.

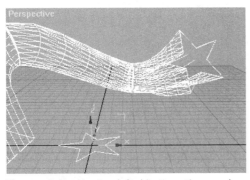

Figure 9.67 To animate a loft object's vertices, work with the shapes used to create the loft.

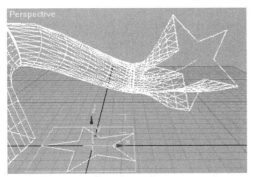

Figure 9.68 Applying a modifier to the original shape affects the shape instance in the loft.

Animating Lofts

You can animate lofts at the object level or at the sub-object level. At the object level, you animate a loft object as you would any other mesh object. At the sub-object level, you animate a loft strictly by animating instances or originals of the loft path and shapes. Applying transforms or modifiers directly to loft sub-objects does not generate any animation keys and has no effect on the loft object over time.

To animate a loft:

1. Select an original or instance of a loft shape or path (**Figure 9.67**).

2. Open the Modify panel.

3. Turn on the Animate button.
   or
   Click the Animate button.

4. Drag the time slider to a new position.

5. Modify the shape or path by changing its creation parameters or applying a modifier. Use Edit Spline to animate vertices. Use the XForm modifier to animate transforms (**Figure 9.68**).

6. Play back the animation.
   The loft changes over time.

Morphing Objects

3D morphing is a method of animation in which a *seed object* changes shape to match a series of *target objects*. It is often used in character animation to change facial expressions and lip-synch voices.

You can apply mesh morphing, patching, or NURBs to objects. The prerequisite for morphing mesh objects is that all target objects must have the same number of vertices as the seed object. This is because morphing moves the vertices of the seed object to corresponding vertices in the target objects. If the number of vertices is unequal, the morph animation will not work.

How do you model objects into different shapes with the same number of vertices? There are three main ways to do this:

◆ Modify clones of a geometry primitive.

◆ Create mesh objects from splines that have identical numbers of vertices using the Extrude, Lathe, or Loft command.

◆ If you want to morph existing mesh models that have unequal vertices, clone a high-density GeoSphere and make Conform objects of each seed or target object.

Once you have learned the basics of morphing, I recommend that you learn how to use the Morpher modifier for more sophisticated tasks. The advantage of the Morpher modifier is that it can be added repeatedly to the modifier stack, and it has over 100 channels for assigning morph targets. To go along with the Morpher modifier, the Morph material assigns materials to different channels of the Morpher modifier, allowing you to morph between materials. For instructions on how to apply Morpher modifiers and Morph materials, see the 3DS MAX online help files.

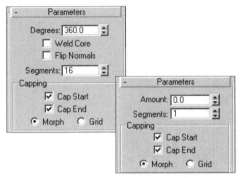

Figure 9.69 Use the General rollout to set a spline's vertex count.

Figure 9.70 (left) Using Extrude to generate morph objects; (right) using Lathe to generate morph objects.

Figure 9.71 Use these Skin Parameters settings when creating morph objects.

To set the number of vertices on a spline:

1. Create a spline object, such as a line.

2. Open the General rollout of the spline (**Figure 9.69**).

3. Uncheck Optimize and Adaptive.

4. Set the number of steps.

   The number of vertices is set.

To extrude or lathe seed and target objects:

1. Select a spline shape.

2. Use the Modeling Toolbar to apply an Extrude or Lathe modifier.

   The Extrude or Lathe rollout appears (**Figure 9.70**).

3. Set the number of segments.

4. If you use the Lathe modifier, make sure Weld Core is unchecked.

5. Set Capping to Morph.

   This arranges cap faces in a predictable pattern for morphing.

6. Repeat steps 1 through 5 using a spline with an equal number of vertices. Make sure that the Segments value is the same each time.

To loft seed and target objects:

1. Select a spline shape.

2. Loft the shape along a path.

3. In the Skin Parameters rollout, uncheck Optimize Shapes and Adaptive Path Steps and set Capping to Morph (**Figure 9.71**).

4. Repeat steps 1 through 3 using loft shapes and paths with the same number of vertices.

MORPHING OBJECTS

To create a morph animation:

1.  Create a seed object and some target objects for morphing.

2. Select the seed object (**Figure 9.72**).

3. Choose Morph Compound Object from the Compounds Toolbar.

   The Compound rollout appears. In the Current Targets rollout, the seed object appears at the top of the Morph Targets list (**Figure 9.73**).

4. Click Pick Target and choose a method for creating targets from your originals: Reference, Move, Copy, or Instance.

5. Click the morph target objects in the viewports.

   The target objects are added to the Morph Targets list (**Figure 9.74**).

6. Highlight the next target to which you want to morph the seed object.

7. Drag the time slider to the frame number or time where you want to set the first morph animation key. Note that it is not necessary to turn on the Animate button.

8. Click Create Morph Key.

   A key appears in the Track Bar at the current frame number or time.

9. To preview the animation, scrub the time slider back and forth. The seed object morphs to the target object automatically (**Figure 9.75**).

10. Repeat steps 6 through 9 until you are finished.

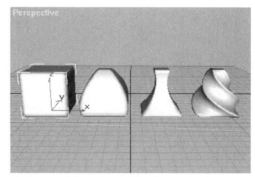

Figure 9.72 The ChamferBox is used as the seed object and thus appears first in the morph animation.

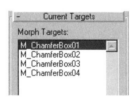

Figure 9.73 The Morph Targets list shows the ChamferBox as the first target.

Figure 9.74 After all the morph targets have been picked, they appear in the list in the order that they'll appear in the morph animation.

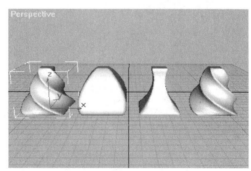

Figure 9.75 The ChamferBox morphs into each shape in turn, ending up as the twisted box.

CAMERAS

In the previous chapters, you learned how to model and animate objects. With cameras, you determine how the audience views the scene.

Cameras make you the director of your own movie. To tell your story, you compose shots to show the part of the scene where the action takes place. As you become more experienced, you begin setting up shots from more informative, beautiful, mysterious, unusual, helpful, or surprising points of view.

This chapter discusses the different types of cameras, how to adjust them, and how to place them. You will also learn how to animate cameras by keyframing and using motion paths.

Creating Cameras

Like other objects in 3D Studio MAX 3, you create cameras in the Create command panel. Shortcuts for creating cameras are found in the Lights & Cameras Toolbar (**Figure 10.1**).

The two types of cameras in MAX are called *target cameras* and *free cameras*. Each one has its own advantages:

◆   **Target cameras** have two components: the camera and a target that it faces (**Figure 10.2**). Each component can move independently of the other, but the camera lens always faces the target. This makes target cameras easy to aim and control. Use target cameras as an all-purpose tool for creating still images and animated scenes.

◆   **Free cameras** are single-object cameras that have an "implied target" in front of them at a target distance that you can set (**Figure 10.3**). The advantage of free cameras is that they can rotate freely to look around a scene. This makes them ideal for animating complex motions. Assign free cameras to follow convoluted motion paths or link them to a hierarchy of dummy objects.

Figure 10.1 Save time by using the Lights & Cameras Toolbar shortcuts.

Figure 10.2 The target camera as seen from overhead; the camera is at the top, and its target is below.

Figure 10.3 The free camera as seen from overhead; it has no target.

Figure 10.4 Use the target camera parameters to set focal length (or lens size), environment ranges, and more.

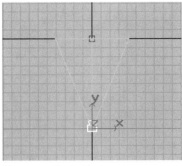

Figure 10.5 To aim the target camera horizontally in your scene, create it in the Top viewport.

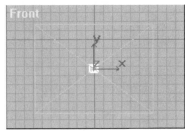

Figure 10.6 To point the free camera into your scene, create it in the Front viewport.

To create a target camera:

1. Open the Lights & Cameras Toolbar.

2. Click Target Camera.

   The target camera Parameters rollout appears in the Create command panel (**Figure 10.4**).

3. In the Top viewport, position the cursor where you want to place the camera.

4. Drag to create the camera and release to position the target (**Figure 10.5**).

5. Position the camera by moving it. To aim the camera, move its target.

   You can also rotate a target camera, but only in its Z (depth) axis.

✔ Tip

■ An easy way to select a target camera's target is by right-clicking the selected camera and choosing Select Target from the pop-up menu.

To create a free camera:

1. Open the Lights & Cameras Toolbar.

2. Click Free Camera.

   The free camera Parameters rollout appears in the command panel.

3. Click the location where you want to place the camera.

   The camera appears in the viewport, facing the active grid (**Figure 10.6**).

4. Move or rotate the camera to position and aim it.

✔ Tip

■ Check AutoGrid in the Creation rollout to align a free camera to the surface of an object as you create the camera. AutoGrid is not available for target cameras.

Activating a Camera view

To see through a camera, you need to change views.

To activate a Camera view:

1. Open a scene that includes a camera (**Figure 10.7**).

2. Activate the viewport you want to change to a Camera view.

3. Type C on your keyboard.

   The viewport changes to the view from the camera (**Figure 10.8**).

✔ Tips

- If the scene includes multiple cameras, clicking in a viewport and typing C opens the Select Camera dialog box (**Figure 10.9**). When you choose a camera, the viewport changes to the view from that camera.

- If a camera is selected already, typing C changes the view to that of the selected camera.

- You can also choose a Camera view by right-clicking a viewport label and selecting the Views menu (**Figure 10.10**).

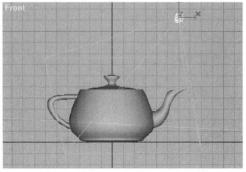

Figure 10.7 Use the orthogonal viewports to set up the camera before activating a Camera view.

Figure 10.8 The view from the camera in Figure 10.7.

Figure 10.9 The Select Camera dialog box lets you choose which camera to use.

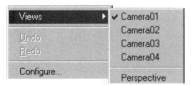

Figure 10.10 The Views sub-menu displays the scene cameras at the top.

CREATING CAMERAS

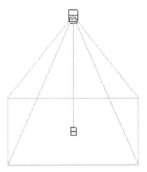

Figure 10.11 The camera cone is a pyramid whose tip is the camera.

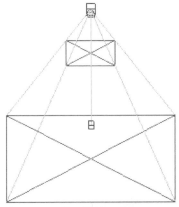

Figure 10.12 The clipping planes indicate which part of the scene the camera can see.

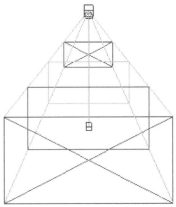

Figure 10.13 The environment range planes show where standard fog will render.

Adjusting Cameras

3D Studio MAX 3 lets you adjust cameras in several ways. The most commonly used settings are Lens Length and Field of View (FOV). These are the main camera parameters:

◆ **Focal length:** The Lens adjustment sets the camera's focal length, just like changing lenses on a real camera does. Focal length is determined by the size of the lens, which is measured in millimeters. You can enter a custom lens size from 9.857mm to 100,000mm or pick from a set of nine stock lenses ranging from 15mm to 200mm. Changing the size of the lens adjusts the FOV setting in an inverse proportion.

◆ **Field of view (FOV):** The FOV setting specifies how large an area the camera sees in degrees of arc from 0 degrees to 175 degrees. It's inversely proportional to the focal length. Field of view is indicated in the viewports by a blue pyramid that fans out from the lens (**Figure 10.11**). Oddly enough, this pyramid is called a *cone*. When you adjust the FOV, the cone and lens size adjust accordingly.

◆ **Clipping planes:** Clipping planes define the region of visibility within a cone. Each camera has two clipping planes that are parallel to the view plane of the camera (**Figure 10.12**). Objects that lie between the clipping planes are visible from the Camera view. Objects that sit in front of or beyond the two planes are invisible to the camera. If a clipping plane intersects an object, the object is cut away.

◆ **Environment ranges:** These settings should really be called standard fog ranges. Environment ranges are two planes that set the near and far limits of standard fog when it is rendered from a Camera view (**Figure 10.13**).

To set the focal length:

1.  Select a camera that views a few objects.

2. Type C to activate the view from that camera (**Figure 10.14**).

3. Open the Modify panel.
   The camera Parameters rollout appears (**Figure 10.15**).

4. Drag the Lens spinner.
   As the focal length increases, the field of view decreases. Objects in the Camera view appear closer, and the perspective flattens (**Figure 10.16**). Decreasing the focal length has the opposite effect (**Figure 10.17**).

✔ Tips

■ Select one of the stock lenses. The 15mm lens provides a wide-angle, fish-eye effect. At the other extreme, the 200mm lens zooms in tightly and flattens perspective.

■ Check Orthogonal Projection to make the Camera viewport flatten the scene as in a User view using orthogonal projection.

To adjust the field of view:

1. Select a camera.

2. Open the Modify panel.

3. Drag the FOV spinner.
   The field of view and lens change size.

✔ Tips

■ The FOV Direction flyout changes the way the program measures the field of view.

■ Check Show Cone to display the FOV cone even when the camera is not selected.

■ You can also adjust the field of view using the Field-of-View button in the Camera viewport controls.

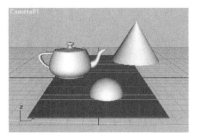

Figure 10.14 Setting the scene for experimenting with focal length.

Figure 10.15 The camera Parameters rollout yields access to the Lens setting.

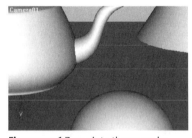

Figure 10.16 Zoom into the scene by increasing the lens size setting.

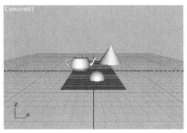

Figure 10.17 Zoom out by decreasing the lens size.

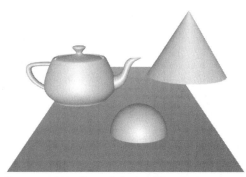

Figure 10.18 Use fog to fade the objects in the scene.

Figure 10.19 Turn on Show in the Environment Ranges group to display the environment range planes.

Figure 10.20 The Top viewport often shows environment range planes best. Here, the Far Range distance is at the rear of the scene.

Figure 10.21 Using environment ranges enhances your control over fog in your scenes.

Setting the environment range

Standard fog gradually fades objects as they move away from a camera. The Environment Range settings determine the near distance at which fog begins to fade objects and the far distance at which it finally obscures them.

To set the environment range:

1. Open or create a scene in which a camera views objects that are placed at different distances.

2. Apply a standard fog effect to the scene and render it (**Figure 10.18**). *(See Chapter 13, "Rendering and Effects," for instructions.)*

3. Select the camera in a non-Camera viewport.

4. Open the Modify panel.

   The camera Parameters rollout appears.

5. In the Environment Ranges group, check Show (**Figure 10.19**).

   The far range plane appears in the camera's field of view cone. The near range plane is set to zero by default, so it probably won't appear immediately.

6. Drag the Near Range spinner to set the beginning of the fog.

   The yellow rectangle of the near range plane moves along the camera's line of sight.

7. Drag the Far Range spinner to set the point of full obscuration (**Figure 10.20**).

   The brown rectangle of the far range plane moves along the camera's line of sight.

8. Change to the Camera view by typing C.

9. Render the scene to view the effect.

   The fog is rendered between the Near Range and the Far Range distances (**Figure 10.21**).

ADJUSTING CAMERAS

Adjusting clipping planes

Clipping planes delimit the visible region within a field of view. Objects that are clipped appear in cross-section.

To adjust clipping planes:

1. Open or create a scene in which a camera views some objects.

2. ![icon] Select a camera.

3. ![icon] Open the Modify panel.

4. In the Clipping Planes group, check Clip Manually (**Figure 10.22**).

   The clipping parameters become available in the rollout. The far clipping plane appears in the cone of the camera as a red rectangle with a red diagonal.

5. Type C to activate the selected camera view.

6. To clip the near side of an object to make it invisible in the Camera view, adjust the Near Clip parameter to intersect the object (**Figure 10.23**). Render the scene in the Camera view (**Figure 10.24**).

7. To clip the far side of the object, adjust the Far Clip parameter so the far clipping plane intersects the object. Render the scene in the Camera view (**Figure 10.25**).

✔ Tip

- You can convert a camera from a target camera to a free camera and vice versa. Just select a camera, open the Modify panel, and choose a camera from the Type drop-down list (**Figure 10.26**).

To change camera types:

1. ![icon] Select a camera.

2. ![icon] Open the Modify panel.

3. Select a new camera type in the Type drop-down list of the Parameters rollout.

Figure 10.22 Turn on Clip Manually to set a specific clipping range.

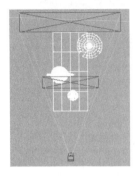

Figure 10.23 Near Clip has been set so that the camera doesn't see the closest object.

Figure 10.24 The sphere doesn't render because it's outside the clipping range, as is the front side of the teapot.

Figure 10.25 Everything past the front side of the teapot is outside the clipping range and thus does not appear.

Figure 10.26 Use the Type drop-down list to change the camera type.

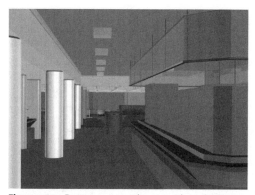

Figure 10.27 Proper camera placement lets viewers feel as if they're a part of the scene.

Figure 10.28 Use a low viewpoint to emphasize the insignificance of the viewer relative to the scene.

Placing Cameras

Camera placement determines the composition of your final rendered image. It tells the viewer what is important and psychologically places the viewer in the scene. By positioning a camera properly, you can transform a scene from mediocre to memorable.

If you want to make viewers feel as if they are participating in a scene, place the camera at eye level. For example, if you are designing an architectural walk-through, the eye-level camera creates the feeling that the viewer is actually taking a tour of the building (**Figure 10.27**).

To create a feeling of insignificance, place the camera close to the ground, so that it is level with an ant's point of view. This gives the viewer the impression that everything is huge and overwhelming by making objects loom steeply overhead (**Figure 10.28**).

PLACING CAMERAS

Maybe you're re-creating a car accident scene and you want to show what led up to the accident. You might position a camera so it gives viewers the idea that they are in a helicopter that is keeping pace with the vehicle. Placing a camera high above a scene creates an omnipotent point of view, like that of a narrator (or lawyer) telling a story (**Figure 10.29**). Adding a second camera at eye level places your witness on the scene (**Figure 10.30**).

Close up shots give the impression of intimacy, like watching a character in a soap opera. Long shots create an impersonal feeling, like gazing across the vast sweep of the Western frontier. If you are working from an existing image, matching the shot—short or long—may be the first step you take to create a digital matte painting.

Like other objects in MAX, cameras can be positioned with the move and rotate transforms. But sometimes it helps to know a trick or two. Align Camera aligns a camera to the surface normal of an object, and Align to View aligns a camera to the view plane of any orthogonal view or perspective-type view.

To align a camera to an object:

1. Select the camera you want to align.

2. Choose Align Camera from the Align flyout in the Main Toolbar.

3. Click the surface of an object with the Align Camera cursor (**Figure 10.31**).

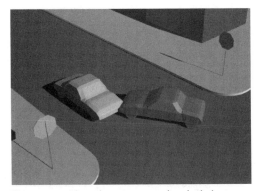

Figure 10.29 Place the camera overhead, aiming downward, for a storytelling viewpoint.

Figure 10.30 Using two vantage points often helps describe an incident better.

Figure 10.31 The mouse cursor contains a movie-camera icon when Align Camera is used.

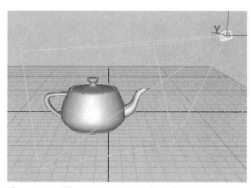

Figure 10.32 The camera points directly at the teapot after you use Align Camera.

Figure 10.33 The Align to View dialog box lets you specify which axis to align.

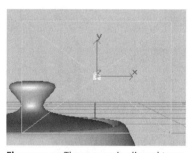

Figure 10.34 The camera is aligned to an orthogonal view.

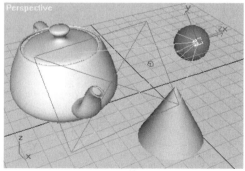

Figure 10.35 The camera is selected in preparation for matching it to the view.

The camera aligns to the surface normal where you clicked the object (**Figure 10.32**).

4. Look through the Camera view to see if you like the alignment. If you don't, realign the camera by repeating steps 2 and 3.

✔ Tip

- Use AutoGrid to align a free camera to the surface of an object upon creation. Remember that you can always swap the free camera for a target camera if you need to do so.

To align a camera to a view:

1. Activate a view.

2. 🔲 Select the camera you want to align.

3. 🔲 Choose the Align to View tool in the Align flyout on the Main Toolbar.

   The Align to View dialog box appears (**Figure 10.33**).

4. Choose an axis of alignment. Check Flip to invert the camera on this axis.

   The camera aligns to the plane of the current view (**Figure 10.34**).

Matching a camera to a view

Match Camera to View both aligns and moves a camera to match any perspective-type view. So if you arc rotate a viewport to a view that you like, you can set a camera there to hold that view.

To match a camera to a view:

1. Activate a viewport that displays a Perspective, Camera, or Light view that you want to match.

2. 🔲 Select a camera (**Figure 10.35**).

(continues on next page)

3. Choose Views > Match Camera to View.

The camera changes position to match the perspective of the active view. If the camera has a target, the target is moved as well (**Figure 10.36**).

Matching a camera to an image

Match a camera to a background image as a first step in creating a digital matte painting.

To match a camera to an image:

1. Place an image in the background of a Camera view. *(To place an image in a background, see Chapter 13, "Rendering and Effects.")*

2. [icon] Select the camera that displays the view.

3. [icon] Open the Modify panel.

4. In the camera Parameters rollout, check Horizon to display the horizon line of the world *XY* plane (**Figure 10.37**).

5. [icons] Position the camera so that its horizon line matches the horizon or vanishing point of the background image.

You can now place in the scene objects that match the perspective of the background image. By adding lights and materials to the scene, you can make objects blend into the background as if they always belonged there (**Figure 10.38**). *(For more information, see Chapter 11, "Lights," and Chapter 12, "Maps and Materials.")*

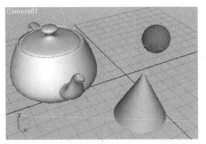

Figure 10.36 After you use Match Camera to View, the camera sees exactly what was in the Perspective viewport.

Figure 10.37 The horizon line lets you align the image horizon to the camera horizon.

Figure 10.38 Top: A box placed in the 3D scene matches the perspective of the one in the background image. Bottom: Lights and materials have been applied to the box to make it look like the building behind it.

PLACING CAMERAS

Figure 10.39 The Camera viewport controls enable interactive camera navigation.

Table 10.1

ICON	NAME	DESCRIPTION
Camera Viewport Controls		
	Dolly Camera	Moves the camera along its line of sight, or depth axis.
	Dolly Camera + Target	Moves the camera and its target along the camera's depth axis.
	Dolly Target	Moves the target toward or away from the camera along the camera's depth axis.
	Perspective	Dollies the camera and changes its FOV (field-of-view) angle at the same time.
	Roll Camera	Rotates the camera around its depth axis.
	Zoom Extents All	Centers selected objects in all viewports except the Camera viewport.
	Zoom Extents All Selected	Centers objects in all viewports except the Camera viewport.
	Field-of-View	Changes the angle of the camera lens.
	Truck Camera	Moves the camera and its target (if any) parallel to the view plane.
	Orbit Camera	Rotates the camera around its target. Free cameras rotate around a point in front of them located at their target distance.
	Pan Camera	Rotates the camera. Targets rotate around their cameras.
	Min/Max Toggle	Toggles between the viewport layout and a full screen display of the active view.

Using Camera Viewport Controls

When you activate a Camera view, the viewport controls change to a new set of navigation buttons called Camera viewport controls (**Figure 10.39**). You use the Camera viewport controls to navigate the camera that displays the current view. It is not necessary to select the camera to navigate it. *(See Chapter 2, "Navigation and Display," for information about viewport controls.)*

Camera viewport commands are based on traditional terms for maneuvering motion picture cameras. For a complete description of Camera viewport controls, see **Table 10.1**.

Dollying a camera

The Dolly command lets you move the camera along its line of sight. You can dolly a camera or a target, or both if you are using a target camera. Roll rotates a camera along its line of sight, causing the scene to spin in the view.

To dolly a camera:

1. Select a camera that views some objects in a scene.

(continues on next page)

2. Type C to change the active viewport to a Camera view (**Figure 10.40**).

3. Click the Dolly Camera button.

4. Drag the dolly cursor up or down in the Camera viewport.

The camera moves along its Z (depth) axis, so that it moves closer toward, or farther away from, the objects it views. The objects grow or shrink in the view (**Figure 10.41**).

✔ Tip

■ Dolly Camera has two additional flyout commands:

◆ **Dolly Target** moves the target of the camera along its depth axis.

◆ **Dolly Camera + Target** moves the camera and target along the Z axis together.

To roll a camera:

1. Select a camera.

2. Type C to change the active viewport to a Camera view.

3. Click Roll Camera.

4. Drag the roll cursor left or right in the Camera viewport.

The camera rotates around its depth axis. The scene rolls in the view (**Figure 10.42**).

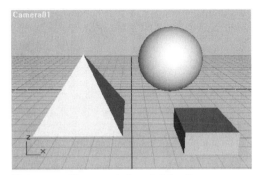

Figure 10.40 The scene before dollying the camera.

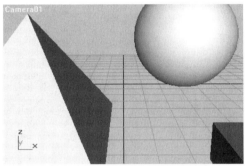

Figure 10.41 After dollying in, the camera is closer, while the center point remains the same.

Figure 10.42 Use Roll to bank, or tilt, the camera.

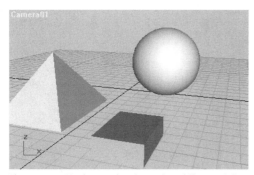

Figure 10.43 To change the viewpoint while remaining aimed at the scene center, use Orbit.

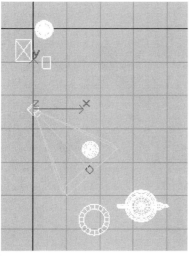

Figure 10.44 The Top view shows the camera after panning to a different set of objects.

Figure 10.45 Pan lets you look at different parts of the scene while remaining in one spot.

Orbiting a camera

Orbit Camera rotates a camera freely around its target. Its companion command, Pan Camera, rotates the target around the camera.

To orbit a camera:

1. ⬚ Select a camera.

2. Type C to change the active viewport to a Camera view.

3. ⬚ Click the Orbit Camera button.

4. Drag the cursor around the Camera viewport.

   The camera rotates around its target. The view revolves around the scene (**Figure 10.43**).

To pan a camera:

1. ⬚ Select a camera.

2. Type C to change the active viewport to a Camera view.

3. ⬚ Click the Pan Camera button, available on the Orbit Camera flyout.

4. Drag the cursor across the Camera viewport.

   In the Top viewport, the camera turns on its axis (**Figure 10.44**). The scene rotates around the camera (**Figure 10.45**).

✔ Tip

■ Dragging the Pan cursor up or down in the Camera view tilts the camera, as if you were looking up and down a tall building.

Changing a perspective

The Perspective command dollies a camera and changes its field of view at the same time. This action preserves the essential composition of the scene, while changing its perspective.

To change perspective:

1. Select a target camera.

2. Type C to change the active viewport to a Camera view (**Figure 10.46**).

3. Click the Perspective button.

4. Drag the cursor up or down in the Camera viewport.

   The view changes perspective and zooms a bit (**Figure 10.47**).

   If you look in the camera Parameters roll-out, you will see the FOV and Lens values change as you drag the perspective cursor (**Figure 10.48**).

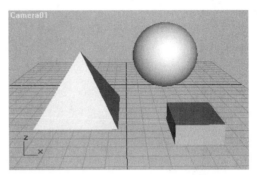

Figure 10.46 The scene with normal perspective. Boring!

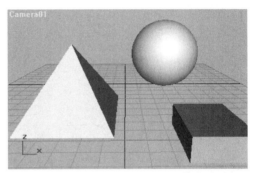

Figure 10.47 Exaggerated perspective adds a dramatic look to the scene.

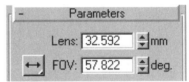

Figure 10.48 As you change the perspective, keep an eye on the Lens and FOV settings.

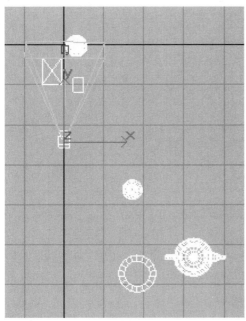

Figure 10.49 Use camera animation to depict looking around the scene. At the beginning, the camera is looking at the box, pyramid, and sphere.

Animating Cameras

You animate cameras by transforming them or changing their parameter settings over time. Camera viewport controls give you a wide range of methods for rotating and moving cameras. You can also animate a camera by assigning it an animation controller such as a Look At, Path, or Expression Controller.

Long, slow camera movements result in a smooth animation. Fast camera movements result in a jumpy animation. To keep your animation as smooth as possible, here are two tips: use plenty of frames, and don't make the camera travel too far in a short period of time.

Whether you use transforms, camera settings, viewport controls, or animation controllers, it all boils down to one of two methods: keyframing or assigning animation controllers.

Keyframing

You keyframe a camera just like you keyframe any other object, except that you can keyframe both a camera and its target. This method takes some fine-tuning to make the motion smooth. *(To review keyframing, see Chapter 6, "Animation.")*

Using a Path controller

The most popular method of animating a camera is assigning the camera to a path. This is usually done with a free camera. A target camera and its target can also be assigned to a path, or to separate paths. A target camera can even be assigned to a different target. *(To review animation controllers, see Chapter 6, "Animation.")*

To keyframe a camera movement:

1. Select a camera (**Figure 10.49**).

2. Type C to change the active viewport to a Camera view.

(continues on next page)

3. ![icon] Click the Animate button.

4. Move the time slider to the right.

5. Move the camera to a new position using move, rotate, or the Camera viewport controls (**Figure 10.50**).

The view of the scene changes. A key appears in the track bar at the current frame (**Figure 10.51**).

6. Repeat steps 3 and 4 to set more keys.

7. ![icon] Turn off the Animate button.

8. ![icon] Play the animation.

✔ Tips

■ The default motion controller for a target camera or target light is the Look At controller. Look At controllers limit rotation to rolling around the Z axis, so that a camera or light will always face its target.

■ If the animation appears to jerk suddenly, try adding more frames between keyframes or adjusting keys in the camera's trajectory. *(See Chapter 6, "Animation," for instructions on adding frames and adjusting keys.)*

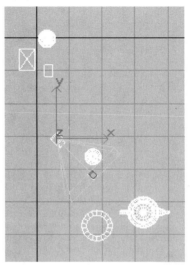

Figure 10.50 The end of the animation shows objects that were out of view before.

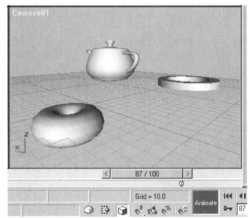

Figure 10.51 A shaded view of the final animation frame shows the torus, tube, and teapot.

Figure 10.52 The Path Parameters rollout lets you assign a spline as the camera path.

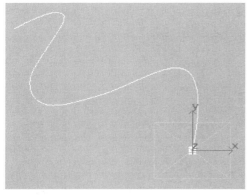

Figure 10.53 The camera starts at the first point in the spline.

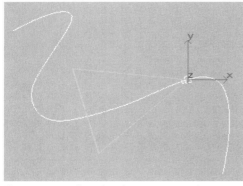

Figure 10.54 As the animation progresses, the camera moves along the spline.

Assigning a camera to a path

Path controllers make an object follow a path.

To assign a camera to a path:

1. Choose a shape from the Shapes Toolbar.

   Choose any open or closed shape. If you choose Line, set the drag type to Smooth.

2. In the Top viewport, draw a spline to represent the camera's motion path.

3. Select or create a free camera.

4. Open the Motion command panel.

5. Assign the position controller to a Path controller.

6. Open the Assign Position Controller rollout.

7. Select the position controller.

8. Click Assign controller.

9. Select Path from the Assign Position Controller list and then click OK.

   The Path Parameters rollout appears (**Figure 10.52**).

10. Click Pick Path and select the spline you drew in step 2.

    The camera jumps to the first vertex of the spline (**Figure 10.53**).

11. Rotate the camera if you want its lens to look down the length of the path.

12. Check Follow if you want the camera to turn with the path.

13. Adjust the position of the camera by dragging the % Along Path spinners.

14. Activate the Camera viewport and play the animation (**Figure 10.54**).

(continues on next page)

✔ Tips

- For a walk-through animation, use a free camera and an open spline. Check Follow and Z-axis in the Path Parameters rollout.

- For fighter planes and roller coaster rides, check Bank to make the camera roll while traversing a 3D path (**Figure 10.55**).

- Move a spline path up or down to change the height of the camera.

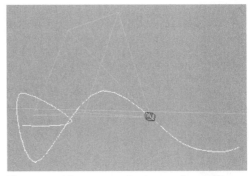

Figure 10.55 The camera rolls along a 3D path.

LIGHTS

In nature, light flows like a luminous tide, revealing and concealing form. Reflection, refraction, radiation, and diffusion effects appear spontaneously. In the digital world, every effect of illumination has to be calculated. Rendering algorithms, normal alignments, G-buffers, and Z-buffers determine the display of light and shadow. Where calculation fails, the eye of the artist must compensate.

The best lighting effects are achieved by artists who make themselves students of nature. Artists who practice painting, photography, and cinematography develop sensitivity, awareness, and a practiced eye.

Working with light and shadow has very practical applications. For instance, suppose you create a model of an office building for a prospective client. The client will want to see what it will look like under different lighting conditions. How will the building cast shadows? How will shadows be cast upon it? At what angle will light enter the windows at different times of the day and year?

This chapter outlines the light sources available in 3D Studio MAX and how to control them.

Creating Lights

You can create five types of lights in 3D Studio MAX 3. As with cameras, the parameters for the different types of lights are nearly identical. By default, all lights are turned on when you create them. Shadows are turned off by default, except for sunlight system shadows.

◆ **Omni lights:** The omni light is the most generic type of light. Its rays shine in all directions from a single point in space, like a lamp that does not have a shade (**Figure 11.1**).

◆ **Default lights:** By default, 3D Studio MAX includes a single, dynamically positioned omnilight at the viewer position in each shaded viewport. Or you can use two omni lights in any viewport. The brighter light, or key light, is positioned above and to the front of the origin. The dimmer light, or fill light, is positioned lower and to the right of the origin. These lights are invisible and unselectable until you add them to the scene.

◆ **Spotlights:** Spotlights illuminate an area within a cone of projection, similar to a stage light. Spotlights, like cameras, come in two varieties. Target spotlights point at a target that you set. Free spotlights have no target, so they can easily be maneuvered (**Figure 11.2**).

◆ **Directional lights:** Directional lights have a cone or projection and light controls similar to spotlights. The difference is that directional lights illuminate an entire scene unidirectionally, as if the source is millions of miles away and the rays are traveling parallel to each other. Like spotlights, directional lights can either be targeted or free (**Figure 11.3**).

Figure 11.1 The omni light looks like this in the viewports.

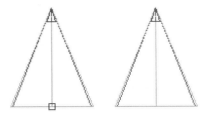

Figure 11.2 The target spotlight (left) and free spotlight (right) both have cones.

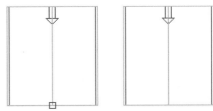

Figure 11.3 The target directional light (left) and free directional light (right) both illuminate the scene with parallel rays, like the sun.

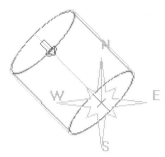

Figure 11.4
The Sunlight System lets you simulate daylight that changes over time.

Figure 11.5 Placing an omni light in the Front viewport.

Figure 11.6 Rendering the scene gives a more accurate picture of the effectiveness of your lighting scheme.

Figure 11.7 You need to use two default lights before you can add default lights to the scene.

◆   **Sunlight System:** This is a hybrid light source that combines a free directional light with a Compass object. The compass helps you orient the light to a specific direction in the scene. The orbital distance, time, and location settings give the sun altitude and place it in the sky at a particular time and geographic location (**Figure 11.4**).

Creating omni lights

Omni lights shine equally in all directions. The default lights in MAX are omni lights. If you want, you can add omni lights to the scene.

To create an omni light:

1. Open a scene file.

2. Click Omni Light on the Lights & Cameras Toolbar.

3. Place the light by clicking in a viewport. The omni light appears where you click (**Figure 11.5**). If it is the first light you add to the scene, it replaces the default lighting.

4. Move the light to better position it.

5. To check the effect of the light more accurately, render the scene (**Figure 11.6**).

To add default lights to a scene:

1. Open the Viewport Configuration dialog box. (You can do this quickly by right-clicking any viewport control button and choosing Configure.)

2. In the Rendering Method panel, check Default Lighting and choose 2 Lights in the Rendering Options group (**Figure 11.7**).

3. Click OK to close the dialog box.

(continues on next page)

4. Choose Views > Add Default Lights to Scene.

The Add Default Lights to Scene dialog box appears (**Figure 11.8**).

5. Check the default lights you want to add. Changing Distance Scaling dollies the lights toward or away from the origin.

6. Click OK.

The default omni lights are added to the scene. They are named DefaultKeyLight and DefaultFillLight.

Creating target lights

Creating a target spotlight or target directional light is a lot like creating a target camera. The first click places the light source, and dragging, then releasing, positions the target.

To create a target spotlight or target directional light:

1. Open a scene file.

2. 🔍 Zoom out of the Front viewport.

3. 📷 Click Target Spot on the Lights & Cameras Toolbar.

or

📷 Click Target Directional Light on the Lights & Cameras Toolbar.

4. Click and hold in the Front viewport to place the light.

5. Drag the cursor toward the objects you want to illuminate.

6. Release the mouse to set the target.

The target and light appear. Default lights are overridden (**Figure 11.9**).

7. Move the light into the desired position.

8. Render the scene (**Figure 11.10**).

The spotlight illuminates the area encompassed by the cone. It is brightest at the center and fades to black at the edge.

Figure 11.8 Several options are available when adding default lights to the scene.

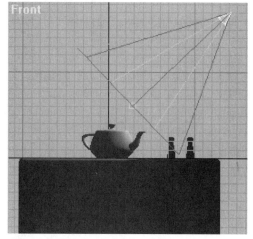

Figure 11.9 Adding a target spotlight in the Front viewport.

Figure 11.10 The spotlight cone indicates the area illuminated by the light.

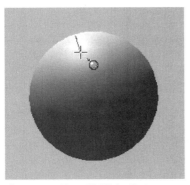

Figure 11.11 Place Highlight gives you precise control over highlight positioning.

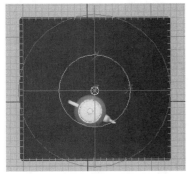

Figure 11.12 Add a free light in the Top viewport to have it point straight down.

Figure 11.13 Illuminating a scene from the top yields stark lighting.

✔ Tip

■ 　To place a light so that it highlights an object from a particular view, select the light and then choose Place Highlight from the Align flyout. Then click the part of the object you want to highlight. The light will move into position to create the highlight (**Figure 11.11**).

Creating free lights

Adding a free spotlight or free directional light to your scene is just like adding a free camera. Free lights are great when you need a lot of light pointing in the same direction, like a row of street lights or lights in an office building.

To create a free spotlight or free directional light:

1. Open a scene file.

2. 　Click Free Spot on the Lights & Cameras Toolbar.

   or

   　Click Free Directional on the Lights & Cameras Toolbar.

3. Click in the Top viewport to place the light (**Figure 11.12**).

   The light is added, and the default lights are overridden.

4. Move the light into the desired position.

5. Render the scene (**Figure 11.13**).

   Since the light is pointing straight down into the scene, it illuminates a perfectly circular area.

To change light types:

1.  Select a light.

2. Open the Modify panel.

3. In the General Parameters rollout, select the Type drop-down list.

   A list of the different light types appears (**Figure 11.14**).

4. Select a light type from the list.

   The new light type replaces the selected light, using the same settings. The name of the light remains unchanged. If the name of the light is Omni01 and you have just changed it to a target spotlight, this is probably a good time to rename it. For better reference, choose a name that indicates both the position and type of light.

Figure 11.14 A new feature in 3D Studio MAX release 3 lets you change the light type on the fly.

Simulating sunlight

A Sunlight System is a combination of a free directional light and a compass. It casts sharp raytraced shadows by default. Use sunlight when you want to know exactly where shadows will fall.

To create a Sunlight System:

1. Open a scene file.

2. Click Sunlight System on the Lights & Cameras Toolbar.

   The Sunlight System rollout appears (**Figure 11.15**).

3. Drag downward in the Perspective viewport to place the compass.

   The compass lets you set the North direction for your world. The size of the compass is for display purposes only.

Figure 11.15 The Sunlight System gives you a range of controls for creating realistic outdoor lighting.

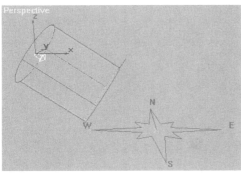

Figure 11.16 Setting up the Sunlight System in the Perspective viewport.

Figure 11.17 Shadows lengthen in the late afternoon (see the settings in Figure 11.15).

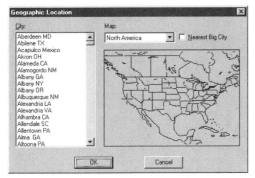

Figure 11.18 The Geographic Location dialog box lets you specify where in the world the scene is.

4. Move the cursor upward and click to set the orbital distance.

This sets the distance of the light from the compass ground (**Figure 11.16**).

5. In the Sunlight Systems rollout, set the time, date, and time zone for the light.

This positions the sun in the sky.

6. Render the scene (**Figure 11.17**).

✔ Tips

■ To position the sun geographically, click Get Location (**Figure 11.18**).

■ After a Sunlight System has been created, you can change its location and orbital setting in the Motion panel.

■ If shadows do not at first appear when you render the scene, open the Modify panel and increase the Falloff setting.

Illuminating Scenes

Lights can illuminate any renderable object that is visible in a scene using the following settings:

◆ **On/Off:** The On checkbox turns a light on or off. Lights are set to On by default.

◆ **Include/Exclude:** This setting determines which objects are illuminated and/or cast shadows.

◆ **Intensity:** Intensity is controlled by a light's multiplier. Reducing the multiplier dims a light. Increasing the multiplier brightens a light.

◆ **Color:** Color is determined by three factors: hue (chroma), saturation (purity), and value (brightness). Choosing a higher value for the color of a light increases its apparent intensity.

◆ **Hot Spot** and **Falloff:** A light cone is actually made up of two concentric cones. The inner cone defines the brightest region of light, called the hotspot. The outer cone defines the edge of illumination, or falloff. Between these two cones, light diminishes gradually or sharply, depending upon the distance between them.

◆ **Attenuation:** Attenuation causes light to fade in and fade out at either end of its range. Attenuation has two main parameters: Near, which sets the beginning of illumination nearest the light source, and Far, which sets the end of illumination farthest from the light source.

◆ **Decay:** Decay causes a light to diminish in intensity over its entire attenuation range. Decay overrides the Far Attenuation Start setting.

◆ **Projector Map:** Projector Maps project images into a scene with a light like a

Setting the Stage

Light radiates, reflects, refracts, reacts, and softly diffuses into air. Light is warm or cool, high or low, near or far, bright or dim, harsh or soft. These qualities make a scene happy or sad, quiet or intense, romantic or dull, mundane or mysterious.

The color and angle of a light place the scene in time and space. For morning or evening scenes, make the sun a warm color such as yellow, orange, or red, and place the light source at a low angle. Cooler white lights placed at a high angle suggest the sun shining at midday. Fill lights above the ground should be blue or gray to match the sky. Fill lights below the ground should be green or brown to match the earth. For night scenes, use a cool blue-white tint to suggest the light of the moon and stars. If there is fog, streetlights create warm, hazy cones of illumination. If there is a large or brightly colored object in the scene, match a nearby light to that color to create the effect of light radiating off of its surface.

Indoor lights also have color. Use warm, yellow colors for incandescent and halogen lights. Use a cold yellow-green color for fluorescent lighting. Be sure to create some fill lights to match the overall colors of the walls and carpets.

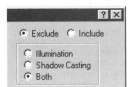

Figure 11.19 Use the On checkbox on the General Parameters rollout to switch the light on and off.

Figure 11.20 Choose Exclude and Both to completely block lights effects on objects.

slide projector or movie projector. They can also project black-and-white silhouettes, like gobos in theatrical lighting. Think of Batman's bat signal, and you get the idea.

◆ **Ambient:** Ambient light sets the minimum level of illumination in a scene. It has no direction and does not create highlights or shadows. Use this setting sparingly, or it will wash out your scene.

For advanced reflection and radiosity effects, consider purchasing a specialty plug-in such as Lightscape or MentalRay.

Turning lights on and off

Turning on a light illuminates all objects within the light's cone and attenuation ranges. Turning off a light removes its illumination from the objects.

To turn a light off and on:

1. Select a light.

2. Open the Modify panel.

3. Uncheck the On checkbox in the General Parameters rollout (**Figure 11.19**).

4. To turn the light back on, recheck the On check box.

To exclude objects from illumination and shadow casting:

1. Select a light that shines on some objects.

2. Open the Modify panel.

3. Click Exclude in the General Parameters rollout.
   The Exclude/Include dialog box appears.

4. Make sure Exclude and Both are selected in the upper-right corner (**Figure 11.20**).

(continues on next page)

ILLUMINATING SCENES

5. Select the names of the objects or group of objects you do not want to be illuminated or to cast shadows.

6. Click the >> button.

The names of the objects are moved to the Exclude list on the right (**Figure 11.21**).

7. Click OK.

8. Render the scene.

The objects you have chosen to exclude neither receive illumination nor cast shadows upon rendering (**Figure 11.22**).

Setting intensity and color

The Multiplier parameter sets the intensity of a light. Higher values create brighter lights. Lower values create dimmer lights.

Color settings assign hue, value, and saturation to a light. The value of a color also affects its intensity. Brighter colors create brighter lights. Darker colors create dimmer lights.

To set intensity:

1. Select a light that shines on some objects.

2. Open the Modify panel.

3. In the General Parameters rollout, increase or decrease the Multiplier value (**Figure 11.23**).

The objects in the scene brighten or dim.

4. Render the scene to see the effect at a higher resolution. If you set the Multiplier value too high, the light will completely wash out the scene (**Figure 11.24**).

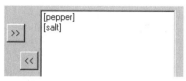

Figure 11.21 Use the list to specify objects to exclude from a light's effects.

Figure 11.22 The salt shakers, having been excluded from the spotlight's effects, are not illuminated, nor do they cast shadows.

Figure 11.23 Increase the Multiplier setting to make the light brighter.

Figure 11.24 With excessive Multiplier values, the rendered scene appears overexposed.

ILLUMINATING SCENES

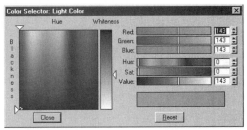

Figure 11.25 The color swatch displays the light's color and lets you change it.

Figure 11.26 3D Studio MAX provides its standard Color Selector dialog box for changing a light's color.

Figure 11.27 By default, the spotlight has a narrow penumbra.

Figure 11.28 To widen the penumbra, make the Hot Spot setting significantly smaller than the Falloff setting.

To set color:

1.   Select a light that shines on some objects. White objects make the best test.

2.   Click the color swatch just to the left of the Exclude button (**Figure 11.25**).
     The Color Selector: Light Color dialog box appears (**Figure 11.26**).

3.   Select a color and render the scene. The color of the light tints the objects.

✔ Tips

■ Negative Multiplier values subtract light from a scene. Use this feature to create your deepest shadows.

■ Animating the multiplier and color settings varies the intensity and color of the light over time.

Setting the hotspot and falloff

A hotspot is the brightest part of a light. It is the inner core of illumination. Falloff is the region at the edge of a pool of light across which illumination gradually diminishes in intensity.

To set the hotspot and falloff:

1.   Select a spotlight or directional light that illuminates a surface.

2.   Render the scene to test the light. The edge of the pool of light is quite sharp (**Figure 11.27**).

3.   Open the Modify menu.

4.   Open the Spotlight or Directional Parameters rollout (**Figure 11.28**).

(continues on next page)

ILLUMINATING SCENES

5. Drag the Hot Spot spinner up or down to enlarge or reduce the hotspot.

   The blue cone of the hotspot within the light cone increases or decreases in size. When the hotspot becomes large enough, the outer cone and the Falloff setting become larger as well. As the hotspot decreases, the region of greatest intensity is likewise reduced (**Figure 11.29**).

6. Drag the Falloff spinner up or down to enlarge or reduce the falloff.

   The outer gray cone that indicates the falloff region increases or decreases in size. When the falloff becomes small enough, the inner cone and hotspot area become smaller as well. As the falloff increases, the total area of illumination and the area of falloff increase accordingly.

7. Render the scene again.

   The edge of the pool of light diminishes across the distance between the hotspot cone and the falloff cone (**Figure 11.30**).

Setting attenuation and decay

Attenuation fades in a light near its source and fades out a light at the far end of its range. Decay diminishes a beam of light along its entire length as it moves away from the source.

To set attenuation:

1. Select a light that illuminates objects that are set at different distances from it.

2. Render the scene (**Figure 11.31**).

3. Open the Modify panel.

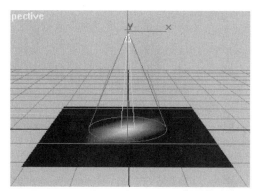

Figure 11.29 You can see the increased falloff region in the viewport.

Figure 11.30 The increased falloff region is most apparent when you render the scene.

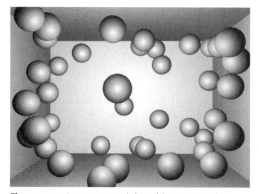

Figure 11.31 A scene containing objects at varying distances from the light source, lighted without attenuation.

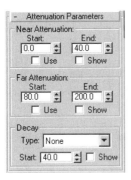

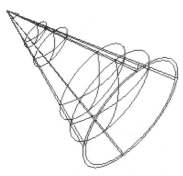

Figure 11.32 The Attenuation Parameters rollout lets you define the way light fades in and out depending on the distances of illuminated objects from the light source.

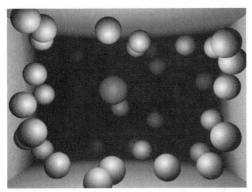

Figure 11.33 3D Studio MAX depicts the attenuation ranges graphically with circles around the light cone.

4. Open the Attenuation Parameters rollout (**Figure 11.32**).

5. In the Near Attenuation and Far Attenuation groups, check Use and Show. The near and far attenuation ranges appear.

6. Set the near and far attenuation using the ranges for reference (**Figure 11.33**).

7. Render the scene to see the result (**Figure 11.34**).

To set decay:

1. Follow steps 1 through 3 under "To set attenuation."

2. Check Show in the Decay group to see the starting point of the decay.

3. Set the Start value.

4. Choose Inverse or Inverse Square decay from the Type drop-down menu. (Inverse light diminishes geometrically with distance. Inverse Square light diminishes faster—with the square of the distance.)

5. Render the scene to see the result.

✔ Tip

■ Because light can continue shining forever, it is a good idea to use far attenuation so that the program won't waste time making unnecessary calculations.

Figure 11.34 When you use attenuation, the illumination level falls off with distance for more realistic lighting.

Projecting maps and setting ambient lighting

Projecting maps into a scene creates the illusion that there is more going on than meets the eye. Ambient light changes the overall color of a scene. Increasing the value of the ambient color reduces contrast throughout the scene.

To project a map:

1. 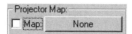 Select a light.

2. Open the Modify panel.

3. Open the second Parameters rollout.

4. Click the Projector Map button (**Figure 11.35**).
   The Material/Map Browser window appears (**Figure 11.36**).

5. Double-click Bitmap.

6. Select a bitmap using the Select Bitmap Image File dialog box. Then click Open.

7. Render the scene (**Figure 11.37**).

✔ Tip

- Try some of the other maps in the Material/Map Browser such as Cellular, Perlin Marble, and Smoke.

To set ambient light:

1. Choose Rendering > Environment.
   The Environment dialog box appears.

2. In the Global Lighting group, click the Ambient light color swatch (**Figure 11.38**).

3. Choose a color in the Color Selector: Ambient Light dialog box.

4. Render the scene to see the results.

Figure 11.35 The name of the light's second Parameters rollout depends on the light type, but the Projector Map rollout is common to all of them.

Figure 11.36 The Projector Map function lets you assign a map the light projects like a photographic slide.

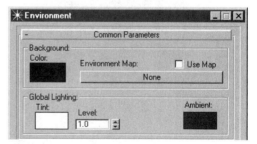

Figure 11.37 You can use Projector Map to simulate complex shadows without incurring additional rendering time.

Figure 11.38 The Environment dialog box's Common Parameters rollout lets you set environmental lighting colors.

ILLUMINATING SCENES

Figure 11.39 The Environment dialog box's Atmospheres & Effects rollout lets you set volume lights.

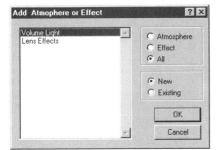

Figure 11.40 After you click Add, the Add Atmosphere or Effect dialog box appears.

Figure 11.41 Volumetric lights simulate the effect of dust in the atmosphere, making spotlights more realistic.

Figure 11.42 When a volumetric light projects an image map, you can see the map throughout the light's volume.

Using Volumetric Lighting

Volumetric lighting is an effect based on the real-world interaction between a light and particulate matter like fog, haze, dust, and smoke. It gives you the hazy glow of street-lights on a misty evening, the sweep of a lighthouse beacon on a foggy morning, or the rays of sunlight streaming through a window.

Volumetric lighting works with all types of light sources, although it is most commonly used with spotlights.

To create a volume light:

1. Select a light.

2. Open the Modify menu.

3. Open the Atmospheres & Effects rollout (**Figure 11.39**). (Note that this does not appear in the Create panel.)

4. Click the Add button.

5. Choose Volume Light from the Add Atmosphere or Effect dialog box (**Figure 11.40**). Then click OK.

6. Render the scene.

    The volumetric light effect appears in the scene (**Figure 11.41**). *(To learn more about setting up volumetric lights, see Chapter 13, "Rendering and Effects.")*

✔ Tips

■ Volume Lights render only from perspec-tive-type viewports, such as the Perspective and Camera viewports.

■ Decreasing the size of the hotspot can make a volume light easier to control.

■ Combining Projector Maps with volume lights creates extraordinary effects (**Figure 11.42**).

Casting Shadows

Any type of light in MAX is capable of projecting shadows from renderable objects. For most displays, you must render a scene with the scanline renderer to see the shadows that are cast and received by objects.

3D Studio MAX 3 lets you set two types of shadows: shadow map and ray traced. A shadow map is a bitmap that is projected from a light. It is created by the scanline renderer during a prerendering pass of the scene. Shadow maps give shadows a soft edge, as if they are being diffused by the atmosphere. Shadow map shadows require less computation to render than do ray-traced shadows.

Ray-traced shadows are more precise and sharp edged than shadow map shadows. They are calculated by tracing a ray from the light source to the object, which uses a lot of calculation. Consequently, they take much longer to render than shadow map shadows. Use ray-traced shadows whenever you need to precisely locate shadows, such as in shadow studies for architectural sitings. To make a transparent or semitransparent object cast shadows, you must use ray-traced shadows.

An interesting innovation in MAX 3 is the ability of lights to cast colored and bitmapped shadows. In addition, you can set the color of a light to mix with the shadow color, giving it a more natural appearance. Volumetric lights and rendering effects may also cast shadows and mix their colors with shadow colors. *(For more information on creating effects, see Chapter 13, "Rendering and Effects.")*

Shadow Parameters

Shadow parameters control the way shadows are calculated in a scene. The default settings are usually sufficient, but here's a list in case you need to tweak them:

- **Bias** controls how close to an object a cast shadow begins. Lower values cause the shadow to move closer to the object. If a shadow makes an object look like it's floating, the Bias setting is too high.

- **Size** controls the sharpness of the edge of a shadow. It measures the number of pixels squared used in the bitmap that generates the shadow. If shadows appear fuzzy along the edge, then the size is too low. Higher values produce cleaner edges.

- **Sample Range** controls the sharpness of shadows by averaging different-size areas of the shadow map. If a shadow smudges, streaks, or creates moiré patterns, the Sample Range setting is probably too high. A Sample Range setting that is too low creates jagged shadows. Recommended values are between 2 and 5. You can also offset a high value by increasing the size of a shadow map or the amount of its bias.

- **Absolute Map Bias** determines how the map bias is computed in relation to the rest of the scene. If you render an animation and notice that the shadows flicker when you replay it, try checking this option to end the flicker.

- **Max Quadtree Depth** controls the accuracy of ray-traced shadows. Lower values use less RAM and take longer to render. Higher values use more RAM but render faster. If a ray-traced shadow does not look accurate enough, increase this setting by just one or two levels.

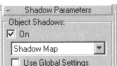

Figure 11.43 Lights don't cast shadows by default, but you can turn on shadow casting on these rollouts.

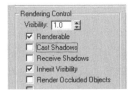

Figure 11.44 A scene rendered with shadows.

Figure 11.46 The salt shakers still cast shadows, but the teapot doesn't.

Turning shadows on and off

Most lights have shadows turned off by default. When they are turned on, renderable objects within the light's range cast shadows as well as receive them. We've already seen how to turn off shadows for individual objects by excluding them from a light. If you want, you can turn off shadow casting as well as shadow receiving using the Object Properties dialog box.

To turn on shadow casting:

1. Select a light that shines on some objects. Make sure there is a surface within the light's range for shadows to fall on.

2. Open the Modify panel.

3. In the General Parameters rollout, check Cast Shadows.

    or

    In the Shadow Parameters rollout, check On in the Object Shadows group (**Figure 11.43**).

4. Render the scene (**Figure 11.44**).

To turn off shadows for an object:

1. Select an illuminated object.

2. Right-click the object.

3. In the pop-up menu, choose Properties.

4. In the Object Properties dialog box, uncheck Cast Shadows and/or Receive Shadows (**Figure 11.45**).

5. Click OK.

6. Render the scene.

    The object no longer casts and/or receives shadows (**Figure 11.46**).

Figure 11.45 The Object Properties dialog box lets you turn off shadow casting on a per-object basis.

Setting the shadow type and shadow color

Shadow maps create soft-edged shadows. They are the default for all types of lights except Sunlight Systems. Ray-traced shadows render more slowly, but they make excellent shadow studies because their edges are so crisp.

You can set shadow color independently of illumination for both types of shadows.

To create ray-traced shadows:

1.  Select a light.

2. Open the Modify menu.

3. Open the Shadow Parameters menu.

4. Turn on Object Shadows.

5. In the Object Shadows drop-down menu, choose Ray Traced Shadows (**Figure 11.47**).

6. Render the scene (**Figure 11.48**).

To set shadow color:

1. Select a light that casts shadows.

2. Open the Modify menu.

3. Open the Shadow Parameters menu.

4. Click the Color swatch (**Figure 11.49**)

5. Choose a color in the Color Selector: Shadow Color dialog box.

6. Render the scene.

7. Repeat steps 5 and 6 until you are satisfied.

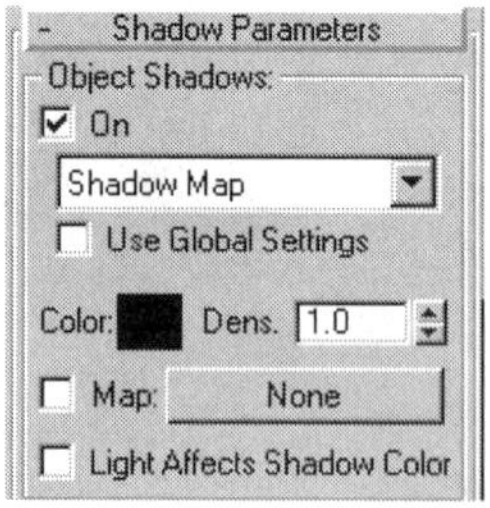

✔ Tips

■ To mix the color of the light with the shadow color, check Light Affects Shadow Color in the Shadow Parameters rollout.

■ To project a map into a shadow, check Map and click the None button.

Figure 11.47 Use the drop-down list to change the shadow type.

Figure 11.48 Ray-traced shadows have hard edges.

Figure 11.49 You can achieve special effects by changing the shadow color.

CASTING SHADOWS

Light Viewport Controls

When you activate a Light view, the viewport controls change to a new set of navigation buttons called Light viewport controls (**Table 11.1**). These controls are very similar to Camera viewport controls. As with camera controls, it is not necessary to select a light in order to navigate it. *(See Chapter 2, "Navigation and Display," for information about viewport controls.)*

Table 11.1

Light Viewport Controls

ICON	NAME	DESCRIPTION
	Dolly Light	Moves the light along its line of sight, or depth axis.
	Dolly Spotlight + Target	Moves the light and its target along its depth axis.
	Dolly Target	Moves the target toward or away from the light along the light's depth axis.
	Light Hotspot	Changes the size of the hotspot by changing the angle of the hotspot cone.
	Roll Light	Rotates the light around its depth axis.
	Zoom Extents All Selected	Centers selected objects in all viewports except the Light viewport.
	Zoom Extents All	Centers objects in all viewports except the Light viewport.
	Light Falloff	Changes the amount of falloff by changing the angle of the falloff cone.
	Truck Light	Moves the light and its target (if any) parallel to the view plane.
	Orbit Light	Rotates the light around its target. Free lights rotate around a point in front of them located at their target distance.
	Pan Light	Rotates the light. Targets rotate around their lights.
	Min/Max Toggle	Toggles between the viewport layout and a full-screen display of the active view.

Changing views

You can look at a scene from the point of view of a spotlight or a directional light.

To change a view to a Light view:

1. Open a scene that has a spotlight or directional light in it.

2. Activate the viewport you want to change.

3. Type $ (Shift+4).

   The view in the viewport changes to the Light view (**Figure 11.50**). The viewport window controls change to Light viewport controls (**Figure 11.51**).

To dolly a light:

1. Change a viewport to a Light view.

2.  Click the Dolly Light button in the Light viewport controls.

3. Drag the dolly cursor up or down in the Light viewport.

   The light moves in or out along its local Z axis, or "line of shine" (**Figure 11.52**).

✔ Tips

- ⊞ To dolly a target, choose Dolly Target from the Dolly Light flyout.

- ⊞ To dolly a light and its target together, choose Dolly Spotlight + Target from the same flyout.

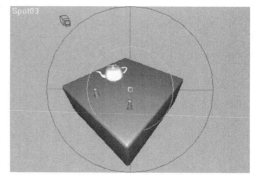

Figure 11.50 You can achieve greater lighting accuracy by setting a viewport to display the view from a light source.

Figure 11.51 The Light viewport controls are similar to the Camera viewport controls.

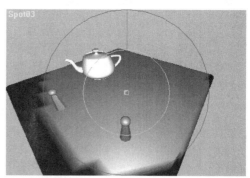

Figure 11.52 With a spotlight, dollying in reduces the area of light coverage.

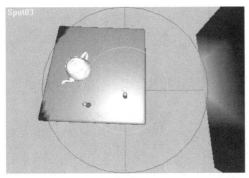

Figure 11.53 Use the Orbit Light control to change the lighting angle while keeping the same lighted area.

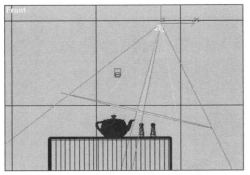

Figure 11.54 While orbiting a light from a Light viewport, it's a good idea to keep an eye on another viewport for comparison.

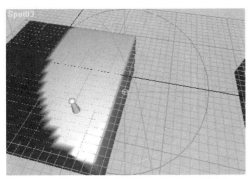

Figure 11.55 Use the Pan Light function to rotate the light's target about the light.

Orbiting a light

The Orbit Light control rotates a spot or directional light around its target. Its companion control, Pan Light, rotates the target around the light. If the light you are navigating does not have a target, it will orbit or pan using an imaginary target located at the light's target distance.

To orbit a light:

1. Change a viewport to a Light view.

2. Click the Orbit Light button in the Light viewport controls.

3. Drag the cursor in the Light viewport.
   The Light view rotates (**Figure 11.53**).
   The light rotates around its target (**Figure 11.54**).

To pan a light:

1. Select a spotlight or a directional light.

2. Change the viewport to the Light view.

3. Click the Pan Light button in the Light viewport controls.

4. Drag the cursor in the Light viewport.
   The Light view pans as the target rotates around the light (**Figure 11.55**).

Animating Lights

Animating lights is a lot like animating cameras. Lights can be animated by setting individual keyframes at various points in time or by assigning them to motion paths. *(Refer to Chapters 6, "Animation," and 10, "Cameras," for details.)* Most of the time, lights are animated by linking them to another object that is doing the movement. Lights may also be set to use a Look At controller that keeps the light on a key subject in the scene.

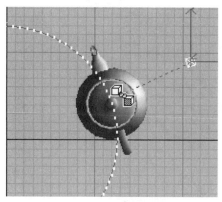

Figure 11.56 Linking a light to a teapot.

Linking lights to animated objects

Linking a light ensures that the light is always properly oriented to an object, such as the headlights of a car. If the light is linked to a camera, the light will always shine on the subject that the camera is viewing.

To link a light to an animated object:

1. Open a scene that contains an animated object.

2. ⌖ Select a light.

3. ⌖ Link the light to the object using the Select and Link tool on the Main Toolbar (**Figure 11.56**).

4. ▶ Play the animation.
   The light follows the object (**Figure 11.57**).

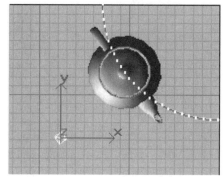

Figure 11.57 Parenting an animated object to a light prevents it from moving into shadow.

Figure 11.58 Setting the teapot as the Look At Target.

Using the Look At controller

The Look At controller turns a light into a searchlight that always points to an object. Moving the target object over time provides an easy way to animate the light. 3DS MAX automatically assigns this controller to spotlights and directional lights, so all you need to do is tell the light what to point to.

To assign a Look At controller to a light:

1. Open a scene that contains an animated object.

2. [icon] Select a spotlight or directional light.

3. [icon] Open the Motion panel.

4. On the Look At Parameters rollout, click the Pick Target button and select the animated object (**Figure 11.58**).

5. [icon] Play the animation.

   The beam of light follows the object (**Figure 11.59**).

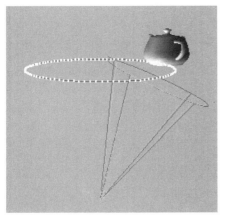

Figure 11.59 Using Look At, the teapot remains in the spotlight as the center attraction.

MAPS AND MATERIALS

Maps and materials dress up a scene by giving objects in it color, texture, pattern, and shine. To give you an idea of their importance, 3D graphics and gaming companies hire people for the sole purpose of building realistic materials and texture maps. Knowledge of 2D paint programs as well as 3D Studio MAX 3 improves your chance of getting a job in this popular field.

Applying materials to objects allows you to quickly create different interpretations of a scene. For example, you can change the paint scheme of a car or change a building material from stucco to brick. Maps that appear as background images can be switched in an instant, giving a totally different look to the scene.

Skillful 3D artists routinely "dirty up" their models to make them look real. To give an old boat the appearance of age, you apply materials that make the paint appear peeled and worn, and make the edges look cracked and broken. A spaceship that has been through the stresses of hyperspace needs burns, dents, shockwave patterns and half-faded insignia.

There is no limit to the illusions you will create by applying maps and materials to your scenes.

About the Material Editor

You create materials in the Material Editor by setting material parameters and by importing bitmap images. As your material evolves, the Material Editor builds a hierarchical structure of parameters called a *material tree*. Materials are saved with the .max scene file, or they may be saved into libraries. The bitmap images that their material trees reference remain external to the scene file.

The Material Editor is visually divided into two main sections. The graphical portion at the top of the window contains a palette of colored material samples and a set of icon-based commands (**Figure 12.1**). These commands help you view and create materials, navigate material trees, and assign materials to objects.

The lower portion of the window contains rollouts with parameters for building materials (**Figure 12.2**). The most important areas for you to get to know are the Basic Parameter rollouts and the Maps rollout.

Learning how to navigate both the Material Editor interface and material hierarchies may prove a bit daunting at first. But once you learn how to get around, I think you will find this to be one of the most creative aspects of the program.

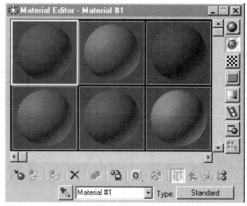

Figure 12.1 The icon menus and sample slots.

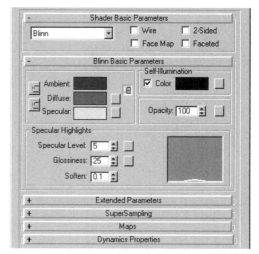

Figure 12.2 The rollouts for assigning unique attributes to the materials.

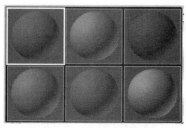

Figure 12.3 The first sample slot is active when you first enter the Material Editor.

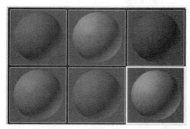

Figure 12.4 The newly selected material slot is now active.

Figure 12.5 The flyout menu that appears when you right-click any sample slot.

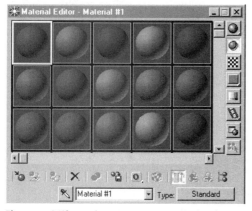

Figure 12.6 Fifteen slots are a common setting that still shows enough detail.

Using Sample Slots

The Material Editor displays materials as you create them in the palette of sample slots. Six slots appear by default, but there are actually 24 slots in all. You view the rest of the slots by scrolling the bar to the right and bottom, or by changing the display.

To activate a sample slot:

1. ▦ Click the Material Editor button in the Main Toolbar. (Or press M on the keyboard.)

    The Material Editor appears. The sample slot in the upper-left corner of the module is selected by default (**Figure 12.3**).

2. Click a sample slot.

    The border of the slot turns white to indicate the slot is activated (**Figure 12.4**).

To change the number of displayed sample slots:

1. ▦ Open the Material Editor.

2. Right-click any active slot.

    The sample slot right-click menu appears (**Figure 12.5**).

3. Choose 5 x 3 Sample Windows or 6 x 4 Sample Windows.

    The display refreshes showing 15 or 24 sample slots (**Figure 12.6**).

✔ Tips

- Sample slots use the same scanline renderer that you use for final output. They show materials at a higher resolution than you see in the viewports.

- To magnify a sample slot, choose Magnify from the sample slot right-click menu. You can increase the magnification by dragging a corner of the window.

Changing the sample slot

The default sample object is a sphere. You can change the sample object type to see how a material will look on an object that more closely matches the shape of your model.

Placing a background behind the sample shape allows you to evaluate the transparency of a material.

To change the sample object:

1. ⊞ Open the Material Editor.

2. Activate a sample slot.

3. ◉ Select a shape from the Sample Type flyout (**Figure 12.7**).

   The sample in the slot changes shape (**Figure 12.8**).

✔ Tips

■ You can assign a custom sample shape based on an actual scene object. See "Creating a Custom Sample Object" in the online help files.

■ The Drag/Rotate setting in the sample slot pop-up menu allows you to rotate the sample object in the slot.

To turn on a background:

1. ⊞ Open the Material Editor.

2. Select a sample slot.

3. ▦ Click the Background button.

   The default background pattern appears in the slot (**Figure 12.9**).

✔ Tip

■ You can also assign a bitmap image to the background. See "Material Editor Options Dialog" in the online help files.

Figure 12.7 The Sample Type flyout menu.

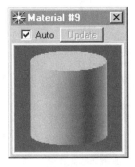

Figure 12.8 The sample sphere is replaced with a sample cylinder.

Figure 12.9 The default background pattern.

USING SAMPLE SLOTS

Figure 12.10 The Material/Map Browser is set to show all material and map types.

Figure 12.11 The Material/Map Navigator lets you access the material hierarchy.

Figure 12.12 The list of materials in the 3dsmax.mat file.

Figure 12.13 Mtl Library is the only heading that gives you all four File selections. Mtl Editor, Selected, and Scene offer only the Save As command.

Using Material Libraries

3D Studio MAX 3 ships with over a dozen libraries of pre-made materials. Using these materials can be a great time-saver that will teach you a lot about creating materials. To browse the materials in external libraries, MAX provides you with a tool called the Material/Map Browser (**Figure 12.10**). The Material/Map Browser allows you to view and manipulate materials and maps. Once you find a material you like, it enables you to bring it into the Material Editor or drag it directly onto an object. In addition to browsing entire libraries, the Material/Map Browser can browse materials that are in the Material Editor, and in the scene. While the Material/Map Browser allows you to work with finished materials, the Material/Map Navigator allows you to view and manipulate the component elements of selected materials within their material trees (**Figure 12.11**).

Opening material libraries

As of this writing, there are 14 different material libraries that ship with the program. They are categorized by content, such as Wood, Brick, Stones, Sky, Ground, Metal, Space, and Backgrounds. The default material library that appears when you first open the browser is called 3dsmax.mat. All material libraries have this .mat extension.

To open a material library:

1. Click Get Material in the row of buttons beneath the sample slot window. The Material/Map Browser appears.

2. Click the Mtl Library radio button. The materials in the current library are displayed in the Material/Map list at right (**Figure 12.12**). On the left, the File group appears in the list of browsing commands (**Figure 12.13**).

(continues on next page)

3. In the File group, click Open.

The Open Material Library dialog box appears (**Figure 12.14**).

4. Select a library from the list and click Open.

The new library of materials opens, replacing the previous library that closes.

✔ Tips

- The Merge command merges materials from a library that you select into the library that is currently loaded.

- Save lets you save the currently loaded material library, including any materials or maps you have added to it.

- Save As lets you save the materials and maps in the list into a new library.

Browsing material libraries

The right side of the Material/Map Browser displays a list of materials, material types, maps, and map types. The default setting shows the names of the materials you have in the library. You can change the display to show materials and maps as thumbnail icons of various sizes.

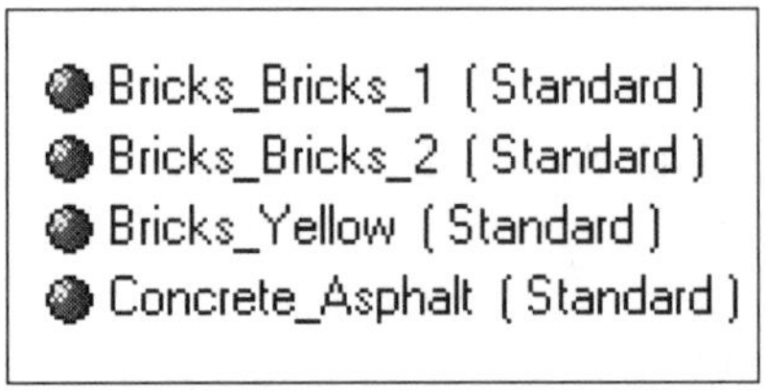

To browse a material library:

1. Open the Material Editor.

2. Click the Get Material button to open the Material/Map Browser.

3. Click the Mtl Library radio button.

The material names and types are listed (**Figure 12.15**).

4. Click the View List + Icons button.

A small thumbnail image appears with the material name and type (**Figure 12.16**).

5. Click the View Small Icons button.

A small thumbnail image appears (**Figure 12.17**).

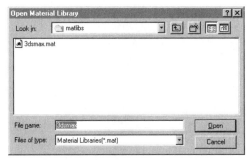

Figure 12.14 The 3dsmax.mat file is the stock material library that ships with 3D Studio MAX.

Figure 12.15 The material type is shown in parentheses.

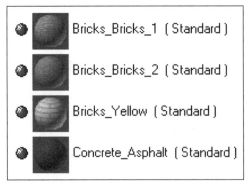

Figure 12.16 This list is bit more descriptive.

Figure 12.17 This display method is not too commonly used unless you're very familiar with the materials in the library.

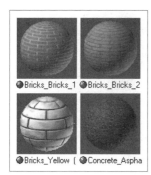

Figure 12.18
This display method is the most descriptive but also uses a lot of system resources for redisplay.

Figure 12.19 The Gold Light Noise material is selected.

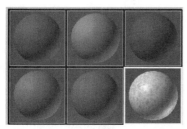

Figure 12.20 Now the material is shown in the active sample slot.

6. ⊙ Click the View Large Icons button.

   A large thumbnail image appears with the material name (**Figure 12.18**).

✔ **Tip**

■ If there are a lot of materials in the library, try not to use the large icons. Loading all the images and refreshing them can take up a lot of time. This is another reason to use smaller, specialized material libraries.

Selecting materials from libraries

There are two ways to load a material from the material library into the Material Editor.

To select a material from a library:

1. ⊞ Open the Material Editor.

2. ⊙ Click the Get Material button to open the Material/Map Browser.

3. Click the Mtl Library radio button.

   The material names and types are listed.

4. Select one of the materials in the library.

   The material sample will appear in the viewer at the upper-left corner (**Figure 12.19**).

5. Double-click the material name.

   The selected material is loaded into the active sample slot of the Material Editor (**Figure 12.20**).

✔ **Tip**

■ You can also load a material by dragging it from the viewer to a sample slot in the Material Editor.

Navigating material trees

The Material/Map Navigator is a great way to see how a material is constructed, and to access all of the settings in the tree

To view a material tree:

1. 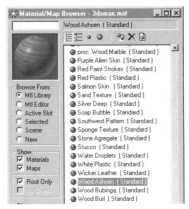 Open the Material Editor.

2. Click the Get Material button to open the Material/Map Browser.

3. Open a material library.

4. Select a material in the library by double-clicking it (**Figure 12.21**).

5. Click the Material/Map Navigator button.

   The Material/Map Navigator appears (**Figure 12.22**).

Figure 12.21 This time, Wood Ashen is selected from the library.

To navigate a material tree:

1. Open the Material/Map Navigator.

2. Click the name of a material in the window.
   The top level of the material tree opens.

3. Click Diffuse Color: Map in the material tree (**Figure 12.23**).

   The Material Editor moves down the material tree. It updates the display to show the parameters of the map type that is used in the Diffuse mapping channel.

4. Click another map type.
   The Material Editor moves to the new branch in the tree (**Figure 12.24**).

✔ Tip

■ You can also navigate a material tree from the controls underneath the sample slots. Move to a deeper level by selecting the level in the drop-down list. Move up or across branches of the tree by clicking the ⬆ Go to Parent and ➡ Go to Sibling arrows.

Figure 12.22 The material hierarchy for the Wood Ashen material.

Figure 12.23 The first map in the hierarchy is selected.

Figure 12.24 The second map in the hierarchy is selected.

Figure 12.25 This teapot is ready for material application.

Figure 12.26. Bricks will look nice.

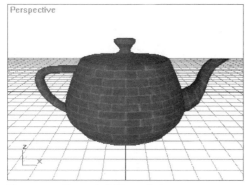

Figure 12.27 The material is applied.

Figure 12.28 The first sample is hot, the second is cold, and the third is not yet assigned to anything.

Assigning a material to an object

There are two ways to assign a material to an object. If the object is selected, you simply click a button. You can also drag a material to an object whether or not it is selected.

If a material has maps in it, the object may need *mapping coordinates* to display the maps. Primitive objects, like the teapot shown at left, have mapping coordinates built in. Otherwise, you must apply a UVW Map modifier. See "Applying Mapped Materials" later in this chapter.

To assign a material to a selected object:

1. Select an object (**Figure 12.25**).

2. Open the Material Editor.

3. Optional: Select a material from a library (**Figure 12.26**).

4. Click the Assign Material to Selection button.

    The material is applied to the teapot (**Figure 12.27**). White triangular tabs appear in the corner of the sample slot to indicate that the material in the slot has been used in the scene (**Figure 12.28**).

To assign a material to an object by dragging:

1. Open the Material Editor.

    Optional: Select a material from a library.

3. Drag the material to an object.
    The material is applied to the object.

✔ Tip

■ When you select an object that has a material assigned to it, the tabs in the sample slot change to a solid white. We say that such a material is "hot."

USING MATERIAL LIBRARIES

Creating a custom library

A custom material library preserves your favorite materials all in one place and keeps the master library from getting too large. I suggest that you create libraries by material category, such as Metallic or Architectural, or create separate libraries for different projects.

To create a library of scene materials:

1. Open a scene file in which materials have been assigned to objects. For practice, use one of the sample scene files that ship with the program.

2. Open the Material Editor.

3. Open the Material/Map Browser.

4. Click the Scene radio button.
   A shorter list of materials appears.

5. Click the Save As button (**Figure 12.29**).
   The Save Material Library dialog appears (**Figure 12.30**).

6. Enter the name of the new library and click Save.
   Your new library contains all materials used in the scene.

✔ Tips

■ You can also create a custom library by loading an existing library, using the ☒ Delete from Library button to get rid of the materials you don't want, and then saving it with a different name.

■ Clicking ⓢ Clear Material Library removes all materials from the currently loaded library. This does not affect the saved library file unless you click Save.

Figure 12.29 Save As is sometimes overlooked, but it provides the best way to save a custom library.

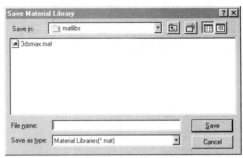

Figure 12.30 Use a logical name such as the name of the project you're working on or a category for specific materials, such as Wood or Metal.

Figure 12.31 The first sample uses unique color settings for Ambient, Diffuse, and Specular; the second uses the same color setting for Ambient and Diffuse; and the third uses the same color setting for Diffuse and Specular.

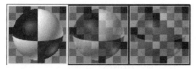

Figure 12.32 Three samples shown against a background pattern displaying different degrees of opacity: 100%, 70%, and 30%.

Figure 12.33 The white areas of the samples show the differences in Self-Illumination settings: none, 50%, and 100%.

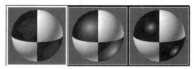

Figure 12.34 The first sample uses the default Specular Level and Glossiness settings of 5 and 25; the dull sheen in the second sample is produced by setting Specular Level to 60; and in the third sample, Glossiness is set to 50 to create a high-gloss finish.

Figure 12.35 Three identical samples shown with different shader types: Blinn, Metal, and Phong.

Creating Basic Materials

Materials begin as solid colors. By manipulating their basic parameters, you affect their hue, value, saturation, opacity, and shininess.

◆ **Color:** Three settings adjust the color of the material (**Figure 12.31**).

Ambient color is the color of a material in the absence of direct light.

Diffuse color is the primary color of a material.

Specular color is the color of its highlight.

◆ **Opacity** changes a material from fully transparent to fully opaque (**Figure 12.32**).

◆ **Self-Illumination** sets the minimum value of a material, regardless of the amount of light falling across its surface. (**Figure 12.33**).

◆ **Specular Level** sets the intensity of the specular highlight. Higher values produce shinier materials.

◆ **Glossiness** controls the size of the specular highlight. Higher values produce a smaller highlight (**Figure 12.34**).

◆ **Shader Type**s use different shading algorithms to determine how light affects the surface of an object when it is rendered.

The most common shader types are Blinn (the default), Metal, and Phong. Blinn gives an object a smooth, realistic surface when rendered. Metal shading creates a shiny, metallic effect. Phong is similar to Blinn, but it creates more distinct highlights (**Figure 12.35**).

Material Types

There are nine different types of materials in addition to the basic Standard material. You select a different material type by clicking on the Type button underneath the sample slots.

- ◆ **Multi/Sub-Object** materials group up to 1,000 materials into a single material. When you assign a multi/sub-object material to an object, it assigns the different materials to different faces based upon the material ID number of each face and material.

- ◆ **Raytrace** materials produce fully raytraced reflections and refractions of the scene that surrounds the object to which it is assigned.

- ◆ **Blend** materials combine two materials by mixing them together.

- ◆ **Composite** materials mix up to 10 different materials. Materials that are set to higher opacity levels affect the mix more strongly than materials that are more transparent.

- ◆ **Double-Sided** materials are made up of two materials: one for the front of a face, and one for the back. Surfaces that are assigned double-sided materials automatically render on both sides.

- ◆ **Matte/Shadow** materials apply an environment map onto the surface of an object. This allows you to add shadows and reflections to the background image and create the illusion of objects moving behind parts of the background.

- ◆ **Morpher** materials shift materials from one to another. Use them in conjunction with the Morph modifier.

- ◆ **Shellac** materials use a base material and shellac material. By adjusting the shellac color blend, you can tint the base material with the color of the shellac material.

- ◆ **Top/Bottom** materials assign different materials to faces based on whether the normals of the material point up or down. The orientation of the normals can be based on either the world coordinates or the object's local coordinates.

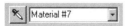

Figure 12.36 The default names are not very intuitive.

Figure 12.37 Descriptive names help you remember what your materials look like; they also help if someone else uses your library.

Naming a material

3D Studio MAX assigns a default name to each material. As with naming objects, giving materials more descriptive titles helps you identify them more easily.

To name a material:

1. Open the Material Editor.

2. Select a sample slot.

   The default name of the material appears below (**Figure 12.36**).

3. Enter a new name that better describes the material (**Figure 12.37**).

4. When you add maps to the material later on, it will help to name each level of the material tree that they generate as an aid to navigation.

Choosing a material color

You instantly recognize a material by its color. MAX allows you to define colors in three ways: by setting red, green, and blue amounts; by setting hue, saturation, and value amounts; or by picking a hue and value from a palette and gradient.

One usually begins by setting the diffuse color of a material, as this will be its predominant color.

To set a color:

1. Open the Material Editor.

2. Select a sample slot.

3. Click the Diffuse color swatch in the Basic Parameters rollout.

   The Color Selector dialog box appears.

(continues on next page)

4. Select a color using any of the three methods mentioned above (**Figure 12.38**). If you are used to working with paint, you may prefer to use the palette and Whiteness slider (**Figure 12.39**).

5. Without closing the Color Selector, click another color swatch and assign it a color.

6. Repeat steps 3 and 4 for the ambient and specular colors. Then close the Color Selector dialog box.

✔ Tip

■ A quick way to create ambient and specular colors is by dragging the diffuse color swatch onto them to create a copy of that color. Then all you need to do is adjust the whiteness slider to make the color lighter or darker.

Setting visibility and contrast

The visibility and contrast of a material are controlled by the Opacity and Self-Illumination settings.

To set opacity:

1. Open the Material Editor.

2. Select a material by clicking a sample slot.

3. Click the Background button.

   A multicolored test pattern appears in the background of the slot (**Figure 12.40**).

4. Drag the Opacity spinner downward (**Figure 12.40**).

   The material becomes more transparent and the background becomes more visible in the slot (**Figure 12.41**). Dragging up on the spinner increases the material's opacity.

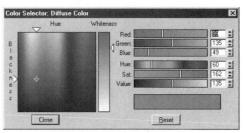

Figure 12.38 Use the Color Selector dialog box to choose the colors of your material.

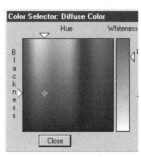

Figure 12.39 The palette and Whiteness slider method is a visually intuitive way to select colors.

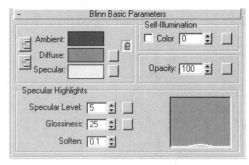

Figure 12.40 The opacity settings are found in the Basic Parameters rollout of a material.

Figure 12.41 The sample material before and after changing its opacity.

Figure 12.42 A new material sample to work on.

Figure 12.43 The illumination appears as if a white light is inside the material, washing out the Diffuse color as the light gets brighter.

Figure 12.44 The material seems to be self-illuminated, as if a light that is the same color as the Diffuse color is inside the material, thus creating a vibrantly colored material.

Figure 12.45 Specular Level affects shininess.

To set self-illumination:

You set self-illumination by changing the whiteness value of its color swatch or by setting a self-illumination percentage value.

1. ▒ Open the Material Editor.

2. Select a sample slot (**Figure 12.42**).

3. Click the black color swatch next to the self-illumination color value.

   The Color Selector dialog box appears with the Whiteness set to black.

4. Drag the Whiteness slider.

   The sample material brightens you increase the whiteness of the color swatch (**Figure 12.43**).

5. Uncheck the box next to the Self-Illumination Color setting to reveal the numerical input field and spinner.

6. Drag the spinner to change the self-illumination of the material (**Figure 12.44**).

Setting shininess

A material's shininess is controlled by two settings: the Specular Level and Glossiness.

1. ▒ Open the Material Editor to set the specular level.

2. Select a sample slot.

3. Change the Specular Level in the Basic Parameters rollout.

   The highlights on the sample material become brighter or dimmer (**Figure 12.45**).

CREATING BASIC MATERIALS

To set glossiness:

◆ Increase the Glossiness value.

The highlights on the sample material become smaller, giving it the appearance of a highly polished surface (**Figure 12.46**).

✔ Tip

■ You must set the Specular Level to a value greater than zero for the material to appear glossy.

Copying materials

Often the fastest way to create a new material is by copying an existing material and adjusting it. Copying is especially useful if materials have similar characteristics but they have different colors or texture maps.

To copy a material:

1. 🔳 Open the Material Editor.

2. Select a sample slot (**Figure 12.47**).

3. Drag the sample to another sample slot. The material is copied (**Figure 12.48**).

4. Rename the material to avoid confusion later.

Creating additional samples

You can create additional samples after the sample slots are all filled up with materials. Eliminating material samples that are assigned to objects has no affect upon the object.

To create a new sample:

1. 🔳 Open the Material Editor.

2. Select a sample slot (**Figure 12.49**).

3. 🔘 Click Get Material.

The Material/Map Browser appears.

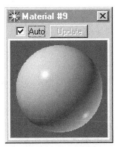

Figure 12.46 Glossiness controls the size of the highlight on the material.

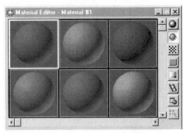

Figure 12.47 The selected sample slot is always surrounded by a heavy white border.

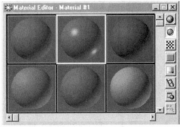

Figure 12.48 Material #1 is copied, and the specular level and glossiness have been increased.

Figure 12.49 Note that the material name matches the material. Remember that other people will be working with your scenes, so logical naming is important.

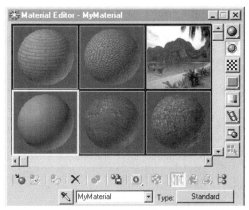

Figure 12.50 The sample slot has been replaced, but as long as the previous material is assigned to something, it will not be overwritten.

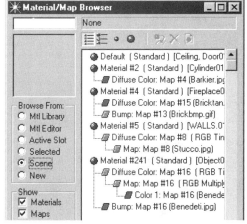

Figure 12.51 The material list shows the materials you have in the currently loaded material library.

Figure 12.52 You can rename your material if a name is already used by a material in the library.

4. Set the Browse From: setting to New.

5. Double-click the Standard material type. The material in the sample slot is replaced by a new, gray sample (**Figure 12.50**).

6. Give the new material a name.

To get a material from a scene:

1. Open a scene that has a material assigned to an object.

2. ▓ Open the Material Editor.

3. ◉ Click Get Material. The Material/Map Browser appears.

4. Set the Browse From setting to Scene. A list of materials used in the current scene appears.

5. Select a material.

Saving materials

Once you've created a material that you like, you can put it in a custom material library.

To save a material to a library:

1. Activate the sample slot of the material you want to save.

2. ◉ Click the Get Material button to display the Material/Map Browser.

3. Change the Browse From setting to Mtl Library (**Figure 12.51**).

4. ▤ Click Put to Library. Confirm the name of the material (**Figure 12.52**). The material is saved.

✔ Tip

■ If you want to delete a material from a library, select the material you don't want and click the ✕ Delete from Library button in the Material/Map Browser.

Adding Maps to Materials

Maps add realistic details to materials. Each time you add a new map to a material, it builds a new level in its material tree.

When you apply a mapped material to an object, the map is projected onto the object's surface. Maps can be repeated across a surface to make a pattern, and they can also be mirrored.

Maps can reference external filters or external bitmap images. When maps reference external bitmaps, they may use the complete color characteristics of the image, or they may just use the light and dark values of those colors. Maps can be generated from within the program as well. These types of maps are called *procedural* maps.

Map Types

3D Studio MAX 3 comes with 35 different types of maps. With the Material/Map Browser, you can select a map type from among the following categories:

◆ **2D Maps** are two-dimensional images or filters that are applied to the surface of an object or to the background of a scene. They include bitmaps plus the following procedural maps: Bricks, Checker, Gradient, Gradient Ramp, Paint, and Swirl. They also include plug-in filters for Adobe Photoshop and Adobe Premiere.

◆ **3D Maps** are procedural maps that project through objects in three dimensions. They include Cellular, Dent, Falloff, Marble, Noise, Particle Age, Particle MBlur, Perlin Marble, Planet, Smoke, Speckle, Splat, Stucco, Water, and Wood.

◆ **Compositors** combine multiple maps or colors into a single map. They include Composite, Mask, Mix, and RGB Multiply.

◆ **Color Modifiers** change the color of a material. They include Output, RGB Tint, and Vertex Color.

◆ **Other** maps create reflection and refraction on the surface of an object. They include Flat Mirror, Raytrace, Reflect/Refract, and Thin Wall Refraction.

◆ **All** includes all of the above categories. This is the default setting for the browser.

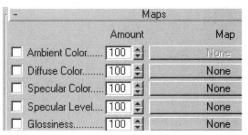

Figure 12.53 The Maps rollout allows you to add maps to a material.

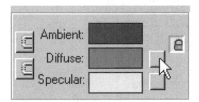

Figure 12.54 Clicking the Diffuse Color map button is a shortcut for assigning a texture map.

Figure 12.55 The Material/Map Browser allows you to choose a map type from five different categories of maps.

You can use a wide variety of bitmap image file formats for maps, including: Windows bitmap (.bmp), JPEG (.jpg), GIF (.gif), Adobe Photoshop (.psd), TIFF (.tif), and Targa (.tga). You can also use animated file formats such as AVI (.avi) and Quicktime (.mov) to create animated materials.

Sources of bitmap images include these:

◆ CD-ROMs

◆ Paint programs

◆ Scanners

◆ Digital cameras

◆ Web sites that give explicit permission

◆ Images you render from MAX scene files

You add maps to a material from the Maps rollout of the Material Editor (**Figure 12.53**). The amount of influence that each map has on a material is set by the Amount spinner.

As a shortcut, you can add maps to basic material parameters by clicking the blank map buttons next to their settings.

Creating texture maps

Diffuse color maps replace the overall diffuse color of a material with a map. You use them to paint or "gift wrap" the surface of the object.

Because diffuse color maps are commonly called *texture maps* in other programs, MAX artists usually call them texture maps instead.

To add a texture map:

1. Open the Material Editor.

2. Select a sample slot.

3. In the Basic Parameters rollout of the shader, click the blank button next to the Diffuse color swatch (**Figure 12.54**).

   The Material/Map Browser appears (**Figure 12.55**).

(continues on next page)

ADDING MAPS TO MATERIALS

4. Double-click the Bitmap map type.

The Select Bitmap Image File dialog box appears.

5. Navigate to the bitmap you want, and then open it.

The bitmap appears as a texture map on the sample object (**Figure 12.56**). A rollout of its parameters appears below. A level is added to the material tree (**Figure 12.57**).

6. ⬆ Click Go to Parent to move back up to the top (i.e., the root) of the material tree.

In the Basic Parameters rollout, an "M" appears on the Diffuse Color map button. In the Maps rollout, the name of the map appears on the button.

✔ Tips

■ To clear a map, drag an empty map button over the map button you want to clear, or click the map button and choose NONE.

■ Any animation file, including animation files you render out from MAX, can be used as a texture map to create an animated material.

Creating bump maps

Bump maps use the dark to light values of a map to create the illusion of recesses or ridges. Darker pixels create the illusion of greater depth while lighter pixels create greater relief.

Artists often add bump maps to texture mapped materials to make a surface look more convincing. So you can see the bump effect more clearly, we will add the bump map first.

Figure 12.56 The sample slot after selecting Bricktan.gif from the 3dsmax3/Maps directory.

Figure 12.57 Bricktan.gif is automatically added to the material tree. It is located one level down from the root.

Figure 12.58 The Bump map button is located in the Maps rollout.

Figure 12.59
Brickbmp.gif ships with the program. The dark lines between the bricks match the mortar in the Bricktan.gif bitmap.

Figure 12.60 The result of increasing the Bump Amount to 185. The recesses are shaded, but the profile is smooth.

Figure 12.61 After adding Bricktan.gif as a texture map.

Figure 12.62 Dragging from one map button to another allows you to copy, instance or swap maps.

To add a bump map:

1. ⁑ Open the Material Editor.

2. Open the Maps rollout.

3. Click the Bump map button (**Figure 12.58**).
   The Material/Map Browser appears.

4. Select any 2D or 3D map type using the 2D and 3D radio buttons in the browser. You can also choose a bitmap made especially to work with a texture map (**Figure 12.59**).

5. 🔼 Click Go to Parent.

6. Increase the Bump amount until bump effect is clearly visible (**Figure 12.60**).

7. Add your texture map to the material to create a more realistic look (**Figure 12.61**).

✔ Tips

- A quick way to create a bump map is to drag an instance of the texture map from the Diffuse Color map button onto the Bump map button (**Figure 12.62**).

- Reducing the Bump Amount to a negative number creates a inverted bump map in which light values indent and dark values are raised.

- Noise and Dent are good choices for making a surface look coarse or dirty. You adjust the default size of the grain in the Parameters rollout of each map.

Creating opacity maps

Opacity mapping uses the light to dark values of a map to calculate transparency. Lighter areas create more opaque surfaces. Darker areas create more transparent surfaces.

Use this map type when you want to change the edges of an object without adding to the complexity of its mesh.

To add an opacity map:

1. ![icon] Open the Material Editor.

2. Select a material and ![icon] click the sample slot background (**Figure 12.63**).

3. In the Basic Parameters rollout, click the small button next to the Opacity spinner (**Figure 12.64**).

    The Material/Map Browser appears.

4. Select a map. Usually you choose a bitmap that you have created specifically for this purpose in a paint program (**Figure 12.65**).

    The dark values of the opacity map make the material transparent. The light values of the opacity map make the material opaque. If there are any gray values in the opacity map, they will create gradual transitions between the areas of transparency and areas of opacity (**Figure 12.66**).

✔ Tips

- If your bitmap has an alpha channel, you can use the same map for both the texture map and the opacity map. All you have to do is set the Mono Channel Output to Alpha in the Parameters rollout of the map. Try this with the 32-bit sample map that ships with the program called Daisy.tif.

- Setting lights to cast ray-traced shadows causes shadows to be cast from the edges of the opacity map instead of from the edges of the object.

Figure 12.63 The texture map in this sample ships with the program. It is called Dfleaf7.jpg.

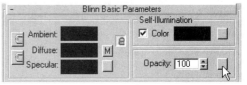

Figure 12.64 Clicking the Opacity map button provides a quick way to select an opacity map.

Figure 12.65 Dleaf7o.gif is a silhouette of Dleaf7.jpg. It also ships with MAX.

Figure 12.66 The result of combining the opacity map with the texture map.

Figure 12.67 Applying a UVW Map modifier from the Modify panel.

Figure 12.68 Displaying a texture map in a viewport.

Applying Mapped Materials

You position mapped materials onto objects using a process known as UVW mapping. UVW mapping projects maps in three dimensions: U positions a map with respect to its width. V positions a map with respect to its height. W positions a map with respect to its depth. The W dimension is used only for 3D procedural maps, such as Marble, Noise, Planet, Smoke, Water, and Wood.

UVW coordinates are automatically generated for mesh primitives when you apply mapped materials to them. For all other objects, you need to apply a UVW Map modifier.

To apply a mapped material to an object:

1. Select an object.

2. If the object you selected is not a mesh primitive, open the Modify panel and apply a UVW Map modifier to it (**Figure 12.67**).

3. Open the Material Editor.

4. Select a mapped material.

5. Click Assign Material to Selection or drag the material to the object.

6. To see a 2D map in the viewports, navigate to the level of that map in the material tree and click Show Map in Viewport. The map appears on the object in the viewport (**Figure 12.68**).

✔ Tips

■ Only 2D maps can be displayed in a viewport. Show Map in Viewport is unavailable for other map types.

■ If an object turns gray when you assign it a map, and Show Map in Viewport is turned on, then you probably forgot to assign it a UVW Map modifier.

Adjusting maps

You can adjust maps in two ways. Adjusting the parameters of the map in the Material Editor changes the coordinates of the map globally for all objects to which the material has been applied. Adjusting the parameters of the UVW Map modifier changes the mapping coordinates locally for the modified object.

Material Editor mapping coordinates include the following:

◆ **UV, VW,** and **WU** select the axes in which the map will be affected by other parameters.

◆ **Offset** positions a map by moving it in its *U*, *V*, or *W* axis.

◆ **Tiling** repeats a map in any direction.

◆ **Mirror** turns on mirror tiling. Mirror tiling creates a copy of a map and flips it around one of its axes to create a symmetrical pattern.

◆ **Tile** turns off mirror tiling.

◆ **Angle** rotates the map in any direction.

UVW Map modifier parameters include the following:

◆ **Mapping** parameters, including:

  ◆ Different shaped mapping gizmos that project a map onto an object.

  ◆ Length, width, and height parameters for scaling the selected mapping gizmo.

  ◆ Tile parameters for U, V, and W.

  ◆ A checkbox to flip the map in each dimension.

Mapping Alignments

Alignment commands align mapping gizmos to the objects they modify. There are eight different alignment commands (*see* Figure 12.73, *later in this chapter*), plus *X*, *Y*, and *Z* alignment options:

◆ **X, Y,** and **Z** align a mapping gizmo to the axes of the world coordinate system.

◆ **Fit** resizes the mapping gizmo to match to the size of the object at the extents of its bounding box. This may distort the proportions of a map.

◆ **Center** realigns the mapping gizmo to the selection center of an object.

◆ **Bitmap Fit** resizes the mapping gizmo in proportion to the size of a bitmap. This prevents distortion in bitmaps that are associated with the material being applied.

◆ **Normal Align** aligns a gizmo to a face normal on the object by dragging the cursor over the surface of the object.

◆ **View Align** aligns the mapping gizmo to the current view.

◆ **Region Fit** allows you to drag out a mapping gizmo. Use the Mapping Length, Width, and Height parameters to fine tune this alignment.

◆ **Reset** returns the gizmo to its default alignment.

◆ **Acquire** obtains the UVW Coordinates from the mapping gizmo of another object and resizes the current mapping gizmo to match.

Figure 12.69 The UVW Map rollout offers seven types of mapping gizmos.

Figure 12.70 Using different mapping gizmos to apply a map. From top to bottom: Planar, Box, Cylindrical, Cylindrical with capping, Spherical, Shrink Wrap, Face, and XYZ to UVW.

◆ **Map Channel** allows you to create up to 99 different mapping coordinates for a single material. To make a map use a map channel, open the Coordinates rollout of the map in the Material Editor and set the Map Channel number to the corresponding channel.

◆ **Alignment** parameters align a mapping gizmo to an object. *See sidebar "Mapping Alignments" on the preceding page.*

Using mapping gizmos

Mapping gizmos determine how a map is projected onto the surface of an object. For two-dimensional mapping, use the Plane gizmo. For three-dimensional mapping, choose a gizmo from Cylinder, Spherical, Shrink Wrap, Box, Face, and XYZ to UVW. Cylindrical mapping gizmos give you the additional option of capping ends of the object with the map.

To change a mapping gizmo:

1. Select an object that has a 2D map applied to it.

2. Click Show Map in Viewport to make the map appear in the viewports.

3. Open the Modify panel and apply a UVW Map modifier to the object.

   or

   Open the Modifiers Toolbar and click UVW Map.

   The UVW Map rollout appears (**Figure 12.69**).

4. Change the mapping gizmo by clicking each of the gizmo radio buttons. (**Figure 12.70** shows results of using different buttons.)

(continues on next page)

APPLYING MAPPED MATERIALS

✔ Tips

- You can use a UVW Map modifier to set the coordinates of any type of map. Texture maps are simply the most visible—and most likely—map you will need to adjust.

- You can apply as many UVW Map modifiers as you like to an object. When the modifier stack is collapsed, the mapping coordinates stay with the object.

- You can assign different mapping coordinates, including different mapping gizmos, to the different mapping channels. Access them by setting the corresponding Mapping Channels parameter in the Coordinates rollout of each map.

Positioning maps

You can change the coordinates of a map in the Material Editor or in the UVW Map modifier. Changing a map's coordinates in the Material Editor affects the placement of the map globally in all objects that use it. Changing a map's coordinates in a UVW Map modifier affects the coordinates of only the map on the selected object in the current mapping channel.

To offset a map globally:

1. ⚏ Open the Material Editor.

2. Select a mapped material.

3. Navigate to the material tree to the level of the map you want to adjust.

   The Coordinates rollout for the map appears (**Figure 12.71**).

4. Change the U or V Offset value.

   The map offsets horizontally or vertically across the material (**Figure 12.72**).

5. To rotate a map, change the Angle settings.

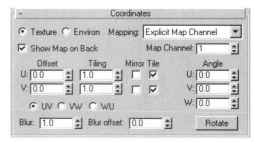

Figure 12.71 The Coordinates rollout of the Material Editor contains parameters for adjusting the position of a map. It affects the U and V map axes by default.

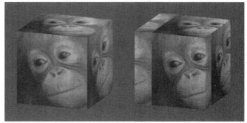

Figure 12.72 The material sample before and after offsetting the map of the monkey's face.

Figure 12.73 You offset a map on a particular object using the alignment commands in the UVW Map modifier.

Figure 12.74 The result of aligning the map to the view.

Figure 12.75 The mapped material of the monkey face in a sample slot.

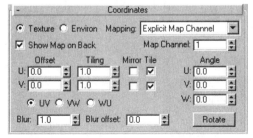

Figure 12.76 The Coordinates rollout of a map provides parameters for tiling and mirroring.

To offset a map locally:

1. ⬚ Select an object that has been mapped using the UVW Map modifier.

2. ✎ Open the Modify panel.

3. Select the UVW Map modifier from the Modifier Stack drop-down list.

4. Using the Alignment buttons, change the alignment of the gizmo in X, Y, or Z (**Figure 12.73**). Use the sidebar at the beginning of this section for reference.

   The map offsets along the surface of the object (**Figure 12.74**).

✔ Tip

■ You can also change the alignment of a map by transforming the mapping gizmo at the sub-object level.

Tiling maps

Tiling causes a map to repeat in a pattern. Mirror causes a map to tile in a symmetrical pattern. You create tiling and mirroring effects in the Material Editor using the Coordinates rollout of a map.

To tile a map:

1. Open the Material Editor.

2. Select a mapped material (**Figure 12.75**).

3. Navigate to the level of the map you want to adjust in the material tree.

   The Coordinates rollout for the map appears (**Figure 12.76**).

   (continues on next page)

4. Make sure that UV is selected and that Tile is checked for the axis in which you want to tile the map.

5. Increase the U and/or V Tiling values.

   The map repeats across the material (**Figure 12.77**).

Figure 12.77 After tiling the map three times in U and V.

To mirror a map:

1. Open the Material Editor.

2. Select a mapped material.

3. Navigate to the level of the map you want to adjust in the material tree.

   The Coordinates rollout for the map appears.

4. Make sure that UV is selected.

5. Check Mirror for the axis in which you want to mirror the map.

6. Increase the U and/or V Tiling values.

   The map repeats and mirrors across the material (**Figure 12.78**).

Figure 12.78 Checking Mirror in U and V reflects the monkey's face in two directions.

Figure 12.79 The Material/Map Browser offers you a choice of 10 different materials.

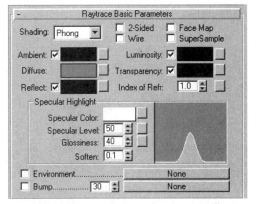

Figure 12.80 The Raytrace Basic Parameters rollout includes settings for color and reflection.

Figure 12.81 Use the Whiteness slider or the Value slider to set the degree of reflectivity.

Creating Reflections

Raytrace materials and reflection maps cause objects to reflect other objects in a scene. Raytracing creates beautiful materials, but reflection maps render faster.

Creating Raytrace materials

Raytrace materials use raytrace shading algorithms to create highly accurate reflections on the surfaces of objects.

To create a raytraced reflection:

1. Select an object.

2. Open the Material Editor.

3. Click a sample slot.

4. Click the Type button.

   The Material/Map Browser appears with a choice of materials (**Figure 12.79**).

5. Double-click Raytrace.

   The Raytrace Basic Parameters rollout appears (**Figure 12.80**). The selected sample material turns gray.

6. Click the Reflect color swatch.

   The Select Color: Reflect dialog box appears.

7. Set the color to a middle gray by dragging the Whiteness slider or the value slider to the middle of its range (**Figure 12.81**).

   Gray creates a moderate amount of reflection. White creates total reflection. Black creates zero reflection.

8. Assign the material to the object.

(continues on next page)

CREATING REFLECTIONS

9. Render the scene.

The object reflects other objects in the scene, as well as the environment map (**Figure 12.82**).

Creating a reflection map

You apply reflection maps to objects with curved or irregular surfaces. They are faster to render than Raytrace materials.

To create a mapped reflection:

1. Select an object that has a curved surface.

2. Open the Material Editor.

3. Select a sample slot.

4. Click the Reset button to change the colors of the material to shades of gray.

5. Open the Maps rollout.

6. Click the Reflection Map button (**Figure 12.83**).

The Material/Map Browser appears with a choice of map types.

7. Select the Reflect/Refract map type.

The Reflect/Refract Parameters rollout appears (**Figure 12.84**).

8. Click the Assign Material to Selected button, or drag the sample to the object.

9. Render the scene.

A reflection of the scene appears on the surface of the object (**Figure 12.85**).

✔ Tips

■ If objects intersect, reflection maps cannot generate a reflection. This includes objects and the plane on which they sit. To remedy this, move the plane slightly downward.

■ Reducing the Reflect Amount in the Maps rollout dims a reflection.

Figure 12.82 After applying the Raytrace material, the teapot reflects the scene around it.

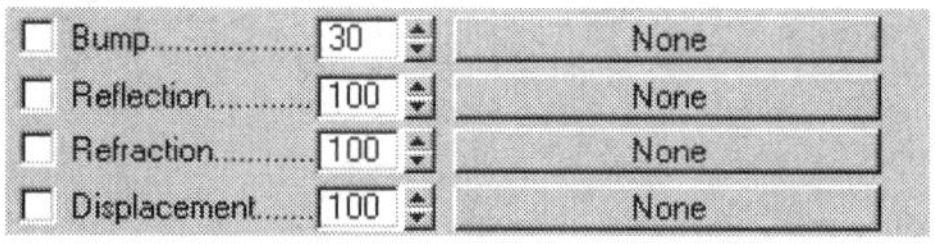

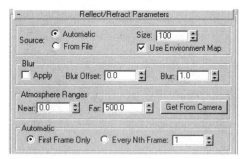

Figure 12.83 The Reflection map button is next to the Refraction map button in the Maps rollout.

Figure 12.84 The Reflect/Refract settings include map size, blurring, turning off the environment map, and atmosphere ranges.

Figure 12.85 The rendered teapot reflects the scene with less accuracy than the Raytrace material.

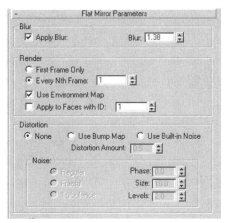

Figure 12.86 Flat Mirror parameters include settings for blurring, reflecting the environment map, and selecting the Material ID of the faces that will reflect.

Figure 12.87 The plane reflects the teapot and teacup.

Creating a Flat Mirror map

You use Flat Mirror maps to turn flat surfaces into mirrors. The easiest way to do this is to assign a Flat Mirror map to a plane object.

To create a flat mirror:

1. Select a plane that has a few objects sitting on it.

2. Open the Material Editor.

3. Select one of the sample slots.

4. Click the Reset button to change the colors of the material to shades of gray.

5. Open the Maps rollout.

6. Click the Reflection Map button.
   The Material/Map Browser appears.

7. Select the Flat Mirror map type.
   The Flat Mirror Parameters rollout appears (**Figure 12.86**).

8. Click the Assign Material to Selection button.

9. Render the scene.
   The planar surface reflects the scene (**Figure 12.87**).

(continues on next page)

CREATING REFLECTIONS

✔ Tips

- Flat Mirror maps work on one of the flat sides of an object only, usually the top side. To change which side of the object reflects, check Apply Faces with ID and change the ID number at right. This number corresponds to the Material ID number of the object's faces and can be reassigned at the face sub-object level of editing.

- An extruded shape also makes a good reflecting surface (**Figure 12.88**).

- Adding a little noise to a flat mirror map creates the appearance of ripples on water (**Figure 12.89**).

Figure 12.88 An extruded circle made the round mirror in this scene. The steam is produced by a plugin called Afterburn, which is made by Afterworks.

Figure 12.89 I created the Taj Mahal for the 3D Studio MAX VIZ 1.0 rollout. A flat mirror map in the foreground created the reflection pool. The ripple on the water was created by adding a small amount of noise.

RENDERING

AND SPECIAL EFFECTS

Rendering produces your final creation in 2D images of your scene. 3D Studio MAX 3 provides you with all the controls you need to produce professional quality prints, posters, Web designs, videos, slide shows, and movies. The images that you render can also be used as background images for scenes or texture maps for models. Fog, volume light, lens effects, glows, and depth of field are all examples of rendered effects that can enhance your images.

The basics of rendering still images were covered at the end of Chapter 3, under the heading "Rendering Objects." This chapter further explains rendering, including how to set image output size, how to render images to different types of file formats, how to view and render a background image, and how to create atmospheric and post-process effects.

Rendering Scenes

Rendering creates a 2D image of a scene using the current view in the active viewport. Rendering an image of a scene is commonly called *rendering a scene*.

Options for rendering scenes are set in the Render Scene dialog box (**Figure 13.1**) and in the Render Type drop-down menu (see the sidebar, "Render Types"). You access the Render Scene dialog box by clicking 🖼 Render Scene on the Main Toolbar or 🖼 Render Scene on the Rendering Toolbar. You can also choose Rendering > Render to open this dialog box.

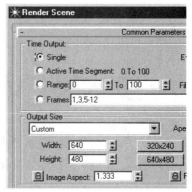

Figure 13.1 The Render Scene dialog box provides a wide range of render settings.

Render Types

3D Studio MAX 3 offers six different ways to render scenes. The default render type is View, which renders the active viewport. You select render types from the Render Type drop-down list in the Main Toolbar (**Figure 13.2**).

Figure 13.2
The Render Type drop-down list gives you six ways to render a scene.

◆ **Selected** renders just the objects that you select. If there is an image in the virtual frame buffer, the Selected type will render the selected objects on top of that image. ✗ Clicking Clear resets the virtual frame buffer.

◆ **Region** renders a rectangular region that you adjust. When you click the Render button, a dotted window appears in the viewport. Anything inside the window will be rendered at the last image resolution setting. Drag the control points around the perimeter to resize the window. Drag from within the window to move the entire window. When you are ready to render, click the OK button in the lower-right corner of the viewport.

◆ **Crop** renders a rectangular region and purges all other image data in the virtual frame buffer.

◆ **Blowup** renders a rectangular region and enlarges the area to fit the current image size.

◆ **Box Selected** renders only the volume specified by the current selection's bounding box, and lets you specify an image resolution for the objects being rendered.

RENDERING SCENES

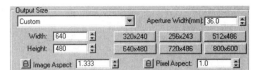

Figure 13.3 The Output Size group gives you presets, customization settings, and more.

The most important groups of options in the Render Scene dialog box include the following:

◆ **Time Output:** Sets the amount of time you want to render from your scene. Time Output defaults to a single frame.

◆ **Output Size:** Sets the resolution of the rendered image. There are six Output Size preset buttons, which you can customize.

◆ **Rendering Output:** Sets the file type and destination of the output image.

There are two shortcuts to rendering:

◆ Quick Render uses the current settings of the Render Scene dialog box. Quick Render has two settings: **Production** and **Draft**. You define these settings by clicking the Production or Draft radio buttons in the lower-left corner of the Render Scene dialog box.

◆ **Render Last** repeats the previous render command. It renders the last view that was produced with the last rendering type that was chosen. If you have changed the settings of the Render Scene dialog box, it will use the new settings, but it never saves an image to a file.

Setting resolution

Output Size sets the resolution of rendered images. The default size is 640 x 480 pixels.

To set the image output size:

1. Click Render Scene.

2. In the Output Size group, select an output size by clicking a preset resolution button or by entering values for width and height (**Figure 13.3**).

   The rendering size of the image is set.

(continues on next page)

✔ Tips

- Clicking the lock icon next to Image Aspect locks the image aspect ratio.

- Right-clicking a preset resolution button brings up the Configure Preset dialog box so you can change the preset (**Figure 13.4**).

- The drop-down list in this group contains a variety of formats and presets for different applications (**Figure 13.5**).

Selecting a name and file format

3D Studio MAX 3 saves up to 10 different still image file formats, as well as three different animation file formats. They are all listed in step 3 below.

To select a name and file format:

1. 🖼 Click Render Scene.

2. In the Render Output group, click Files. The Render Output File dialog box appears (**Figure 13.6**).

3. Choose a file format from the Save as Type drop-down list (**Figure 13.7**). BMP, Kodak Cineon, Encapsulated PostScript, JPEG, PNG, SGI, RLA, RPF, Targa, and TIF are all still image file formats. AVI, Autodesk Flic, and MOV are animation file formats.

4. Enter a name for the image. You do not need to type the file extension.

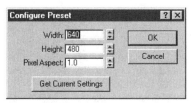

Figure 13.4 The Configure Preset dialog box lets you customize a preset output size.

Figure 13.5 If you're rendering for a standard cinematic or video resolution, such as IMAX, choose from the Output Size drop-down list.

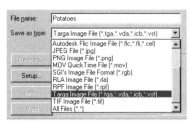

Figure 13.6 The Render Output File dialog box is similar to Save dialog boxes in other programs.

Figure 13.7 Choose your desired output file format from the Save as Type list.

RENDERING SCENES

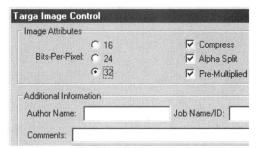

Figure 13.8 The Targa Image Control dialog box is an example of a configuration dialog box that gives you additional options specific to the output file format you choose.

Figure 13.9 You can turn file saving on and off with the checkbox next to Save File.

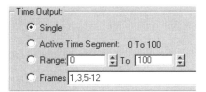

Figure 13.10 Save still image files by choosing Single in the Time Output group.

Figure 13.11 The Virtual Frame Buffer window displays the rendered image.

5. Click Save.

Some file formats require extra configuration settings so a configuration dialog box may appear (**Figure 13.8**).

A check appears in the Save File checkbox of the Render Scene dialog box to let you know that the next rendering will be saved to a file (**Figure 13.9**).

✔ Tips

- For Web graphics, use the JPEG format and accept the default image controls settings.

- For uncompressed, full-color images, use the Targa format. If you check Alpha Split in the Targa Image Control dialog box, MAX will automatically save an additional alpha channel file called A_*filename*.tga.

- The most widely used animation formats are AVI and MOV.

Rendering still images

Rendering defaults to a single image of the current frame. For testing, use a small image output size such as 320 x 240 pixels.

To render an image to a file:

1. 🖼 Click Render Scene.

2. Choose an image size in the Output Size group.

3. Click the Files button and then specify a name and still image file format.

4. In the Time Output group, make sure that Single is selected (**Figure 13.10**).

5. Click Render.

The current frame renders to the Virtual Frame Buffer and to the file you selected (**Figure 13.11**).

(continues on next page)

RENDERING SCENES

✔ Tips

- To render a series of still frames that are sequentially numbered, with the format *filename. ####* —where *####* is the frame number, prepended with zeros—choose a still image file format and select Active Time Segment or Range in the Time Output group.

- If you select Range, specify the extent of the range by entering the numbers of the frames you want to render. Separate each frame with a comma or define sub-ranges using a hyphen between frame numbers.

- Sequentially numbered files can be used to create animated bitmaps in the Material Editor. See "IFL files" in the online help files for more information about this option.

- Remember to uncheck Save File in the Render Scene dialog box if you don't want the program to save the next rendering.

Figure 13.12 Use Make Preview to quickly produce a test rendering of your animation.

Rendering animations

The Time Output group sets the amount of time or the number of frames to render, using the time code chosen in the Time Configuration dialog box. *(See Chapter 6, "Animation," for a complete description of how to set time codes.)*

You can render an entire active time segment or any range of frames that you specify. Take advantage of the Range and Preview options to test-render different parts of your animation.

To render a preview animation:

1. Open the Rendering Toolbar.

2. Click Preview.

   The Make Preview dialog box appears (**Figure 13.12**).

Figure 13.13 You can see the preview as it renders frame by frame in the preview window.

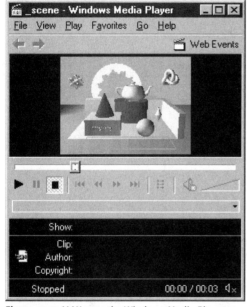

Figure 13.14 MAX uses the Windows Media Player to play back the preview.

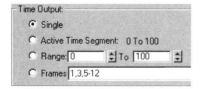

Figure 13.15 To render an animation, choose Active Time Segment or Range.

3. Set the Preview Range, Frame Rate, and Image Size parameters, or accept the defaults.

4. Click Create. If necessary, choose a compression.

The preview window replaces the viewports. The preview renders in the center of the window (**Figure 13.13**).

5. When the preview has finished rendering, the Windows Media Player appears. It automatically plays back the preview (**Figure 13.14**).

✔ Tip

■ Previews are named _scene.avi and saved in the 3dsmax3/Preview folder by default. Use the Rendering > Rename Preview command if you want to save the preview to a new file that won't be saved over.

To render an animation:

1. 🖳 Click Render Scene.

2. Choose an image size in the Output Size group.

3. In the Time Output group, select Active Time Segment or Range (**Figure 13.15**).

4. If you chose Range, specify a range.

(continues on next page)

5. Choose a name and animation file format by clicking the Files button. When you click Save, the program prompts you to select a compression method or color palette (**Figure 13.16**).

6. Click Render.

The active time segment or range renders to a movie file. To play back the movie, choose File > View File and navigate to the file you just saved.

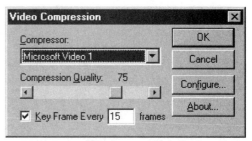

Figure 13.16 Microsoft Video 1 is the default compression option for .avi files, but not the best one.

✔ Tips

■ Render uncompressed AVI files if you are going to process and compress the file later in another application.

■ One of the best codecs, or compression methods, for MOV files is Sorensen Video.

■ Use the Flic format to render 8-bit files.

■ If you increase the value of Every Nth Frame, the program will render frames at intervals of N (**Figure 13.17**).

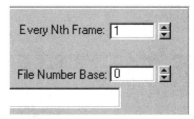

Figure 13.17 For test rendering of animations at a higher quality than the preview, render every second or third frame.

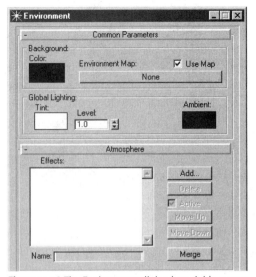

Figure 13.18 The Environment dialog box yields access to various special effects and background settings.

Figure 13.19 Use the Material/Map Browser to specify a background image.

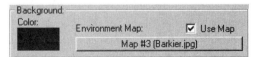

Figure 13.20 The Background group displays the name of the background map.

Adding Backgrounds

Background images add interest to a scene and provide it with a context. Adding a background image is a great way to save time, because you don't have to build the objects in the image.

You can display background images in a viewport or render a background image as part of a scene environment. In a viewport, backgrounds make a great reference for building realistic models. In a rendering, environment backgrounds provide a backdrop for your scene. If you know you are going to render a background image with your scene, placing the same background in a viewport helps you build models to match it.

Background images can be generated procedurally within the program, obtained from a material library, or imported from any image file on your system. For your convenience, MAX ships with an extra CD-ROM full of images called The World Creating Toolkit.

To add a background image to the environment:

1. Open the Rendering Toolbar.

2. Click the Environments button.
   The Environment dialog box appears (**Figure 13.18**).

3. Click the Environment Map button (labelled "None").
   The Material/Map Browser appears (**Figure 13.19**).

4. Double-click Bitmap.
   The Select Bitmap Image File dialog box appears.

5. Select an image and click OK.
   The name of the bitmap image appears on the Environment Map button (**Figure 13.20**).
   (continues on next page)

6.  Render the scene.

The environment map appears in the background (**Figure 13.21**).

✔ Tips

- To adjust the appearance of the environment map, drag an instance of the map from the Environment Map button to a sample slot in the Material Editor. Then make your adjustments. The instanced map automatically updates in the environment.

- You can drag maps to and from any map button or sample slot in the Material Editor, the Environment dialog box, projector map buttons, the displacement map button, and so on.

Adding a background image to a viewport

There are two ways to obtain backgrounds for a viewport. You can import an image file from your system, or you can use the environment map. For rotoscoping and matte painting, use the environment map.

To add a background image to a viewport:

1. Choose Views > Viewport Background.

The Viewport Background dialog box appears (**Figure 13.22**).

2. Click the Files button and use the Select Background Image dialog box to find a background image (**Figure 13.23**).

or

Check the Use Environment Background checkbox.

Figure 13.21 Using a background map can enhance your rendered images quite a bit.

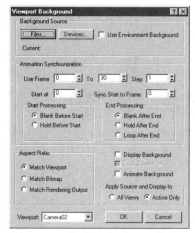

Figure 13.22 Placing a background image in a viewport helps you preview the way the scene will render with the same image.

Figure 13.23 Use the Select Background Image dialog box to load an image file.

Figure 13.24 To display a background image in a viewport, turn on Display Background in the Viewport Background dialog box.

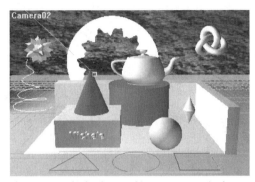

Figure 13.25 The background image appears in the viewport just as it does in the rendered image.

3. Make sure that Display Background is checked (**Figure 13.24**).

4. Click OK.

The image appears in the background of the active viewport (**Figure 13.25**).

✔ Tips

■ You can add different background images to each of the viewports.

■ If you are using a background image as a reference for modeling, be sure to check Match Bitmap in the Aspect Ratio group.

■ To temporarily turn off the display of a background image, right-click the viewport label and uncheck Show Background.

ADDING BACKGROUNDS

Adding Atmospheric Effects

Atmospheric effects are visual effects that create the illusion of fog, fire, smoke, and clouds. These effects appear when your render your scene. Some of the newer video display cards display atmospheric effects in the viewports.

Using the Environment dialog box, you can create the following effects:

- **Fog:** Adds smoke and fog effects to a scene. Fog gradually fades objects toward the front, back, top, or bottom of a view. You can also make fog constant throughout the view.

- **Volume Fog:** Creates swirling smoke, fog, and cloud effects. By adding a gizmo to the scene, you can confine volume fog to a certain region of the scene.

- **Volume Light:** Adds swirling smoke and fog to a light beam, creating the illusion of headlights on a foggy night or spotlights in a smoky theater.

- **Combustion:** Creates smoke, fire, and explosion effects, including candles, campfires, fireballs, nebulae, and clouds. Combustion is animated by default.

Atmospheric effects can be animated.

For advanced atmospheric effects, such as self-shadowing smoke, consider purchasing the Afterburn plug-in. To see examples of the highly realistic effects it creates, check www.afterworks.com.

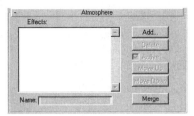

Figure 13.26 Use the Atmosphere rollout to add effects like fog and combustion.

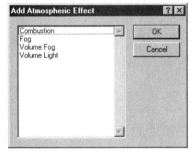

Figure 13.27 Choose the atmospheric effect from the Add Atmospheric Effect list.

Figure 13.28 The Effects list lets you activate and deactivate individual effects.

To add an atmospheric effect:

1. Open the Rendering panel.

2. Click the Environments button.

   The Environment dialog box appears. The Atmosphere rollout appears at the bottom (**Figure 13.26**).

3. Click the Add button.

   The Add Atmospheric Effect dialog box appears (**Figure 13.27**).

4. Select an effect and click OK.

   The name of the effect appears in the Effects list of the Environment dialog box (**Figure 13.28**). Active is checked by default. The Parameters rollout for the effect appears below the Effects list.

✔ Tips

■ To delete an effect, select the name of the effect from the Effects list and click the Delete button.

■ To disable an effect temporarily, select the name of the effect and uncheck Active.

ADDING ATMOSPHERIC EFFECTS

Adding fog

You can create two kinds of fog: standard fog, which fades the scene along your line of sight, and layered fog, which fades the scene between the earth and sky. Standard fog renders in any type of view. Layered fog renders only in Perspective and Camera views.

To add standard fog:

1. ![icon] Create a targeted camera.

2. Set the Environment ranges of the camera to define the region that will be affected by the fog.

3. Set and activate a Camera viewport.

4. Open the Environment dialog box.

5. Add the Fog effect.
   The Fog Parameters rollout appears (**Figure 13.29**).

6. Select Standard type fog.

7. ![icon] Render the scene to see the effect of the default settings (**Figure 13.30**).

8. Adjust the parameters of the Fog.
   Choose Near or Far to fade a scene from the Near Range to Far Range or vice versa.
   Check Exponential to increase the rate at which the fog effect obscures the scene.

9. ![icon] Render the scene to see the result (**Figure 13.31**).

✔ Tips

- You can change the color of the fog by clicking the color swatch in the Fog Parameters rollout.

- Uncheck Fog Background if you don't want the fog to fade out the background (**Figure 13.32**).

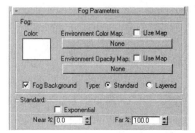

Figure 13.29 Use the Fog Parameters rollout to change the fog color, its extents, and other parameters.

Figure 13.30 This scene uses the default settings for standard fog.

Figure 13.31 In this rendering, the fog becomes denser more quickly, so the teapots are partially obscured.

Figure 13.32 Turn off Fog Background for an unrealistic effect in which the scene objects are affected by fog, but the background is not.

Figure 13.33 Layered fog parameters include Top and Bottom, letting you create a fog that can be seen from outside the fog, as in flying over a misty city.

Figure 13.34 Here the fog falls off toward the bottom.

Figure 13.35 This scene uses horizon noise to produce an uneven edge where the fog meets the sky.

Figure 13.36 Fog can be used for special effects, like adding mundane objects to an unusual environment.

To add layered fog:

1. Activate a Perspective or Camera viewport.

2. Open the Environment dialog box.

3. Add the Fog effect.
   The Fog Parameters rollout appears.

4. Select Layered fog.
   The Layered group becomes enabled in the Parameters rollout (**Figure 13.33**).

5. 🖼 Render the scene to see the effect of the default settings (**Figure 13.34**).

6. Set the extent of the fog in world units from the top to the bottom of the scene, using the parameters on the left.
   On the right, specify whether the fog will fade the scene top to bottom or vice versa.
   Check Horizon Noise to add a rough edge to the fog.

7. 🖼 Render the scene to see the result (**Figure 13.35**).

✔ Tips

- Adding a map to the environment color map channel applies a texture map to fog. If you use the same texture map in the background, it can make objects appear to sink into the environment (**Figure 13.36**).

- Adding a map to the environment opacity map channel varies the opacity of the fog.

Adding volumetric fog

Volume fog distributes the fog effect unevenly. You can also confine it within the bounds of an atmospheric apparatus, or gizmo.

To add volume fog:

1. Open the Environment dialog box.

2. Add the Volume Fog effect.

   The Volume Fog Parameters rollout appears (**Figure 13.37**).

3. ![icon] Render the scene to see the effect of the default settings (**Figure 13.38**).

4. Adjust the size, density, and granularity of the fog using the Size, Density, and Step Size spinners. For low density values, reduce the Max Steps value so the fog doesn't take forever to render.

5. ![icon] Render the scene to see the results (**Figure 13.39**).

To confine volume fog to a gizmo:

1. Open the Helpers Toolbar.

2. ![icon] Choose a gizmo.

3. Drag out a gizmo in a Perspective or Camera view.

4. Open the Environment dialog box.

5. Select the Volume Fog effect from the Effects list.

6. Click Pick Gizmo.

7. ![icon] Render the scene to see the result (**Figure 13.40**).

✔ Tip

■ For a complete description of the volume fog parameters, see the online help files.

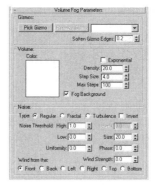

Figure 13.37
The Volume Fog Parameters rollout appears.

Figure 13.38 This scene uses the default settings for volumetric fog.

Figure 13.39 This fog is less dense and finer grained than the one in Figure 13.38.

Figure 13.40 Volume fog is confined within a region.

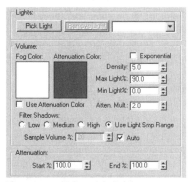

Figure 13.41 Volumetric light uses an effect much like fog but confines it to a beam of light.

Figure 13.42 The directional light in this scene uses the default volumetric settings.

Figure 13.43 This scene uses a denser volumetric light.

Adding volumetric light

In Chapter 11, you added volumetric light by modifying a light. Now you will learn how to add light from the Environment dialog box and make some adjustments to the effect.

To add volumetric light:

1. Open the Environment dialog box.

2. Add the Volume Light effect.
   The Volume Lights Parameters rollout appears (**Figure 13.41**).

3. Click Pick Light and select a light.

4. 🖼 Render the scene to see the effect of the default settings (**Figure 13.42**).

5. Adjust the fog color, density, minimum and maximum percentages, and attenuation multiplier.

6. Adjust the attenuation start and end percentages. If you want, you can also use and set an attenuation color that is different from the fog color.

7. 🖼 Render the scene to see the result (**Figure 13.43**).

✔ Tip

■ For a complete description of the volume light parameters, see the online help files.

Adding combustion

Combustion requires a gizmo in order to render. It renders only in Perspective and Camera views.

To add combustion:

1. Activate a Perspective or Camera viewport.

2. Open the Helpers Toolbar.

3. ▽ 🗑 ◎ Choose a gizmo.

4. Drag out a gizmo in a Perspective or Camera view.

5. Open the Environment dialog box.

6. Add the Combustion effect.
   The Combustion Parameters rollout appears (**Figure 13.44**).

7. Click Pick Gizmo and click the gizmo.

8. 🗔 Render the scene to see the effect of the default settings (**Figure 13.45**).

9. Adjust the shape and characteristics of the flame.

10. 🗔 Render the scene to see the results (**Figure 13.46**).

✔ Tip

■ Use the Motion and Explosion parameters to animate the combustion effect. You will find an excellent description of all the combustion parameters, including illustrations of flames and explosions, in the online help files.

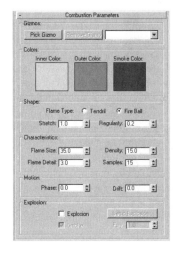

Figure 13.44
The Combustion Parameters rollout lets you create fire, explosions, and other special effects.

Figure 13.45 The combustion effect, confined to a spherical gizmo, uses the default settings in this scene.

Figure 13.46 Here the combustion effect produces a more realistic fire, thanks to tweaked parameters.

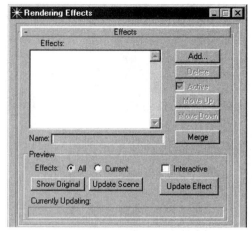

Figure 13.47 Use the Rendering Effects dialog box's Add button to create new effects.

Adding Render Effects

The Rendering Effects dialog box adds effects to your scene that are processed in the virtual frame buffer after an image has been rendered. Render effects include the following:

◆ **Blur:** Blurs the contents of a rendered image.

◆ **Brightness and Contrast:** Changes the brightness and/or contrast of a rendered image.

◆ **Color Balance:** Shifts the color balance of a rendered image using CMY/RGB sliders.

◆ **Depth of Field:** Blurs scene objects and the background along a camera's Z axis— that is, your line of sight.

◆ **File Output:** Takes a snapshot of a scene and saves the image to a file or returns the image to the Effects stack for further processing.

◆ **Film Grain:** Applies noise to a rendered image. This effect may be used to create the appearance of grain on old film.

◆ **Lens Effects:** Simulates effects that are created by a camera lens and a bright light. Use this effect to create glows around a light, starburst effects, streaking, or rainbow rings.

(Note: The Effects list is sometimes referred to as the Effects stack, because the effects in the list are evaluated in a certain order.)

Most effects give you the option of including or excluding background images from the effect.

To add a render effect:

1. Open the Rendering Toolbar.

2. Click the Effects button.

   The Rendering Effects dialog box appears (**Figure 13.47**).

(continues on next page)

3. Click Add.

The Add Effect dialog box appears (**Figure 13.48**).

4. Select the effect you want and click OK.

The effect is added to the Effects list. The parameters for the effect appear below the list (**Figure 13.49**).

The effect is applied to the scene (**Figure 13.50**).

Figure 13.48
Choose the Blur effect from the Add Effect dialog box.

5. In the Preview group, check Interactive.

The virtual frame buffer appears. The view from the active viewport renders in the window, using the image size specified in the Render Scene dialog box.

If you added Blur or Film Grain, the render effect is applied to the image after a short pause (**Figure 13.51**).

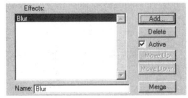

Figure 13.49 The effect is added to the Effects List.

6. Adjust the parameters of the effect.

The virtual frame buffer automatically updates to show the change.

7. To render the effect from a different view, activate the viewport that displays that view and click Update Scene.

Figure 13.50 In this rendering, the scene is heavily blurred.

Figure 13.51 Here the effect has been diminished, producing a less pronounced blurring.

Figure 13.52 Use Film Grain Parameters to simulate the look of movie film.

Figure 13.53 A fine grain appears throughout the image.

Figure 13.54 Here the film grain effect is more obvious.

Adding film grain

Film grain makes a rendered image look old and weathered, like the graininess you see on old movie films.

To create a film grain effect:

1. Open the Render Effects dialog box.

2. Add a Film Grain effect.

   The Film Grain Parameters rollout appears (**Figure 13.52**).

3. Check Interactive.

   The scene renders in the virtual frame buffer (**Figure 13.53**).

4. Increase the Grain setting.

   The image gets grainier (**Figure 13.54**).

5. Check the Ignore Background checkbox if you do not want the background image to be affected by the grain.

Creating depth of field

A depth of field effect selectively blurs the foreground or background of a scene. You can also choose to blur around an object, while keeping the object in focus.

To create depth of field:

1. Open the Render Effects dialog box.

2. Add the Depth of Field effect.
   The Depth of Field Parameters rollout appears (**Figure 13.55**).

3. Click Update Scene to see the initial results (**Figure 13.56**).

4. Click Pick Camera and pick a camera in the scene.

5. Click Pick Node and click an object in the scene.

6. Click Update.

7. The scene renders in the virtual frame buffer (**Figure 13.57**).

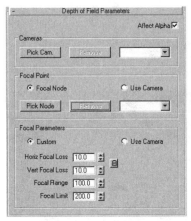

Figure 13.55 The depth of field effect simulates a camera lens that blurs parts of the scene out of the focus point.

Figure 13.56 You can see a test rendering with the Update Scene feature.

Figure 13.57 The depth of field effect is more apparent when rendered in the virtual frame buffer.

INDEX

B

INDEX

INDEX

L

M

INDEX

INDEX

INDEX

INDEX